*This is the tenth of twelve
books which together make up
the first complete paper-
back edition of Sir Winston
Churchill's classic memoirs,* The
History of the Second World
War. *Here, full and unabridged,
is the greatest Englishman of
our time, describing in unfor-
gettable words the follies which
brought about the most terrible
war known to mankind, and the
sacrifices, determination and
matchless courage by which it
was brought to an end.*

The Moral of the Work

In War: RESOLUTION
In Defeat: DEFIANCE
In Victory: MAGNANIMITY
In Peace: GOODWILL

Winston S. Churchill

THE SECOND WORLD WAR
10. Assault from the Air

CASSELL · LONDON

CASSELL & COMPANY LTD
35 Red Lion Square · London WC1

and at Melbourne, Sydney, Toronto,
Johannesburg, Cape Town, Auckland

Assault from the Air
was first published as Book 2 of 'Closing the Ring',
the fifth volume of Sir Winston Churchill's
The Second World War

First published 1952
All rights reserved
First published in this edition September 1964
Second edition March 1965

Set in 9 point Intertype Times and
printed in Great Britain by Cox and Wyman Ltd.,
London, Reading and Fakenham.
1064

Preface

(From the Preface to the original edition)

I must regard these volumes as a continuation of the story of the First World War which I set out in The World Crisis, The Eastern Front *and* The Aftermath. *Together they cover an account of another Thirty Years War.*

I have followed, as in previous volumes, the method of Defoe's Memoirs of a Cavalier, *as far as I am able, in which the author hangs the chronicle and discussion of great military and political events upon the thread of the personal experiences of an individual. I am perhaps the only man who has passed through both the two supreme cataclysms of recorded history in high executive office. Whereas however in the First World War I filled responsible but subordinate posts, I was in this second struggle with Germany for more than five years the head of His Majesty's Government. I write therefore from a different standpoint and with more authority than was possible in my earlier books. I do not describe it as history, for that belongs to another generation. But I claim with confidence that it is a contribution to history which will be of service for the future.*

These thirty years of action and advocacy comprise and express my life-effort, and I am content to be judged upon them. I have adhered to my rule of never criticising any measure of war or policy after the event unless I had before expressed publicly or formally my opinion or warning about it. Indeed in the afterlight I have softened many of the severities of contemporary controversy. It has given me pain to record these disagreements with so many men whom I liked or respected; but it would be wrong not to lay the lessons of the past before the future. Let no one look down on those honourable, well-meaning men whose actions are chronicled in these pages without searching his own heart, reviewing his own discharge of public duty, and applying the lessons of the past to his future conduct.

It must not be supposed that I expect everyone to agree with what I say, still less that I only write what will be popular. I gave my testimony according to the lights I follow. Every possible care has been taken to verify the facts; but much is constantly coming to light from the disclosure of captured documents and other revelations which may present a new aspect to the conclusions which I have drawn.

One day President Roosevelt told me that he was asking publicly for suggestions about what the war should be called. I said at once 'The Unnecessary War'. *There never was a war more easy to stop than that which has just wrecked what was left of the world from the previous struggle. The human tragedy reaches its climax in the fact that after all the exertions and sacrifices of hundreds of millions of people and the victories of the Righteous Cause we have still not found Peace or Security, and that we lie in the grip of even worse perils than those we have surmounted. It is my earnest hope that pondering upon the past may give guidance in days to come, enable a new generation to repair some of the errors of former years, and thus govern, in accordance with the needs and glory of man, the awful unfolding scene of the future.*

WINSTON SPENCER CHURCHILL

Chartwell,
Westerham,
Kent.

March 1948

Acknowledgments

I have been greatly assisted in the establishment of the story in its military aspect by Lieutenant-General Sir Henry Pownall; in naval matters by Commodore G. R. G. Allen; in presenting the Air aspect by Air Chief Marshal Sir Guy Garrod; and on European and general questions by Colonel F. W. Deakin, of Wadham College, Oxford, who has helped me with my work Marlborough: His Life and Times. *I have had much assistance from the late Sir Edward Marsh, Mr. Denis Kelly, and Mr. C. C. Wood. I must in addition make my acknowledgments to the very large number of others who have kindly read these pages and commented upon them.*

Lord Ismay has also given me his invaluable aid, as have my other friends.

I record my obligations to Her Majesty's Government for the permission to reproduce the text of certain official documents of which the Crown Copyright is legally vested in the Controller of Her Majesty's Stationery Office. At the request of Her Majesty's Government, on security grounds, I have paraphrased some of the telegrams I have quoted. These changes have in no way altered the sense or substance of the telegrams.

I am indebted to the Roosevelt Trust for the use they have permitted me of the President's telegrams I have quoted; to Captain Samuel Eliot Morison, U.S.N.R., whose books on naval operations give a clear presentation of the actions of the United States Fleet; and also to others who have allowed their private letters to be published.

The publishers wish to thank the owners, named and unnamed, of the photographs used to illustrate this book.

Contents

Illustrations

The Teheran Conference—Churchill in Persian head-dress

His Majesty King George VI

A flotilla of tank landing-craft massed in a North African harbour

Monte Cassino Monastery before and after the Allied bombing

A 'V2' rocket ready to be fired

A Sherman tank crossing the Volturno

Churchill and Alexander watch an Allied attack in Italy

Yugoslav partisans taken prisoner by the Germans

A wounded Army dog is taken to a dressing station, the Solomon Islands

Maps and Diagrams

Theme of the Book

HOW
NAZI GERMANY WAS
ISOLATED AND
ASSAILED ON
ALL SIDES

CHAPTER 1

Cairo

Voyage in the 'Renown' – A Stay at Malta – Khartoum an Impossible Meeting-place – We All Gather Round the Pyramids – The President Arrives – I Meet Chiang Kai-shek and His Wife – My Indictment of Our Mismanagement of Military Operations Since Salerno – Unreal Division of Forces and Responsibilities in the Mediterranean – German Mastery of the Eastern Ægean – The Shadow of 'Overlord' – The First Plenary Meeting of the Cairo Conference, November 23 – Chiang Kai-shek's Request for British Naval Support – Our Second Meeting, November 24 – Mr. Eden Joins Us after Conference with the Turks – The Question of the High Command – United States Proposal for One Supreme Commander Against Germany – Adverse Memorandum by the British Chiefs of Staff – I Support Them – Our Allies Remain Silent – A Family Party on Thanksgiving Day, November 25 – Off for Teheran, November 27.

On the afternoon of November 12 I sailed in the *Renown* from Plymouth with my personal staff on a journey which was to keep me from England for more than two months. With me came Mr. Winant, the American Ambassador, Admiral Cunningham, First Sea Lord, and General Ismay and other members of the Defence Office. I was feeling far from well, as a heavy cold and sore throat were reinforced by the consequences of inoculations against typhoid and cholera. I stayed in bed for several days. My Cabinet colleagues had expressed the kindly wish that my daughter Sarah should come with me, and it gave me pleasure to defer to their request. She was serving in the Air Force, and became my aide-de-camp. We had an uneventful voyage across the Bay, and I was able to go on deck as we passed the Straits of Gibraltar. While we stopped for a few hours at Algiers on the 16th I had a long talk with General Georges about the French situation in Africa. As darkness fell we resumed our course for Malta, which we reached on the 17th.

Here I found Generals Eisenhower and Alexander, and other important personages. After the conclusion of the Tunisian campaign I had suggested to the King that General Alexander should receive the distinction of the North Africa ribbon with the numerals 1 and 8 upon it, representing the two victorious British armies of the campaign. I felt that as Eisenhower had been the Supreme Commander this was also his by right, and I sought and obtained the King's approval. I had the honour of investing these two Commanders with this unique decoration. They were both taken by surprise, and seemed highly gratified when I pinned the ribbons on their coats. I arrived in Malta quite ill with a new cold and temperature, but I had sufficient strength to attend the dinner at the Governor's war-time palace, the real one being uninhabitable from bombardment.

Although I continued to conduct business without cessation I had to remain in bed all the time I was in Malta, except for a Staff conference and a final tour of the frightfully battered dockyard, where the whole of the people and workmen gathered with great enthusiasm. At midnight on November 19 we sailed again on our voyage to Alexandria.

A telegram had reached me from the President saying that his security advisers thought that Cairo was too dangerous for the Conference. They feared a German air attack from Greece or Rhodes, and suggested Khartoum instead. Roosevelt of course had nothing to do with this himself, as he was entirely indifferent to his personal safety. Khartoum would have been quite unequal to handling the great staffs we were bringing, amounting altogether to nearly five hundred. I therefore asked Ismay to examine the resources of Malta. He reported that owing to air damage the accommodation was not only inadequate for our considerable gathering, but also extremely primitive. I therefore decided that we had better stick to Cairo, where all arrangements had been perfected. The eight squadrons of British aircraft based on Alexandria would certainly intercept and destroy any German attack. The enclave near the Pyramids which we were to occupy was to be guarded by more than a brigade of infantry, and there were upward of five hundred anti-aircraft guns hard by. Accordingly I wirelessed the *Iowa*, which was bringing the President across the ocean:

Prime Minister to President   21 Nov 43
    See St. John, chapter xiv, verses 1 to 4.

On reading this through more carefully after it had gone I was a little concerned lest, apart from a shadow of unintended profanity, it should be thought I was taking too much upon myself and thus giving offence. However, the President brushed all objections aside and our plans continued unchanged. In the event no German aeroplanes ever came within several hundred miles of the Pyramids.

*   *   *

The *Renown* reached Alexandria on the morning of November 21, and I flew at once to the desert landing-ground near the Pyramids. Here Mr. Casey had placed at my disposal the agreeable villa he was using. We lay in a broad expanse of Kasserine woods, thickly dotted with the luxurious abodes and gardens of the cosmopolitan Cairo magnates. Generalissimo Chiang Kai-shek and Madame had already been ensconced half a mile away. The President was to occupy the spacious villa of the American Ambassador Kirk, about three miles down the road to Cairo. I went to the desert airfield to welcome him when he arrived in the 'Sacred Cow' from Oran the next morning, and we drove to his villa together.

The Staffs congregated rapidly. The headquarters of the Conference and the venue of all the British and American Chiefs of Staff was at the Mena House Hotel, opposite the Pyramids, and I was but half a mile away. The whole place bristled with troops and anti-aircraft guns, and the strictest cordons guarded all approaches. Everyone set to work at once at their various levels upon the immense mass of business which had to be decided or adjusted.

What we had apprehended from Chiang Kai-shek's presence now in fact occurred. The talks of the British and American Staffs were sadly distracted by the Chinese story, which was lengthy, complicated, and minor. Moreover, as will be seen, the President, who took an exaggerated view of the Indian–Chinese sphere, was soon closeted in long conferences with the Generalissimo. All hope of persuading Chiang and his wife to go and see the Pyramids and enjoy themselves till we returned from Teheran fell to the ground, with the result that Chinese business occupied first instead of last place at Cairo. The President, in spite of my arguments, gave the Chinese the promise of a considerable amphibious operation across the Bay of Bengal within the next few months. This would have cramped 'Overlord' for landing- and tank-landing craft, which had now become the bottle-neck, far more than any of my Turkey and Ægean projects. It would also have hampered grievously the immense operations we were carrying out in Italy. On November 29 I wrote to the Chiefs of Staff: 'The Prime Minister wishes to put on record the fact that he specifically refused the Generalissimo's request that we should undertake an amphibious operation simultaneously with the land operations in Burma.' It was not until we returned from Teheran to Cairo that I at length prevailed upon the President to retract his promise. Even so, many complications arose. Of this more anon.

I of course took occasion to visit the Generalissimo at his villa, where he and his wife were suitably installed. This was the first time I had met Chiang Kai-shek. I was impressed by his calm, reserved, and efficient personality. At this moment he stood at the height of his power and fame. To American eyes he was one of the dominant forces in the world. He was the champion of 'the New Asia'. He was certainly a steadfast defender of China against Japanese invasion. He was a strong anti-Communist. The accepted belief in American circles was that he would be the head of the great Fourth-Power in the world after the victory had been won. All these views and values have since been cast aside by many of those who held them. I, who did not in those days share the excessive estimates of Chiang Kai-shek's power or of the future helpfulness of China, may record the fact that the Generalissimo is still serving the same causes which at this time had gained him such wide renown. He has however since been beaten by the Communists in his own country, which is a very bad thing to be.

I had a very pleasant conversation with Madame Chiang Kai-shek, and found her a most remarkable and charming personality. I told her how much I had regretted that we could not find an occasion for a meeting at the time when we had both been in America together, and we agreed that no undue formalities should stand in the way of our talks in the future. The President had us all photographed together at one of our meetings at his villa, and although both the Generalissimo and his wife are now regarded as wicked and corrupt reactionaries by many of their former admirers I am glad to keep this as a souvenir.

*   *   *

During the outward voyage I had prepared what was in effect an indictment of our mismanagement of operations in the Mediterranean during the two months which had passed since our victory at Salerno. I gave this to the Chiefs of Staff, and they, while agreeing in principle, made a number of comments in detail upon it. The final version read as follows:

For a year from Alamein and the landings in North-West Africa the British and Americans have had virtually unbroken success in every theatre, and there is no doubt that our methods of war direction, through the Combined Chiefs of Staff, working under the heads of the two Governments, have enabled our commanders in the field to gain resounding victories and achieve solid results. In all the history of alliances there never has been such harmony and mutual comprehension not only in the high direction of the war but among the commanders and troops in the field. Our combined operations from the beginning of the Battle of Alamein to the end of the Battle of Naples and the deployment of the Army in Italy may well be regarded as an extremely well-managed and prosperous affair.

2. However, since then there has been a change. We have been overtaken and in a sense outrun by our own successes. Certain divergences of view, of emphasis rather than principle, have opened between the British and American Staffs. We must not allow ourselves to be prevented by victories already gained from subjecting ourselves severally and jointly to searching self-examination with a view to improving our methods and giving an increasingly high standard of service.

3. Since the successful landing and deployment of the Army in Italy in September the war in the Mediterranean has taken an unsatisfactory course. Both the build-up and advance of the Army in Italy, making allowance for bad weather, must be considered extremely slow. There is not a sufficient preponderance over the enemy in the front line. Many of the divisions have been continuously in action since the landing without any spell of relief. At the same time, two of the best British divisions, the 50th and 51st, which stood in Sicily close to the battlefield, were first stripped of their equipment and have since been withdrawn to the United Kingdom. It has not been found possible to assist the forward movement of the Army to the extent that might have been hoped by making amphibious scoops along either coast. Some of the vitally needed landing-craft have been sent home, losing heavily from the weather on the way. A large number of others have been withdrawn and assembled in preparation for their homeward journey. These orders have now been arrested till December 15, but this is a useless date for Mediterranean purposes. The landing-craft have done nothing in October and

November except assist in bringing vehicles ashore. At the same time the build-up of the Strategic Air Force in Italy has hampered the reinforcement of the fighting front. Thus the whole campaign on land has flagged. There is no prospect of Rome being taken in 1943. . . .

5. Side by side with this we have failed to give any real measure of support to the Partisans and Patriots in Yugo-slavia and Albania. These guerrilla forces are containing as many [German] divisions as are the British and American Armies put together. Hitherto they have been nourished only by supplies dropped from the air. It is now more than two months since we have had air and naval superiority in the mouth of the Adriatic, yet no ships with supplies have entered the ports taken by the Partisans. On the contrary, the Ger-mans are systematically driving them from these ports and acquiring mastery of the whole Dalmatian coast. It was not possible to prevent the Germans obtaining Corfu and Argos-toli, and they actually hold these islands at the moment. Thus the Germans have weathered the difficulties caused by the Italian collapse and desertion, and with great severity are mopping up many of the Patriot forces and cutting them off from the sea.

6. How has it happened? An imaginary line has been drawn down the Mediterranean which relieves General Eisenhower's armies of all responsibility for the Dalmatian coast and the Balkans. These are assigned to General Wilson, of the Middle East Command, but he does not possess the necessary forces. One command has the forces but not the responsibilities, the other the responsibilities but not the forces. This can hardly be considered an ideal arrangement.

7. Most unfortunate of all has been the Dodecanese and the Ægean. Immediately after the fall of Italy a number of islands held by the Italians were occupied by us with Italian consent. Of these the two most important were Cos and Leros. We did not succeed in getting Rhodes, which is of course the master key to the Ægean. Hitler was not slow to recognise the naval and political importance of the fortress of Leros, which had fallen so cheaply into our hands, and with great stubborn-ness and tenacity he personally set himself to restore the situation in the Ægean. A very large proportion of the Ger-man air forces which would have been available to fight in Italy was moved into the Ægean theatre, and sea transport was improvised.* It was evident early in October that attacks on Leros and Cos were imminent, and on October 4 Cos, where we had only one battalion, was retaken by the Ger-

* German records show that during this period their Ægean air forces were increased by nearly three hundred aircraft, while those in Italy were reduced by about two hundred.

mans. In spite of unexpectedly prolonged defence Leros fell on November 16, the British losses in the whole business being about 5,000 and the enemy scoring his first success since Alamein. All this of course is outside the parish of the High North African Command. . . .

9. The Germans are now complete masters of the Eastern Ægean. Although already outmatched in the air in Italy, they have not hesitated to reduce their air-power there, and have transferred to the Ægean forces sufficient to dominate this theatre. Although the United States and British air forces in the Mediterranean have a first-line strength of over 4,000— *i.e.*, practically equal to the whole of the German Air Force —the Germans have been able to reproduce in the Ægean theatre all the old technique of the days of our air nakedness, and with their Stuka dive-bombers have broken down the resistance of our best troops and sunk or damaged our ships. . . .

11. There are two causes for these misfortunes. The first has been mentioned—the artificial line of division between East and West in the Mediterranean, absolving the Western commanders, who have the forces, of all responsibility for the vital interests at stake in the East. The second cause of course is the shadow of 'Overlord'. The decisions at Quebec were taken before the consequences of the collapse of Italy were apparent and before the surrender of the Italian Fleet and the successful invasion of the mainland of Europe. Nevertheless they have been maintained until a fortnight ago with inflexible rigidity. It has not been found possible to meet together earlier. We are now faced with the prospect that a fixed target date for 'Overlord' will continue to hamper and enfeeble the Mediterranean campaign, that our affairs will deteriorate in the Balkans, and that the Ægean will remain firmly in German hands. All this is to be accepted for the sake of an operation fixed for May upon hypotheses that in all probability will not be realised at that date, and certainly not if the Mediterranean pressure is relaxed.

12. Nor must we overlook the discouraging and enfeebling effect upon the whole of the operations in the Mediterranean of the fact that it is now common knowledge in the Armies that the theatre is to be bled as much as necessary for the sake of an operation elsewhere in the spring. The fact of troops and landing-craft being withdrawn from the very battlefield and of units being put under orders for home is in itself injurious. The intense desire to concentrate upon the enemy which carried us from Alamein and sustained us in Tunisia has been impaired. Yet in the Mediterranean alone are we in contact with the enemy and able to bring superior

numbers to bear upon him now. It is certainly an odd way of helping the Russians, to slow down the fight in the only theatre where anything can be done for some months.

*　　　*　　　*

The first plenary meeting of the Cairo Conference (which was given the code-name 'Sextant') was held at the President's villa on Tusday, November 23. Its purpose was to outline formally to Chiang Kai-shek and the Chinese delegation the proposed operations in South-East Asia, as drawn up by the Combined Chiefs of Staff at Quebec. Admiral Mountbatten, with his officers, had flown from India, and he first gave a description of the military plans he had been given and was executing for 1944 in that theatre. To this I added the general naval picture. Owing to the surrender of the Italian Fleet and other naval events of a favourable character a British fleet would be established soon in the Indian Ocean. There would be ultimately no fewer than five modernised capital ships, four heavy armoured cruisers, and up to twelve auxiliary carriers. Chiang Kai-shek intervened to say that he thought that the success of operations in Burma depended not only on the strength of our naval forces in the Indian Ocean, but on the simultaneous co-ordination of naval action with land operations. I pointed out that there was no necessary connection between the land campaign and fleet action in the Bay of Bengal. Our main fleet base would be able to exercise its influence in sea-power from areas 2,000 to 3,000 miles away from the scene where the armies were operating. There was therefore no comparison between these operations and those carried out in Sicily, where the Fleet had been able to work in close support of the Army.

This meeting was brief, and it was agreed that Chiang Kai-shek should discuss further details with the Combined Chiefs of Staff.

*　　　*　　　*

On the following day a second meeting of our Combined Chiefs of Staff was held by the President, without the presence of the Chinese delegation, to discuss operations in Europe and the Mediterranean. We sought to survey the relations of the two theatres and to exchange our views before going on to Teheran. The President opened upon the effect on 'Overlord' of any possible action we could take in the meantime in the Mediterranean, including the problem of Turkey's entry into the war.

When I spoke I said 'Overlord' remained top of the bill, but this operation should not be such a tyrant as to rule out every other activity in the Mediterranean ; for example, a little flexibility in the employment of landing-craft ought to be conceded. General Alexander had asked that the date of their leaving for 'Overlord' should be deferred from mid-December to mid-January. Eighty additional L.S.T.s had been ordered to be built in Britain and Canada. We should try to do even better than this. The points which were at issue between the American and British Staffs would probably be found to affect no more than a tenth of our common resources, apart from the Pacific. Surely some degree of elasticty could be arranged. Nevertheless I wished to remove any idea that we had weakened, cooled, or were trying to get out of 'Overlord'. We were in it up to the hilt. To sum up, I said that the programme I advocated was to try to take Rome in January and Rhodes in February ; to renew supplies to the Yugoslavs, settle the Command arrangements, and to open the Ægean, subject to the outcome of an approach to Turkey ; all preparations for 'Overlord' to go ahead full steam within the framework of the foregoing policy for the Mediterranean.

This is a faithful record of my positon on the eve of Teheran.

*　　*　　*

Mr. Eden had now joined us from England, whither he had flown after his discussions in Moscow. His arrival was a great help to me. On the way back from the Moscow Conference he and General Ismay had met the Turkish Foreign Minister and other Turks at Cairo. At these talks Mr. Eden pointed out that we had urgent need of air bases in the south-west of Anatolia. He explained that our military situation at Leros and Samos was precarious, owing to German air superiority. Both places had since been lost. Mr. Eden also dwelt on the advantages that would be derived from Turkey's entry into the war. In the first place, it would oblige the Bulgarians to concentrate their forces on the frontier, and thus would compel the Germans to replace Bulgarian troops in Greece and Yugoslavia to the extent of some ten divisions. Secondly, it would be possible to attack the one target which might be decisive—Ploesti. Thirdly, Turkish chrome would be cut off from Germany. Finally, there was the moral advantage. Turkey's entry into the war might well hasten the process of disintegration in Germany and among her satellites. By all this argument the Turkish delegation were unmoved. They said, in effect, that the granting of bases in Anatolia would amount to intervention in the war, and that if they intervened in the war there was nothing to prevent a German retaliation on Constantinople, Angora, and Smyrna. They refused to be comforted by the assurances that we would give them sufficient fighters to deal with any air attack that the Germans could launch and that the Germans were so stretched everywhere that they had no divisions available to attack Turkey. The only result of the discussions was that the Turkish delegation promised to report to their Government. Considering what had been happening under their eyes in the Ægean, the Turks can hardly be blamed for their caution.

* * *

As I had heard no more about the plans for the combined command of 'Overlord' and the Mediterranean I assumed that the British view had been accepted. But on November 25, during our stay in Cairo, the proposal for one overall Supreme Command was presented to us by the American Chiefs of Staff in a formal memorandum. From this it was apparent that the President and the American High Command felt strongly that a Supreme Commander should be appointed to command all the United Nations' operations against Germany, both from the Mediterranean and the Atlantic. They still wished to see a commander for North-West European operations, a commander of the Allied forces in the Mediterranean, and above both a supreme figure who would not only plan and conduct the war in both theatres, but move the forces from one to the other as he might think best. It must be remembered that we not only had at that time, and were bound to have for many months to come, a very large superiority in all the forces, Army, Navy, and Air, but also that with Alexander's and Montgomery's victories in Tunis and the Desert our reputation stood high.

The American memorandum immediately encountered strong opposition from the British Chiefs of Staff. Both they and I recorded our views in writing. The rejoinder of the British Chiefs of Staff was as follows:

COMMAND OF BRITISH AND UNITED STATES FORCES OPERATING AGAINST GERMANY
MEMORANDUM BY THE BRITISH CHIEFS OF STAFF

25 Nov 43

The British Chiefs of Staff have given careful consideration to the proposal put forward by the United States Chiefs of Staff that 'a Supreme Commander be designated at once to command all United Nations operations against Germany from the Mediterranean and the Atlantic'. This proposal has immense political implications, and is clearly a matter for the most earnest consideration of the United States and British Governments. Nevertheless the British Chiefs of Staff must say at once that, from the military point of view, they profoundly disagree with the proposal. Their reasons are set out in the paragraphs that follow.

Total war is not an affair of military forces alone, using the word 'military' in the widest sense of the term. There are political, economic, industrial, and domestic implications in almost every big war problem. Thus it seems clear that the Supreme Commander for the war against Germany will have to consult both the United States and the British Governments on almost every important question. In fact, it boils down to this, that he will only be able to make a decision without reference to high authority on comparatively minor and strictly military questions, such as the transfer of one or two divisions, or a few squadrons of aircraft, or a few scores of landing-craft, from one of his many fronts to another. He will thus be an extra and unnecessary link in the chain of command.

There is no real analogy between the position of Marshal Foch in the last war and the position now contemplated for the Supreme Commander against Germany. Marshal Foch was responsible only for the Western Front and the Italian Front. His authority did not extend to the Salonika Front, the Palestine Front, or the Mesopotamian Front. Under the arrangements now contemplated the Supreme Commander will have not only 'Overlord' and the Italian Front under his authority, but also the Balkan Front and the Turkish Front (if this is opened). There must be some limit to the responsibilities which Allied Governments can delegate to a single soldier, and the sphere now proposed seems to exceed these limits considerably.

The United States Chiefs of Staff propose that the decisions of the Supreme Commander should be 'subject to reversal by the Combined Chiefs of Staff'. If the main object of this new arrangement is to ensure rapid decisions, it looks as though the above proviso will lead to deplorable consequences. Instances will occur in which the Supreme Commander has issued orders and the troops have marched in accordance with these orders, only to be followed by a reversal of the order by the Combined Chiefs of Staff and consequent confusion. Again, it may happen that the British Chiefs of Staff agree with a decision taken by the Supreme Commander, while the United States Chiefs of Staff totally disagree with it. What happens then? Or, again, the Combined Chiefs of Staff may wholeheartedly support, on military grounds, a decision taken by the Supreme Commander, only to find that one or other of the Governments concerned is not prepared to ratify it. Then what happens?

If the Supreme Commander is going to exercise real control he will need to assemble the whole paraphernalia of Intelligence, Planning, and Administration on an unprecedented scale. This staff will merely be a great pad between the theatre commanders and the Combined Chiefs of Staff. . . .

If the well-tried machinery that had led us safely through the last two years has failed in the smaller problems, it would be better to examine that machinery and see how it can be speeded up and adjusted, rather than to embark upon an entirely novel experiment, which merely makes a cumbrous and unnecessary link in the chain of command, and which will surely lead to disillusionment and disappointment.

*   *   *

The American Chiefs of Staff were impressed by the arguments used. They realised that their proposal meant virtually the end of Combined Chiefs of Staff control, since the Super-Supreme Commander would to a large extent take the authority from their hands. They therefore dropped the subject from the Staff discussions on the understanding that it must be settled between the heads of Governments.

*   *   *

I warmly approved of the Chiefs of Staff paper, and developed the arguments still further in a note which I wrote the next day.

SUPREME COMMANDER OF ALL OPERATIONS AGAINST GERMANY

NOTE BY THE PRIME MINISTER AND MINISTER OF DEFENCE

26 Nov 43

The difficulties and shortcomings in our conduct of the war since the Battle of Salerno have arisen from divergences of view between our two Staffs and Governments. It is not seen how these divergences would be removed by the appointment of a Supreme Commander working under the Combined

Chiefs of Staff and liable to have his decisions reversed by them. The divergences, which are political as much as military, would still have to be adjusted by the present methods of consultation between the Combined Staffs and the heads of the two Governments. Thus the Supreme Commander, after being acclaimed as the World War winner, would in practice find his functions restricted to the narrow ground between the main decisions of policy and strategy, which can only be dealt with by the present methods, and the spheres of the two chief regional commanders.

2. This would certainly not be sufficient to justify arousing all the expectations and setting up all the apparatus inseparable from the announcement of a 'Supreme Commander for the defeat of Germany'.

3. On the other hand, if the power of decision is in fact accorded to the Supreme Commander the work of the Combined Chiefs of Staff would be virtually superseded, and very great stresses would immediately arise between the Governments and the Supreme Commander. Without going into personalities, it is greatly to be doubted whether any single officer exists who would be capable of giving decisions over the vast range of problems now dealt with by the heads of Governments assisted by the Combined Chiefs of Staff.

4. The principle which should be followed as far as possible between allies of equal status is that the command in any theatre should go to the ally who has the largest forces deployed or about to be deployed there. On this it would be natural that the command in the Mediterranean should be British and that the command of 'Overlord' should be American.

5. If the two commands are merged under a Supreme Commander the British would have available against Germany in May [1944] decidedly larger forces than the United States. It would therefore appear that the Supreme Command should go to a British officer. I should be very reluctant, as head of His Majesty's Government, to place such an invidious responsibility upon a British officer. If, on the other hand, disregarding the preponderance of forces involved, the Supreme Command was given to a United States officer and he pronounced in favour of concentrating on 'Overlord' irrespective of the injury done to our affairs in the Mediterranean, His Majesty's Government could not possibly agree. The Supreme Commander, British or American, would therefore be placed in an impossible position. Having assumed before the whole world the responsibility of pronouncing and being overruled by one Government or the other, he would have little choice but to resign. This might bring about a most

serious crisis in the harmonious and happy relations hitherto maintained between our two Governments.

6. It is not seen why the present arrangement should not continue, subject to any minor improvements that can be suggested. Under this arrangement an American commander would conduct the immense cross-Channel operation and a British commander would conduct the war in the Mediterranean, their action being concerted and forces assigned by the Combined Chiefs of Staff, working under the heads of the two Governments. ... More frequent meetings of the Combined Chiefs of Staff should also be arranged, and possibly monthly visits of one week's duration by the chairman of each Chiefs of Staff Committee alternately to London and Washington.

This paper I handed to the President before we left for Teheran, and I was not aware during the Conference at Teheran what his answer would be. I understood from private sources that the American Chiefs of Staff realised fully the clash of authority that might arise between our Combined Staff organisation and the new supreme general, and that after weighing our arguments they were by no means wedded to the plan. Neither the President nor any of his immediate circle referred to the matter in any way on the occasions, formal and informal but always friendly, when we came into contact. I therefore rested under the impression that General Marshall would command 'Overlord', that General Eisenhower would succeed him in Washington, and that it would fall to me, representing His Majesty's Government, to choose the Mediterranean commander, who at that time I had no doubt would be Alexander, already waging the war in Italy. Here the issue rested till we returned to Cairo.

*   *   *

Thanksgiving Day, which fell on November 25, is a feature in American life. Every soldier in the American armies is supposed to eat turkey on that date, and most of them did in 1943. Ample supplies of turkeys for all the United States Staffs at Cairo had been brought out in the President's ship. Mr. Roosevelt invited me to join him at dinner in his villa. 'Let us make it a family affair,' he said. So Sarah was asked too, and also 'Tommy' (Commander Thompson), to whom he had taken a great liking. The President's guests included his personal circle, his son, Elliott, his son-in-law, Major Boettiger, and Harry Hopkins and his son Robert. We had a pleasant and peaceful feast. Two enormous turkeys were brought in with all ceremony. The President, propped up high in his chair, carved for all with masterly, indefatigable skill. As we were about twenty, this took a long time, and those who were helped first had finished before the President had cut anything for himself. As I watched the huge platefuls he distributed to the company I feared that he might be left with nothing at all. But he had calculated to a nicety, and I was relieved, when at last the two skeletons were removed, to see him set about his own share. Harry, who had noted my anxiety, said, 'We have ample reserves.' Speeches were made of warm and intimate friendship. For a couple of hours we cast care aside. I had never seen the President more gay. After the meal was over we returned to the big room in which we had held so many conferences. Dance music—from gramophone records—began to play. Sarah was the only woman present, and she had her work cut out, so I danced with 'Pa' Watson (Roosevelt's trusted old friend and aide), to the delight of his chief, who watched us from the sofa. This jolly evening and the spectacle of the President carving up the turkeys stand out in my mind among the most agreeable features of the halt at Cairo.

*　　　*　　　*

At last all the puzzles had been solved. The difficulties of the American Constitution, Roosevelt's health, and Stalin's obduracy, the complications of a journey to Basra and the Trans-Persian railway, were all swept away by the inexorable need of a triple meeting, and the failure of every other alternative but a flight to Teheran. So we sailed off into the air from Cario at crack of dawn on November 27 in perfect weather for the long-sought meeting-place, and arrived safely by different routes at different times.

CHAPTER 2

Teheran: The Opening

Security Arrangements – Recapitulation of My Views – Stalin
and the President Confer – The First Plenary Meeting, Novem-
ber 28 – The President Opens the Discussion – Stalin's Account
of the Situation on the Soviet Front – I State the British View –
The Position of Turkey – Thirty-five Divisions for 'Overlord' –
Stalin Favours the Invasion of Southern France as the Secondary
Objective – I Insist upon the Capture of Rome – The President
and the Timing of Operations – The Proper Course for Tur-
key.

I could not admire the arrangements which had been made for
my reception after landing in Teheran. The British Minister met
me in his car, and we drove from the airfield to our Legation. As
we approached the city the road was lined with Persian cavalry-
men every fifty yards, for at least three miles. It was clearly
shown to any evil people that somebody of consequence was
coming, and which way. The men on horseback advertised the
route, but could provide no protection at all. A police car driving a hundred yards in advance gave warning of our approach.
The pace was slow. Presently large crowds stood in the spaces
between the Persian cavalry, and as far as I could see there were
few, if any, foot police. Towards the centre of Teheran these
crowds were four or five deep. The people were friendly but
non-committal. They pressed to within a few feet of the car.
There was no kind of defence at all against two or three determined men with pistols or a bomb. As we reached the turning
which led to the Legation there was a traffic block, and we
remained for three or four minutes stationary amid the crowded
throng of gaping Persians. If it had been planned out beforehand
to run the greatest risks and have neither the security of quiet
surprise arrival nor an effective escort the problem could not
have been solved more perfectly. However, nothing happened.
I grinned at the crowd, and on the whole they grinned at me. In
due course we arrived at the British Legation, which lay within
a strong cordon of British-Indian troops.

The Legation and its gardens lay almost adjoining the Soviet

Embassy, and as the Anglo-Indian brigade entrusted with our safety was in direct contact with the still larger Russian force that encircled their own domain both soon joined and we became an isolated area with all the precautions of war. The American Legation, which was guarded by United States forces, was a mile or more away, and this meant that either the President or else Stalin and I would have to traverse the narrow streets of Teheran two or three times a day, back and forth, during the Conference. Meanwhile Molotov, who had been in Teheran twenty-four hours before our arrival, produced a story that the Soviet Secret Intelligence had unearthed a plot to kill one or more of the 'Big Three', as we were regarded, and the idea of one or other of us continually going to and fro through the streets filled him with deep alarm. 'If anything like that were to happen,' he said, 'it could produce a most unfortunate impression.' This could not be denied. I strongly supported Molotov in his appeals to the President to move forthwith inside the Soviet Embassy, which was three or four times as big as the others, and stood in extensive grounds, now ringed by Soviet troops and police. We prevailed upon Mr. Roosevelt to take this good advice, and next afternoon he moved, with his personal staff, including the excellent Filipino cooks from his yacht, into the Russian domain, where ample and comfortable quarters were provided for him. Thus we were all within a circle, and could discuss the problems of the World War without any chance of annoyance. I was made very comfortable in the British Legation, and had only to walk a couple of hundred yards to reach the Soviet palace, which might be said to be for the time being the centre of the world. I continued to be far from well, and my cold and sore throat were so vicious that for a time I could hardly speak. However, Lord Moran with sprays and ceaseless care enabled me to say what I had to say—which was a lot.

* * *

There have been many misleading accounts of the line I took, with the full agreement of the British Chiefs of Staff, at this Conference. It has become a legend in America that I strove to prevent the cross-Channel enterprise called 'Overlord', and that I tried vainly to lure the Allies into some mass invasion of the Balkans, or a large-scale campaign in the Eastern Mediterranean, which would effectively kill it. Much of this nonsense has already in previous chapters been exposed and refuted, but it may be worth while to set forth what it was I actually sought, and what, in a very large measure, I got.

'Overlord', now planned in great detail, should be launched in May or June, or at the latest in the opening days of July 1944. The troops and all the ships to carry them still had first priority. Secondly, the great Anglo-American army in action in Italy must be nourished to achieve the capture of Rome and advance to secure the airfields north of the capital, from which the air attack on Southern Germany became possible. After these were gained there should be no advance in Italy beyond the Pisa-Rimini line—*i.e.*, we should not extend our front into the broader part of the Italian peninsula. These operations, if resisted by the enemy, would attract and hold very large German forces, would give the Italians the chance to 'work their passage', and keep the flame of war burning continually upon the hostile front.

I was not opposed at this time to a landing in the south of France, along the Riviera, with Marseilles and Toulon as objectives, and thereafter an Anglo-American advance northwards up the Rhone valley in aid of the main invasion across the Channel. Alternatively, I preferred a right-handed movement from the north of Italy, using the Istrian peninsula and the Ljubljana Gap, towards Vienna. I was delighted when the President suggested this, and tried, as will be seen, to engage him in it. If the Germans resisted we should attract many of their divisions from the Russian or Channel fronts. If we were not resisted we should liberate at little cost enormous and invaluable regions. I was sure we should be resisted, and thus help 'Overlord' in a decisive manner.

My third request was that the Eastern Mediterranean, with all the prizes that it afforded, should not be neglected, provided no strength which could be applied across the Channel should be absorbed. In all this I adhered to the proportions which I had mentioned to General Eisenhower two months earlier—namely, four-fifths in Italy, one-tenth in Corsica and the Adriatic, and one-tenth in the Eastern Mediterranean. From this I never varied—not an inch in a year.

We were all agreed, British, Russians, and Americans, upon the first two, involving nine-tenths of our available strength. All I had to plead was the effective use of one-tenth of our strength in the Eastern Mediterranean. Simpletons will argue, 'Would it not have been much better to centre all upon the decisive operation and dismiss all other opportunities as wasteful diversions?' But this ignores the governing facts. All the available shipping in the Western Hemisphere was already committed to the last ton to the preparation of 'Overlord' and the maintenance of our front in Italy. Even if more shipping had been found it could not have been used, because the programmes of disembarkation filled to the utmost limit all the ports and camps involved. As for the Eastern Mediterranean, nothing was needed that could be applied elsewhere. The Air Force massed for the defence of Egypt could equally well or better discharge its duty if used from a forward frontier. All the troops, two or three divisions at the outside, were already in that theatre, and there were no ships, except local vessels, to carry them to the larger scenes. To get the active, vigorous use of these forces, who otherwise would be mere lookers-on, might inflict grave injury upon the enemy. If Rhodes were taken the whole Ægean could be dominated by our Air Force and direct sea contact established with Turkey. If, on the other hand, Turkey could be persuaded to enter the war, or to strain her neutrality by lending us the airfields we had built for her, we could equally dominate the Ægean and the capture of Rhodes would not be necessary. Either way it would work.

And of course the prize was Turkey. If we could gain Turkey it would be possible without the subtraction of a single man, ship, or aircraft from the main and decisive battles to dominate the Black Sea with submarines and light naval forces, and to give a right hand to Russia and carry supplies to her armies by a route far less costly, far more swift, and far more abundant than either the Arctic or the Persian Gulf.

This was the triple theme which I pressed upon the President and Stalin on every occasion, not hesitating to repeat the arguments remorselessly. I could have gained Stalin, but the President was oppressed by the prejudices of his military advisers and drifted to and fro in the argument, with the result that the whole of these subsidiary but gleaming opportunities were cast aside unused. Our American friends were comforted in their obstinacy by the reflection that 'at any rate we have stopped Churchill entangling us in the Balkans'. No such idea had ever crossed my mind. I regard the failure to use otherwise unemployable forces to bring Turkey into the war and dominate the Ægean as an error in war direction which cannot be excused by the fact that in spite of it victory was won.

*   *   *

Shortly after the President's move into his new quarters in the Soviet Embassy Stalin came to greet him, and they had a friendly talk. According to the Hopkins biography the President informed Stalin of his promise to Chiang Kai-shek of active operations in Burma. Stalin expressed a low opinion of the fighting quality of the Chinese troops. The President 'referred to one of his favourite topics, the education of the peoples of the Far Eastern colonial areas in the arts of self-government. ... He cautioned Stalin against bringing up the problems of India with Churchill, and Stalin agreed that this was undoubtedly a sore subject. Roosevelt said that reform in India should begin from the bottom, and Stalin replied that reform from the bottom would mean revolution.' I passed the morning peacefully in bed nursing my cold and dealing with many telegrams from London.

*   *   *

The first plenary meeting was held at the Soviet Embassy on Sunday, November 28, at 4 p.m. The conference room was spacious and handsome, and we seated ourselves at a large, round table. I had with me Eden, Dill, the three Chiefs of Staff, and Ismay. The President had Harry Hopkins, Admiral Leahy, Admiral King, and two other officers. General Marshall and General Arnold were not present: 'they had misunderstood the time of the meeting,' says Hopkins' biographer, 'and had gone off on a sight-seeing tour round Teheran.' I had my admirable interpreter of the previous year, Major Birse. Pavlov again performed this service for the Soviets, and Mr. Bohlen, a new figure, for the United States. Molotov and Marshal Voroshilov alone accompanied Stalin. He and I sat almost opposite one another. We had agreed beforehand that the President should preside at this first meeting, and Roosevelt consented to do so. He opened the proceedings in a felicitous speech, saying, according to our record, that the Russians, the British, and the Americans were sitting round the table for the first time as members of the same family, with the single purpose of winning the war. No fixed agenda had been drawn up for the meeting, and it was open to anybody to discuss whatever they liked and to leave undiscussed whatever they did not like. Everyone could speak as freely as he wished on the basis of friendship, and nothing would be published.

In my opening remarks I also stressed the importance of the occasion. This meeting, I said, probably represented the greatest concentration of worldly power that had ever been seen in the history of mankind. In our hands lay perhaps the shortening of the war, almost certainly victory, and, beyond any shadow of doubt, the happiness and fortunes of mankind.

Stalin said that he appreciated our references to the friendship of the three Powers. It was indeed true that a great opportunity had been given to them, and he hoped they would make good use of it.

The President then began the discussion with a brief account of the war situation from the American point of view. He first dealt with the Pacific, which had particular importance for the United States, since American forces there were bearing the main load, assisted by Australia, New Zealand, and China. The United States had concentrated in the Pacific the greater part of their Navy and the best part of a million men. The vast extent of that theatre could be gauged by the fact that a supply ship could do only three trips a year. The United States were pursuing a policy of attrition, which up to the present had been successful. It was certain that Japanese ships, both naval and mercantile, were being sunk more rapidly than new construction could replace them. Mr. Roosevelt then explained the plans for the recapture of Northern Burma. Anglo-American forces would co-operate with the Chinese, and would be under the command of Admiral Lord Louis Mountbatten. Plans were also being discussed for an amphibious operation against the Japanese lines of communication from Bangkok. Considerable forces were to be employed, although every effort had been made to keep them down to the minimum required to achieve our essential objectives. Those objectives were to keep China actively in the war, to open the Burma Road, and to establish positions from which Japan could be vanquished with the greatest possible speed, once Germany had collapsed. It was hoped to secure bases in China which would enable Tokyo to be attacked in the coming year.

The President then turned to Europe. There had been many Anglo-American conferences and many plans. A year and a half ago it had been decided to launch an expedition across the English Channel, but owing to transportation and other difficulties it was still impossible to decide a definite date for the operation. An adequate force must be assembled in England, not only for the actual landing, but also for marching inland. The English Channel had proved such a disagreeable body of water that it was impossible to stage an expedition before May 1, 1944. This was the date decided upon at Quebec. He explained that landing-craft were the limiting factor in all landings, and if it were decided to mount a very big expedition in the Mediterranean we should have to give up the cross-Channel operation altogether. If a lesser operation in the Mediterranean were decided upon the delay would amount to one, two, or perhaps three months. Consequently both he and I wished in this military conference to hear from Marshal Stalin and Marshal Voroshilov what action would be of the greatest service to the Soviets. Many plans had been mooted—increasing the strength of our attack in Italy, the Balkans, the Ægean, Turkey, and so forth. The most important task of the Conference would be to decide which of these to adopt. The governing object would be for the Anglo-American armies to draw the greatest weight off the Soviet forces.

*   *   *

Stalin, speaking next, welcomed the successes of the United States in the Pacific, but said that the Soviets could not join in the struggle against Japan at the present time, since practically all their forces were required against Germany. The Soviet forces in the Far East were more or less sufficient for defence, but they would have to be at least trebled in order to attack. The moment for joining their friends in this theatre would be the moment of Germany's collapse: then they would march together.

As for Europe, Stalin said that he would like to begin with a few words about the Soviet experiences in the conduct of the war. Their attack in July had been anticipated by the Germans; but when sufficient troops and equipment had been collected the Soviets had found it comparatively easy to pass to the offensive. He frankly admitted that they had not expected the successes which were gained in July, August, and September. The Germans had proved weaker than had been thought.

He then gave details of the latest situation on the Soviet front. On some of the sectors they had been slowed down, on others they had stopped altogether, while in the Ukraine, west and south of Kiev, the initiative had passed to the Germans within the last three weeks. The Germans had recaptured Jitomir, and would probably recapture Korosten. Their objective was the recapture of Kiev. Nevertheless in the main the initiative still rested with the Soviet armies.

He had been asked, he said, how the Anglo-American forces could best help Russia. The Soviet Government had always felt that the Italian campaign had been of great value to the Allied cause in that it opened the Mediterranean. But Italy was not a suitable jumping-off ground for the invasion of Germany. The Alps stood between. Therefore nothing was to be gained by concentrating large numbers of troops in Italy for the invasion of Germany. Turkey would be a better point of entry than Italy ; but it was a long way from the heart of Germany. He believed that North or North-West France was the place for Anglo-American forces to attack, though it was of course true that the Germans there would resist desperately.

*   *   *

Though invited to speak earlier, I had hitherto said nothing. I now stated the British position.

It had long been agreed, I said, with the United States that we should invade North or North-West France across the Channel. The enterprise was absorbing most of our preparations and resources. A long dissertation on facts and figures would be necessary to show why it had been impossible to carry out this operation in 1943, but we were resolved to do it in 1944. Instead of the cross-Channel invasion of 1943 a series of operations had been launched in the Mediterranean. This had been done with full recognition that they were of a secondary character ; but we had felt that they were the best contribution we could make in 1943, having regard to our resources and to transportation. The British and American Governments had now set themselves the task of carrying out a cross-Channel invasion in the late spring or summer of 1944. The forces which could be accumulated by that time amounted to about sixteen British and nineteen United States divisions—a total of thirty-five divisions. These divisions were much stronger both in numbers and equipment than the German divisions.

Stalin here observed that he never regarded the operations in the Mediterranean as being of a secondary character. They were of the first importance, but not from the point of view of invading Germany.

I replied that none the less the President and I had both re-garded them as stepping-stones to the decisive cross-Channel operation. Having regard to the British forces engaged in the Mediterranean and India, the sixteen British divisions which were being put into the cross-Channel operation were the most that could be provided by a country with a total population of forty-five millions. These divisions could be kept up to strength in the line, but the number could not be increased. It would have to be left to the United States, who had a large number of reserve divisions, to broaden the front and nourish the battle. The early spring and summer of 1944 were still six months away however, and the President and I had been asking our-selves what could be done during these six months with the resources available in the Mediterranean that would best take the weight off Russia, without postponing 'Overlord' for more than perhaps a month or two. Seven of the best Anglo-American divisions and a certain number of landing-craft had already been, or were being, moved from the Mediterranean to the United Kingdom. The result had been a weakening of effort on the Italian front. The weather had been bad, and it had not yet been possible to take Rome; but it was hoped to take it by January; and General Alexander, who, under General Eisen-hower, was commanding the Fifteenth Army Group in Italy, aimed not only at taking Rome, but at destroying or capturing ten or eleven German divisions.

I explained that we had not contemplated going into the broad part of the leg of Italy, still less invading Germany across the Alps. The general plan was first to capture Rome and seize the airfields north of it, which would enable us to bomb Southern Germany, and then to establish ourselves on a line towards Pisa–Rimini. After that the possibility of establishing a Third Front in conformity with, but not in substitution for, the cross-Channel operation would have to be planned. One of the pos-sibilities was to move into Southern France, and the second, suggested by the President, was to move from the head of the Adriatic north-east towards the Danube.

Meanwhile what should be done in the next six months? There was much to be said for supporting Tito, who was holding a number of German divisions and doing much more for the Allied cause than the Chetniks under Mihailović. There would clearly be great advantage in supporting him with supplies and guerrilla activities, and the Balkan theatre was one of the areas where we could stretch the enemy to the utmost. This brought us to the biggest problem which would have to be decided after consideration by the military staffs, namely, how to bring Turkey into the war and open communications through the Ægean to the Dardanelles and thence to the Black Sea. Once Turkey was in the war and we had the use of her air bases we could capture the islands in the Ægean with comparatively small forces, say two or three divisions, and the air forces already in that theatre. If we had access to the Black Sea ports convoys could be run continuously. At present we had had to limit ourselves to four convoys by the Northern route, as the escorts were required for 'Overlord'; but once the Dardanelles were open the escort vessels already in the Mediterranean could keep up a ceaseless flow of supplies to the Soviet Black Sea ports.

How could we persuade Turkey to come into the war? If she came in, what should she be asked to do? Should she merely give us her bases, or should she attack Bulgaria and declare war on Germany? Should she move forward or should she stay on the Thracian frontier? What would be the effect on Bulgaria, who owed a profound debt to Russia for rescuing her in former days from the Turkish yoke? How would Roumania react? They were already putting out genuine peace-feelers for unconditional surrender. Then there was Hungary. Which way would she go? There might well be a political landslide among the satellite States which would enable the Greeks to revolt and hustle the Germans out of Greece. All these were questions on which the Soviets had a special point of view and special knowledge. It would be invaluable to know what they thought about it all. Would these plans in the Eastern Mediterranean be of sufficient interest to the Soviet Government to make them wish us to go ahead, even if it meant a delay of one to two months from May 1 in launching 'Overlord'? The British and American Governments had deliberately kept their minds open on the subject until they knew what the Soviet Government felt about these problems.

The President here reminded me of the further project of moving up to the Northern Adriatic and then north-east to the Danube. I agreed and said that once we had taken Rome and destroyed the German armies south of the Apennines in the narrow part of Italy the Anglo-American armies would advance far enough to make contact with the enemy. We could then hold the line with the minimum forces and keep the option to strike with the remainder either in the South of France, or, in accordance with the President's idea, north-east from the head of the Adriatic. Neither of these problems had been considered in detail, but if Stalin should look upon them with favour a technical sub-committee could be set up to examine ways and means and facts and figures and to report to the Conference.

The discussion now came to a crucial point. The record says:

Marshal Stalin addressed the following questions to the Prime Minister:

Question: 'Am I right in thinking that the invasion of France is to be undertaken by thirty-five divisions?'

Answer: 'Yes. Particularly strong divisions.'

Question: 'Is it intended that this operation should be carried out by the forces now in Italy?'

Answer: 'No. Seven divisions have already been, or are in process of being, withdrawn from Italy and North Africa, to take part in "Overlord". These seven divisions are required to make up the thirty-five divisions mentioned in your first question. After they have been withdrawn about twenty-two divisions will be left in the Mediterranean for Italy or other objectives. Some of these could be used either for an operation against Southern France or for moving from the head of the Adriatic towards the Danube. Both these operations will be timed in conformity with "Overlord". Meanwhile it should not be difficult to spare two or three divisions to take the islands in the Ægean.'

*   *   *

I then explained that it would be quite impossible to transfer any divisions from the Mediterranean to the United Kingdom over and above the seven mentioned. Shipping would not run to it. Thirty-five Anglo-American divisions would be assembled in the United Kingdom for the initial assault. Thereafter the British could do no more than maintain in Northern France their sixteen divisions, but the United States would continue to pump in further troops until the Expeditionary Force in Northern France amounted all told to fifty or sixty divisions. Both the British and American divisions, if line of communication troops, corps troops, flak, etc., were taken into account, amounted gross to about 40,000 men each. There were already very considerable Anglo-American air forces in the United Kingdom, but even so the United States Air Force was going to be doubled, or perhaps trebled, in the next six months. Thus there would be a tremendous weight of air-power concentrated in an area from which the enemy could be easily reached. All the forces and equipment were being built up according to a prearranged schedule, which would be shown to the Soviet authorities if they so desired.

Stalin asked me about the operation against the South of France. I said it had not yet been planned in detail, but the idea was that it might be done in conformity or simultaneously with 'Overlord'. The assault force would consist of troops now in Italy. I added that it would also be necessary to examine the President's idea of moving north-east from the head of the Adriatic.

Stalin next asked how many Anglo-American troops would have to be allotted if Turkey came into the war.

Observing that I spoke for myself alone, I said that two or three divisions at the most would be required to take the islands in the Ægean, and that, in addition, we should probably have to give Turkey about twenty squadrons of air forces and several regiments of flak to defend herself. Both the air forces and the flak could be provided without prejudice to other operations.

Stalin thought it would be a mistake to send part of our forces to Turkey and elsewhere and part to Southern France. The best course would be to make 'Overlord' the basic operation for 1944, and, once Rome had been captured, to send all available forces in Italy to Southern France. These forces could then join hands with the 'Overlord' forces when the invasion was launched. France was the weakest spot on the German front. He did not himself expect Turkey to agree to enter the war.

I asked whether the Soviet Government was not very anxious to get Turkey into the war. We had tried once and had failed, but was it not intended that we should renew the effort?

'I am all in favour of trying again,' said Stalin. 'We ought to take them by the scruff of the neck if necessary.'

I then said that I entirely agreed with Marshal Stalin's observations about the undesirability of dispersion, but all that I suggested was that a handful of divisions—say two or three—would be very well employed in making contact with Turkey, while the air forces which would come into play were those which were already defending Egypt and would merely be advancing their line. Thus there was no appreciable diversion of effort, either from the Italian front or from 'Overlord'.

Stalin thought it would be well worth while to take the islands if this could be done with three or four divisions.

What I particularly dreaded, I said, was an interval of six months' inactivity between the capture of Rome and 'Overlord'. We ought to be fighting the enemy all the time, and the operations which I had suggested, although admittedly of a secondary character, should be the subject of careful consideration.

Stalin repeated that 'Overlord' was a very serious operation, and that it was better to help it by invading the South of France. He would even prefer to assume a defensive rôle in Italy and forgo the capture of Rome for the present if this would admit the invasion of Southern France by, say, ten divisions. Two months later 'Overlord' would follow, and the two invasions could then join hands.

I replied that we should be no stronger if we pulled out of the advance on Rome, and once we had taken the city we should be in a much stronger position through having destroyed or badly mutilated ten or eleven German divisions. Moreover, we required the airfields north of Rome for the bombing of Germany. It would be impossible for us to forgo the capture of Rome. To do so would be regarded on all sides as a crushing defeat, and the British Parliament would not tolerate the idea for a moment.

* * *

The President now suggested that the timing of operations required the most careful consideration. Any operation undertaken in the Eastern Mediterranean would probably put off 'Overlord' until June or July. He himself was opposed to such a delay if it could possibly be avoided. He therefore suggested that the military experts should examine the possibility of operations against Southern France on the timing put forward by Stalin, *i.e.*, two months before 'Overlord', the governing factor being that 'Overlord' should be launched at the prescribed time.

Stalin said that the experience gained by the Soviets during the last two years of fighting was that a big offensive, if undertaken from only one direction, rarely yielded results. The better course was to launch offensives from two or more directions simultaneously. This compelled the enemy to disperse his forces and at the same time gave an opportunity for the attacks, provided they were close enough to each other, to make contact and increase the power of the offensive as a whole. He suggested that this principle might well be applied to the problem under discussion.

I did not disagree in principle with these views. The suggestions that I had made for minor help to Yugoslavia and Turkey did not, I said, conflict in any way with that general conception. At the same time, I wished it to be placed on record that I could not in any circumstances agree to sacrifice the activities of the armies in the Mediterranean, which included twenty British and British-controlled divisions, merely in order to keep the exact date of May 1 for 'Overlord'. If Turkey refused to come into the war it could not be helped. I earnestly hoped that I should not be asked to agree to any such rigid timing of operations as the President had suggested. Would it not be right for the Conference to meditate over all that had been said and to continue their discussions on the following day? The President agreed, and suggested that the Staffs should set to work the following morning.

Stalin then observed that he had not expected that military questions would be discussed at the Conference, and he had not brought his military experts with him. Nevertheless Marshal Voroshilov would do his best.

I asked how it was proposed to discuss the question of Turkey. The problem was probably as much political as military. The questions to which the Conference should address itself were as follows:

(a) What do we want Turkey to do?
(b) What are we prepared to offer her to bring her into the war?
(c) What will be the consequences of any such offer?

Stalin agreed. Turkey was an ally of England and on terms of friendship with the United States. It was for them to persuade her to take the proper course. When I said that Turkey would be mad if she declined Russia's invitation to come in on the winning side, and at the same time lost the sympathy of Great Britain, Stalin rejoined that a number of people preferred to be mad, and all neutrals regarded those who were waging war as fools to fight when they might be doing nothing.

I concluded the meeting by saying that, although we were all great friends, it would be idle for us to delude ourselves that we saw eye to eye on all matters. Time and patience were necessary.

Here ended our first talk.

CHAPTER 3

Conversations and Conferences

The formal conferences were interspersed with what may be thought to be even more important talks between Roosevelt, Stalin, and myself at luncheons and dinners. Here there were very few things that could not be said and received in good-humour. On Sunday night the 28th the President was our host for dinner. We were a party of ten or eleven, including the interpreters, and conversation soon became general and serious.

After dinner on this first evening, when we were strolling about the room, I led Stalin to a sofa and suggested that we talk for a little on what was to happen after the war was won. He assented, and we sat down. Eden joined us. 'Let us,' said the Marshal, 'first consider the worst that might happen.' He thought that Germany had every possibility of recovering from this war, and might start on a new one within a comparatively short time. He feared the revival of German nationalism. After Versailles peace had seemed assured, but Germany had recovered very quickly. We must therefore establish a strong body to prevent Germany starting a new war. He was convinced that she would recover. When I asked, 'How soon?' he replied, 'Within fifteen to twenty years.' I said that the world must be made safe for at least fifty years. If it was only for fifteen to twenty years then we should have betrayed our soldiers.

Stalin thought we should consider restraints on Germany's

manufacturing capacity. The Germans were an able people, very industrious and resourceful, and they would recover quickly. I replied that there would have to be certain measures of control. I would forbid them all aviation, civil and military, and I would forbid the General Staff system. 'Would you,' asked Stalin, 'also forbid the existence of watchmakers' and furniture factories for making parts of shells? The Germans produced toy rifles which were used for teaching hundreds of thousands of men how to shoot.'

'Nothing,' I said, 'is final. The world rolls on. We have now learnt something. Our duty is to make the world safe for at least fifty years by German disarmament, by preventing rearmament, by supervision of German factories, by forbidding all aviation, and by territorial changes of a far-reaching character. It all comes back to the question whether Great Britain, the United States, and the U.S.S.R. can keep a close friendship and supervise Germany in their mutual interest. We ought not to be afraid to give orders as soon as we see any danger.'

'There was control after the last war,' said Stalin, 'but it failed.'

'We were inexperienced then,' I replied. 'The last war was not to the same extent a national war, and Russia was not a party at the Peace Conference. It will be different this time.' I had a feeling that Prussia should be isolated and reduced, that Bavaria, Austria, and Hungary might form a broad, peaceful, unaggressive confederation. I thought Prussia should be dealt with more sternly than the other parts of the Reich, which might thus be influenced against throwing in their lot with her. It must be remembered that these were war-time moods.

'All very good, but insufficient,' was Stalin's comment.

Russia, I continued, would have her Army, Great Britain and the United States their Navies and Air Forces. In addition, all three Powers would have their other resources. All would be strongly armed, and must not assume any obligation to disarm. 'We are the trustees for the peace of the world. If we fail there will be perhaps a hundred years of chaos. If we are strong we can carry out our trusteeship. There is more,' I went on, 'than merely keeping the peace. The three Powers should guide the future of the world. I do not want to enforce any system on other nations. I ask for freedom and for the right of all nations to develop as they like. We three must remain friends in order to ensure happy homes in all countries.'

Stalin asked again what was to happen to Germany.

I replied that I was not against the toilers in Germany, but only against the leaders and against dangerous combinations. He said that there were many toilers in the German divisions who fought under orders. When he asked German prisoners who came from the labouring classes (such is the record, but he probably meant 'Communist Party') why they fought for Hitler they replied that they were carrying out orders. He shot such prisoners.

* * *

I suggested that we should discuss the Polish question. He agreed and invited me to begin. I said that we had declared war on account of Poland. Poland was therefore important to us. Nothing was more important than the security of the Russian western frontier. But I had given no pledges about frontiers. I wanted heart-to-heart talks with the Russians about this. When Marshal Stalin felt like telling us what he thought about it the matter could be discussed and we could reach some agreement, and the Marshal should tell me what was necessary for the defence of the western frontiers of Russia. After this war in Europe, which might end in 1944, the Soviet Union would be overwhelmingly strong and Russia would have a great responsibility in any decision she took with regard to Poland. Personally I thought Poland might move westwards, like soldiers taking two steps 'left close'. If Poland trod on some German toes that could not be helped, but there must be a strong Poland. Poland was an instrument needed in the orchestra of Europe.

Stalin said the Polish people had their culture and their language, which must exist. They could not be extirpated.

'Are we to try,' I asked, 'to draw frontier lines?'

'Yes.'

'I have no power from Parliament, nor, I believe, has the President, to define any frontier lines. But we might now, in Teheran, see if the three heads of Governments, working in agreement, could form some sort of policy which we could recommend to the Poles and advise them to accept.'

We agreed to look at the problem. Stalin asked whether it would be without Polish participation. I said 'Yes', and that when this was all informally agreed between ourselves we could go to the Poles later. Mr. Eden here remarked that he had been much struck by Stalin's statement that afternoon that the Poles could go as far west as the Oder. He saw hope in that and was much encouraged. Stalin asked whether we thought he was going to swallow Poland up. Eden said he did not know how much the Russians were going to eat. How much would they leave undigested? Stalin said the Russians did not want anything belonging to other people, although they might have a bite at Germany. Eden said that what Poland lost in the east she might gain in the west. Stalin replied that possibly she might, but he did not know. I then demonstrated with the help of three matches my idea of Poland moving westwards. This pleased Stalin, and on this note our group parted for the moment.

* * *

The morning of the 29th was occupied by a conference of the British, Soviet, and American military chiefs. As I knew that Stalin and Roosevelt had already had a private conversation, and were of course staying at the same Embassy, I suggested that the President and I might lunch together before the second plenary meeting that afternoon. Roosevelt however declined, and sent Harriman to me to explain that he did not want Stalin to know that he and I were meeting privately. I was surprised at this, for I thought we all three should treat each other with equal confidence. The President after luncheon had a further interview with Stalin and Molotov, at which many important matters were discussed, including particularly Mr. Roosevelt's plan for the government of the post-war world. This should be carried out by the 'Four Policemen', namely, the U.S.S.R., the United States, Great Britain, and China. Stalin did not react favourably to this. He said the 'Four Policemen' would not be welcomed by the small nations of Europe. He did not believe that China would be very powerful when the war ended, and even if she were European States would resent having China as an enforcement authority for themselves. In this the Soviet leader certainly showed himself more prescient and possessed of a truer sense of values than the President. When Stalin proposed as an alternative that there should be one committee for Europe and another for the Far East—the European committee to consist of Britain, Russia, the United States, and possibly one other European nation—the President replied that this was somewhat similar to my idea of regional committees, one for Europe, one for the Far East, and one for the Americas. He does not seem to have made it clear that I also contemplated a Supreme United Nations Council, of which the three regional committees would be the components. As I was not informed till much later of what had taken place I was not able to correct this erroneous presentation.

*   *   *

Before our second plenary session began at four o'clock I presented, by the King's command, the Sword of Honour which His Majesty had had specially designed and wrought to commemorate the glorious defence of Stalingrad. The large outer hall was filled with Russian officers and soldiers. When, after a few sentences of explanation, I handed the splendid weapon to Marshal Stalin he raised it in a most impressive gesture to his lips and kissed the scabbard. He then passed it to Voroshilov, who dropped it. It was carried from the room in great solemnity, escorted by a Russian guard of honour. As this procession moved away I saw the President sitting at the side of the room, obviously stirred by the ceremony. We then moved to the conference chamber and took our seats again at the round table, this time with all the Chiefs of Staff, who were now to report the result of their morning's labours.

The C.I.G.S. said that they had surveyed various operations, and they realised that unless something was done in the Mediterranean between now and the launching of 'Overlord' the Germans would be able to transfer troops from Italy to Russia or Northern France. They had considered carrying the advance up the leg of the Italian peninsula, strengthening the Partisans in Yugoslavia so that they could hold German divisions in the Balkans, and getting Turkey into the war. They had also discussed a landing in Southern France to coincide with 'Overlord'. Portal had reviewed our bombing offensive and Marshall the United States build-up in Britain.

General Marshall said that the problem confronting the Western Allies in Europe was not one of troops or material, but of ships and landing-craft and getting fighter airfields close enough to the scene of operations. Landing-craft were particularly short, and the most vital need was for the L.S.T.s, which carried forty tanks apiece. So far as 'Overlord' was concerned, the flow of troops and supplies was proceeding according to schedule. The variable and questionable factor in almost every one of the problems facing the Allies was landing-craft. The building programme had been accelerated both in the United Kingdom and in the United States, with two objects: first, to in-

crease the scale of the initial assault for 'Overlord', and, secondly, to enable us to undertake the operations which we
thought right in the Mediterranean.

* * *

Stalin then put the crucial question, 'Who will command
"Overlord"?' The President replied that this had not yet been
decided. Stalin said bluntly that the operation would come to
nought unless one man was placed in charge of all the preparations for it. Roosevelt explained that this had already been
done. General Morgan, a British officer, had been given a combined Anglo-American staff and had been planning the operation
for some considerable time. Everything, in fact, had already
been decided, except the name of the Supreme Commander.
Stalin declared it essential that a man should be appointed at
once to be responsible not only for the planning, but also for the
execution. Otherwise, although General Morgan might say that
everything was ready, the Supreme Commander, when appointed,
might have very different ideas and wish to alter everything.

I said that General Morgan had been appointed some months
before by the Combined Chiefs of Staff, with the approval of the
President and myself, to be Chief Staff Officer to the Supreme
Commander (Designate). His Majesty's Government had expressed their willingness to serve under a United States Commander, since the United States would be responsible for the
build-up of the invasion force and would have the proponder-
ance in numbers. In the Mediterranean, on the other hand,
practically all the naval forces were British and we had also a
considerable preponderance in Army forces. We therefore felt
that the command of this theatre should properly go to the
British. I suggested that the appointment of a Supreme Commander was more appropriate for discussion by the three heads
of Governments than in a somewhat large conference. Stalin
said that the Soviet Government laid no claim to a voice in the
appointment. They merely wanted to know who it would be.
It was vital that this appointment should be made as soon as
possible and that the general chosen should be responsible not
only for the preparation of the plan, but also for carrying it out.
I agreed that the decision who was to command 'Overlord' was
one of the most important points to be dealt with, and said it
would be settled within the next fortnight at latest.

* * *

I then set out the British case. I said that I was somewhat concerned at the number and complexity of the problems which confronted us. The Conference represented some twelve to fourteen hundred millions of the human race, who depended upon our reaching right conclusions. It was therefore imperative that we should not separate until the great military, political, and moral problems confronting us had been firmly resolved ; but I proposed to confine myself to a few specific points which might be studied by a military sub-committee.

First, what help could be given to 'Overlord' by the large forces already assembled in the Mediterranean? In particular, what was the scale of operations which could be launched against Southern France by the troops in Italy? This project had been mentioned by both the President and Stalin, but it had not yet been studied in sufficient detail for anyone to express a final view. Stalin had very rightly stressed the value of pincers opera-tions, but it was obviously useless to attack with a small force which could be annihilated before the main body came on the scene. Speaking entirely for myself, I said I thought that suffi-cient landing-craft to transport at least two divisions should be retained in the Mediterranean. With a landing-craft force of this size we could help forward the advance up the leg of Italy by seaborne outflanking movements, and thus avoid the slow, labori-ous methods of frontal attack. Secondly, these landing-craft would enable us to take Rhodes and open the Ægean simultane-ously with the entry of Turkey into the war. This same force of landing-craft would enable us five or six months hence to make a descent upon Southern France in concert with 'Overlord'.

Clearly, all these operations would require the most careful timing and study, but there seemed to be a good hope that all those I had mentioned could be carried through. On the other hand, it was obvious that landing-craft sufficient to transport two divisions could not be kept in the Mediterranean without setting back the date of 'Overlord' for perhaps six to eight weeks, or alternatively, without recalling from the East the assault craft and ships which had been sent there for operations against the Japanese. This placed us in a dilemma. It was a case of balancing one problem against the other. I said I should be grateful to hear the views of Marshal Stalin and Marshal Voro-shilov on these points, since their military record inspired their British Allies with so much admiration and respect.

The second main point was the question of Yugoslavia and

the Dalmatian coast. No fewer than twenty-one German divisions were held in the Balkans by Partisan forces. There were, in addition, nine Bulgarian divisions in Greece and Yugoslavia. Thus thirty enemy divisions were being contained by these gallant guerrillas. Surely therefore the Balkan theatre was one of the areas in which we could stretch the enemy to the utmost and give ourselves relief in the heavy battles which lay ahead. We ourselves had no ambitions in the Balkans. All we wanted to do was to nail down these thirty hostile divisions. M. Molotov, Mr. Eden, and a representative of the President should meet together and advise the Conference on all the political points at issue. For example, did our Soviet friends and Allies see any political difficulty in the course advocated? If so, what? We were determined to work harmoniously with them. From the military point of view there was no question of using large forces in this area. All that was required was to help the Partisans with supplies and equipment and Commando operations.

The third and last point was Turkey. Great Britain was Turkey's ally, and had accepted the task of trying to persuade or induce Turkey to enter the war before Christmas. If the President was prepared to come in at this point and take the lead the British Government would be entirely happy to leave it to him. I said I was prepared, on behalf of His Majesty's Government, to give an assurance that Great Britain would go a long way towards bringing Turkey into the war. From the military point of view the entry of Turkey into the war would not mean the diversion of more than two or three Allied divisions at most.

I then asked what the Soviet Government felt about Bulgaria. Would they be prepared to tell Bulgaria that if Turkey found herself at war with Germany and Bulgaria were to attack Turkey the Soviets would at once regard Bulgaria as an enemy? I suggested that Molotov and Eden and a representative of the President might meet to advise the Conference on the best way of getting Turkey into the war. If we could only bring this about it would be a terrible blow to Germany. Bulgaria would be weakened, Roumania was already trying desperately hard to surrender unconditionally, and the effects on Hungary would be considerable. The object of all the operations in the Mediterranean which I had contemplated was to take the weight off Russia and to give the best possible chance to 'Overlord'.

*   *   *

I had spoken for about ten minutes. There was a pause. Stalin then said: 'The Soviet Government will consider themselves at war with Bulgaria if, as a result of Turkey's entry into the war, Bulgaria threatens Turkey.' I thanked him for this assurance, and inquired whether I could inform the Turks. Stalin said that he was quite agreeable to this. He then proceeded to give his own ideas on the Balkans. He said there seemed to be no difference of opinion, and he was all in favour of help being given to the Partisans. But he added bluntly that the entry of Turkey into the war, the support of Yugoslavia, and the capture of Rome were, to the Russian way of thinking, relatively unimportant. If the Conference had been convened to discuss military matters 'Overlord' must come first.

If a military commission was to be set up as had been suggested it would clearly have to be given precise instructions as to the task it was required to perform. The Russians needed help, and urgent help, in their great struggle against the German Army. This could best be given by the early and vigorous prosecution of Operation 'Overlord'. There were three main matters to be decided. First, the date. This should be some time in May and no later. Secondly, it should be supported by a landing in the South of France. If this could be carried out two or three months before 'Overlord' so much the better, but, if not, it might coincide with it, and, if it could not coincide, it would still help if it took place a little after it. The assault on the South of France as a supporting operation would be definitely helpful to 'Overlord'. The capture of Rome and other operations in the Mediterranean could only be regarded as diversions.

The third matter to be decided was the appointment of a Commander-in-Chief for 'Overlord'. He said he would like to see this made before the Conference ended, or at least within a week thereafter. Preparations for 'Overlord' could not be carried on successfully unless there was a Supreme Commander. Choosing the man was of course a matter for the British and American Governments, but the Soviet Government would be glad to know his name.

* * *

The President said that we were all agreed on the importance of 'Overlord', but not about its date. If 'Overlord' was to be carried out during May one at least of the Mediterranean operations would have to go by the board. If however landing-craft and other equipment were retained in the Mediterranean, then it would have to be postponed till June or July. There were obvious dangers in delaying 'Overlord'. If we launched expeditions in the Eastern Mediterranean, even with only two or three divisons, there was always the possibility of their developing into bigger commitments involving the dispatch of larger forces. If this happened even the later date of 'Overlord' would be prejudiced.

Mr. Roosevelt then referred to my point about the thirty German and Bulgarian divisions which were contained in the Balkans. He recommended that we should intensify the process of keeping them pinned down by Commando forces. It was important to hold them in this area and prevent them from doing harm elsewhere. There was clearly general agreement that Tito should be supported, but that this should be done without subtracting from the 'Overlord' operation.

Stalin said that, according to his information, the Germans had eight divisions in Yugoslavia, five in Greece, and three in Bulgaria, and twenty-five divisions in France. He was not prepared to agree to any delay in 'Overlord' beyond the month of May.

I said I could not agree to give any such undertaking. Nevertheless I did not think there was any fundamental divergence in the views so far expressed. I was willing to do everything in the power of His Majesty's Government to begin 'Overlord' at the earliest possible moment, but I did not consider that the very great possibilities in the Mediterranean should be ruthlessly sacrificed and cast aside as if they were of no value, merely to save a month or so in the launching of 'Overlord'. There was a large British army in the Mediterranean, and I could not agree that it should stand idle for nearly six months. It should be fighting the enemy with the greatest vigour alongside its American Allies. I had every hope that, together, British and American forces would destroy a large force of Germans in Italy, and, having advanced northward of Rome, would hold a considerable German army on the Italian front. To be quiescent in Italy and remain inert for nearly six months would be an improper use of our forces and lay us open to the reproach that the Russians were bearing almost the entire burden of the land war.

Stalin said that he had never contemplated a complete cessation of all operations in Italy during the winter.

I explained that if landing-craft were taken away from the

Mediterranean this would mean a definite curtailment of our operations there. I reminded Stalin of the three conditions on which the success of 'Overlord' depended. First, there must be a satisfactory reduction in the strength of the German fighter force in North-West Europe between now and the assault. Secondly, German reserves in France and the Low Countries must not be more on the day of the assault than about twelve full-strength first-quality mobile divisions. Thirdly, it must not be possible for the Germans to transfer from other fronts more than fifteen first-quality divisions during the first sixty days of the operation. To obtain these conditions we should have to hold as many Germans as possible in Italy and Yugoslavia. If Turkey entered the war, this would be an added help, but not an essential condition. The Germans now in Italy had for the most part come from France. If we slackened off our pressure in Italy they would go back again. We must continue to engage the enemy on the only front where at present we could fight them. If we engaged them as fiercely as possible during the winter months in the Mediterranean this would make the best possible contribution towards creating the conditions needed for a successful 'Overlord'.

Stalin asked what would happen if there were thirteen or fourteen mobile German divisions in France and more than fifteen available from other fronts. Would this rule out 'Overlord'?

I said, 'No, certainly not.'

*   *   *

I then turned the discussion back to Turkey. We had agreed to press her to enter the war by the end of the year. If she did, the only military operations needed would be to establish our planes on the Turkish airfields in Anatolia and capture the island of Rhodes. One assault division and some garrison troops would suffice. Once in possession of Rhodes and the Turkish air bases we could starve out all the other Ægean islands at our leisure. These operations would not involve us in an unlimited liability, and could be regarded as a commitment of a strictly limited character. If our efforts to bring Turkey in were unsuccessful, that would be the end of the matter. Nevertheless, failure to bring Turkey in would also be a relief to the Germans. There was a further point about Turkey. If she came in and we captured Rhodes and subsequently turned the Germans out of the other Ægean islands our troops and air forces in Egypt could all move forward into action to the northward instead of remaining in their present defensive *rôle*.

The issue of Turkey should not be lightly turned aside. As the President and General Marshall had stated, the scale, nature, and timing of our operations all turned upon the availability of landing-craft and transportation of forces across the sea. I said I was prepared to go into this question at any time and at any length and in any detail, but if the small number of landing-craft involved could not be retained in the Mediterranean or found from some other theatre no operations on any scale would be possible in the Mediterranean area, and this ban included an assault on the South of France. These arguments should be very carefully weighed before decisions were taken. I told Stalin that I agreed with him that a definite reference should be given to the Technical Military Committee, and I suggested that the terms of reference should be drawn up severally by the heads of the three Governments.

Stalin said that, on thinking it over, he did not feel that a Military Committee was necessary. In order to take decisions it was not necessary to go into detail. The issues at stake were the date of 'Overlord', the appointment of the Commander-in-Chief, and whether any supporting operations could be carried out in the South of France. All this had to be decided by the plenary Conference. Nor did he see any necessity for a Committee of the Foreign Secretaries. The appointment of these committees would delay the completion of the Conference, and he, for his part, could not extend his visit to Teheran beyond December 1, or at the latest December 2.

The President said that he had drawn up tentative terms of reference in simple form for the Military Committee, if it was decided that this body should get to work. The terms were in two sentences, namely: 'Paragraph 1: The Committee of three Staffs will assume that Operation "Overlord" is the dominating operation in 1944. Paragraph 2: The Committee will make recommendations as to subsidiary operations to be carried out, taking into most careful account any delay on Operation "Overlord".' This was agreed.

Stalin said that the Soviet Government was vitally concerned with the date of 'Overlord', particularly because of the need for co-ordinating operations on the Russian front. The President observed that the 'Overlord' date had been fixed at the Quebec

Conference, and it was only the important developments which had occurred since then that had caused any change to be contemplated.

Before we separated Stalin looked at me across the table and said, 'I wish to pose a very direct question to the Prime Minister about "Overlord". Do the Prime Minister and the British Staff really believe in "Overlord"?' I replied, 'Provided the conditions previously stated for "Overlord" are established when the time comes, it will be our stern duty to hurl across the Channel against the Germans every sinew of our strength.' On this we separated.

*　　　*　　　*

Stalin was our host at dinner. The company was strictly limited—Stalin and Molotov, the President, Hopkins, Harriman, and Clark Kerr, myself and Eden, and our interpreters. After the labours of the Conference there was a good deal of gaiety, and many toasts were proposed. Presently Elliott Roosevelt, who had flown out to join his father, appeared at the door and somebody beckoned him to come in. He therefore took his seat at the table. He even intervened in the conversation, and has since given a highly coloured and extremely misleading account of what he heard. Stalin, as Hopkins recounts, indulged in a great deal of 'teasing' of me, which I did not at all resent until the Marshal entered in a genial manner upon a serious and even deadly aspect of the punishment to be inflicted upon the Germans. The German General Staff, he said, must be liquidated. The whole force of Hitler's mighty armies depended upon about fifty thousand officers and technicians. If these were rounded up and shot at the end of the war German military strength would be extirpated. On this I thought it right to say, 'The British Parliament and public will never tolerate mass executions. Even if in war passion they allowed them to begin they would turn violently against those responsible after the first butchery had taken place. The Soviets must be under no delusion on this point.'

Stalin however, perhaps only in mischief, pursued the subject. 'Fifty thousand,' he said, 'must be shot.' I was deeply angered. 'I would rather,' I said, 'be taken out into the garden here and now and be shot myself than sully my own and my country's honour by such infamy.'

At this point the President intervened. He had a compromise to propose. Not fifty thousand should be shot, but only forty-nine thousand. By this he hoped, no doubt, to reduce the whole matter to ridicule. Eden also made signs and gestures intended to reassure me that it was all a joke. But now Elliott Roosevelt rose in his place at the end of the table and made a speech, saying how cordially he agreed with Marshal Stalin's plan and how sure he was that the United States Army would support it. At this intrusion I got up and left the table, walking off into the next room which was in semi-darkness. I had not been there a minute before hands were clapped upon my shoulders from behind, and there was Stalin, with Molotov at his side, both grinning broadly, and eagerly declaring that they were only playing, and that nothing of a serious character had entered their heads. Stalin has a very captivating manner when he chooses to use it, and I never saw him do so to such an extent as at this moment. Although I was not then, and am not now, fully convinced that all was chaff and there was no serious intent lurking behind, I consented to return, and the rest of the evening passed pleasantly.

CHAPTER 4

Teheran: The Crux

My Sixty-ninth Birthday – I See Stalin Alone – Earnestness of Our Preparations for 'Overlord' – The Effect in the Mediterranean – The Supreme Command – Everything Turns on Landing-craft – The Forces Gathered for 'Overlord' – A Great Battle impending in Italy – Stalin Emphasises the Need for 'Overlord' – He Offers a Russian Offensive in May or June – The President's Luncheon for 'Three Only' – Russia's Claim to Warm-Water Ports – The Third Plenary Session, November 30 – The Main Military Decisions Taken – A Communiqué Agreed – Dinner at the British Legation – Compliments All Round and Many Speeches – General Brooke's Rejoinder to Stalin.

November 30 was for me a crowded and memorable day. It was my sixty-ninth birthday, and was passed almost entirely in transacting some of the most important business with which I have ever been concerned. The fact that the President was in private contact with Marshal Stalin and dwelling at the Soviet Embassy, and that he had avoided ever seeing me alone since we left Cairo, in spite of our hitherto intimate relations and the way in which our vital affairs were interwoven, led me to seek a direct personal interview with Stalin. I felt that the Russian leader was not deriving a true impression of the British attitude. The false idea was forming in his mind that, to put it shortly, 'Churchill and the British Staffs mean to stop "Overlord" if they can, because they want to invade the Balkans instead.' It was my duty to remove this double misconception.

The exact date of 'Overlord' depended upon the movements of a comparatively small number of landing-craft. These landing-craft were not required for any operation in the Balkans. The President had committed us to an operation in the Bay of Bengal. If this were cancelled there would be enough landing-craft for all I wanted, namely, the amphibious power to land against opposition two divisions at a time on the coasts of Italy or Southern France, and also to carry out 'Overlord' as planned in May. I had agreed with the President that May should be the

month, and he had, for his part, given up the specific date of
May 1. This would give me the time I needed. If I could persuade the President to obtain relief from his promise to Chiang
Kai-shek and drop the Bay of Bengal plan, which had never
been mentioned in our Teheran conferences, there would
be enough landing-craft both for the Mediterranean and for a
punctual 'Overlord'. In the event the great landings began on
June 6, but this date was decided much later on, not by any
requirements of mine, but by the moon and the weather. I also
succeeded when we returned to Cairo, as will be seen, in persuading the President to abandon the enterprise in the Bay of
Bengal. I therefore consider that I got what I deemed imperative. But this was far from certain at Teheran on this November
morning. I was determined that Stalin should know the main
facts. I did not feel entitled to tell him that the President and I
had agreed upon May for 'Overlord'. I knew that Roosevelt
wanted to tell him this himself at our luncheon which was to
follow my conversation with the Marshal.

The following is founded upon the record made by Major
Birse, my trusted interpreter, of my private talk with Stalin.

*   *   *

I began by reminding the Marshal that I was half American
and had a great affection for the American people. What I was
going to say was not to be understood as disparaging to the
Americans, and I would be perfectly loyal towards them, but
there were things which it was better to say outright between
two persons.

We had a preponderance of troops over the Americans in the
Mediterranean. There were two or three times more British
troops than American there. That was why I was anxious that
the armies in the Mediterranean should not be hamstrung if it
could be avoided. I wanted to use them all the time. In Italy
there were some thirteen to fourteen divisions, of which nine
or ten were British. There were two armies, the Fifth Anglo-
American Army, and the Eighth Army, which was entirely
British. The choice had been represented as keeping to the date
of 'Overlord' or pressing on with the operations in the Mediterranean. But that was not the whole story. The Americans wanted
me to undertake an amphibious operation in the Bay of Bengal
against the Japanese in March. I was not keen about it. If
we had the landing-craft needed for the Bay of Bengal in the

Mediterranean we should have enough to do all we wanted there and still be able to keep to an early date for 'Overlord'. It was not a choice between the Mediterranean and the date of 'Overlord', but between the Bay of Bengal and the date of 'Overlord'. However, the Americans had pinned us down to a date for 'Overlord' and operations in the Mediterranean had suffered in the last two months. Our army in Italy was somewhat disheartened by the removal of seven divisions. We had sent home three divisions, and the Americans were sending four of theirs, all in preparation for 'Overlord'. That was why we had not been able to take full advantage of the Italian collapse. But it also proved the earnestness of our preparations for 'Overlord'.

It was vital to get an early decision on the appointment of the Commander-in-Chief. Up till August we British were to have had the Supreme Command in 'Overlord', but at Quebec I had told the President that I would agree to the appointment of an American, while we should have the Supreme Command in the Mediterranean. I was content with this because the Americans, although equal in numbers to the British when we landed, would soon have a preponderance, and their stake would be greater after the first few months. On the other hand, as the British had the preponderance in the Mediterranean and I had my own ideas about the war there I considered it right that we should have the Supreme Command in that theatre. The President had accepted this arrangement, and it now rested with him to nominate the Commander-in-Chief for 'Overlord'. As soon as the President did so I would nominate the Mediterranean Commander-in-Chief and other commanders. The President had delayed the appointment for domestic reasons connected with high personages, but I had urged him to decide before we all left Teheran. Stalin said that was good.

I then turned to the question of landing-craft, and explained once again how and why they were the bottle-neck. We had plenty of troops in the Mediterranean, even after the removal of the seven divisions, and there would be an adequate invading British and American army in the United Kingdom. All turned on landing-craft. When the Marshal had made his momentous announcement two days before about Russia's coming into the war against Japan after Hitler's surrender I had immediately suggested to the Americans that they might find more landing-craft for the operations we had been asked to carry out in the Indian Ocean, or that they might send some landing-craft from

the Pacific to help the first lift of 'Overlord'. In that case there
might be enough for all. But the Americans were very touchy
about the Pacific. I had pointed out to them that Japan would
be beaten much sooner if Russia joined in the war against
her, and that they could therefore afford to give us more
help.

The issue between myself and the Americans was in fact a
very narrow one. It was not that I was in any way lukewarm
about 'Overlord'. I wanted to get what I needed for the Mediterranean and at the same time keep to the date for 'Overlord'.
The details had to be hammered out between the Staffs, and I
had hoped that this might be done in Cairo. Unfortunately
Chiang Kai-shek had been there and Chinese questions had
taken up nearly all the time. But I was sure that in the end enough
landing-craft would be found for all.

Now about 'Overlord'. The British would have ready by the
date fixed in May or June nearly sixteen divisions, with their
corps troops, landing-craft troops, anti-aircraft, and services, a
total of slightly over half a million men. These would consist of
some of our best troops, including battle-trained men from the
Mediterranean. In addition the British would have all that was
needed from the Royal Navy to handle transportation and to
protect the Army, and there would be the metropolitan Air
Forces of about 4,000 first-line British aircraft in continuous
action. The American import of troops was now beginning. Up
till now they had sent mainly air troops and stores for the Army,
but in the next four or five months I thought 150,000 men or
more would come every month, making a total of seven to
eight hundred thousand men by May. The defeat of the submarines in the Atlantic had made this movement possible. I was
in favour of launching the operation in the South of France
about the same time as 'Overlord' or at whatever moment was
found correct. We should be holding enemy troops in Italy, and
of the twenty-two or twenty-three divisions in the Mediterranean as many as possible would go to the South of France and
the rest would remain in Italy.

A great battle was impending in Italy. General Alexander
had about half a million men under him. There were thirteen or
fourteen Allied divisions against nine to ten German. The
weather had been bad and bridges had been swept away, but in
December we intended to push on, with General Montgomery
leading the Eighth Army. The amphibious landing would be

made near the Tiber. At the same time the Fifth Army would be fiercely engaged holding the enemy. It might turn into a miniature Stalingrad. We did not intend to push into the wide part of Italy, but to hold the narrow leg.

Stalin said he must warn me that the Red Army was depending on the success of our invasion of Northern France. If there were no operations in May 1944 then the Red Army would think that there would be no operations at all that year. The weather would be bad and there would be transport difficulties. If the operation did not take place he did not want the Red Army to be disappointed. Disappointment could only create bad feeling. If there was no big change in the European war in 1944 it would be very difficult for the Russians to carry on. They were war-weary. He feared that a feeling of isolation might develop in the Red Army. That was why he had tried to find out whether 'Overlord' would be undertaken on time as promised. If not, he would have to take steps to prevent bad feeling in the Red Army. It was most important.

I said 'Overlord' would certainly take place, provided the enemy did not bring into France larger forces than the Americans and British could gather there. If the Germans had thirty to forty divisions in France I did not think the force we were going to put across the Channel would be able to hold on. I was not afraid of going on shore, but of what would happen on the thirtieth, fortieth, or fiftieth day. However, if the Red Army engaged the enemy and we held them in Italy, and possibly the Turks came into the war, then I thought we could win.

Stalin said that the first steps of 'Overlord' would have a good effect on the Red Army, and if he knew that it was going to take place in May or June he could already prepare blows against Germany. The spring was the best time. March and April were months of slackness, during which he could concentrate troops and material, and in May and June he could attack. Germany would have no troops for France. The transfer of German divisions to the east was continuing. The Germans were afraid of their Eastern Front, because it had no Channel which had to be crossed and there was no France to be entered. The Germans were afraid of the Red Army advance. The Red Army would advance if it saw that help was coming from the Allies. He asked when 'Overlord' would begin.

I said that I could not disclose the date for 'Overlord' without the President's agreement, but the answer would be given at lunch-time, and I thought he would be satisfied.

*　　　*　　　*

After a short interval the Marshal and I separately proceeded to the President's quarters for the luncheon of 'Three Only' (with our interpreters) to which he had invited us. Roosevelt then told Stalin that we were both agreed that 'Overlord' should be launched during the month of May. The Marshal was evidently greatly pleased and relieved by this solemn and direct engagement which we both made. The conversation turned on lighter subjects, and the only part of which I have a record was the question of Russia's outlet upon the seas and oceans. I had always thought it was a wrong thing, capable of breeding disastrous quarrels, that a mighty land-mass like the Russian Empire, with its population of nearly two hundred millions, should be denied during the winter months all effective access to the broad waters.

When Marshal Stalin raised this question of warm-water ports for Russia I said there were no obstacles. He also asked about the Dardanelles and the revision of the Treaty of Sèvres. I said that I wanted to get Turkey into the war, and this was an awkward moment for raising the question. Stalin replied that the time would come later. I said I expected Russia would sail the oceans with her Navy and merchant fleet, and we would welcome her ships. At this Stalin remarked that Lord Curzon had had other ideas. I said that in those days we did not see eye to eye with Russia.

The President said that the Baltic should be free to all nations for merchant shipping. There should be free zones in the ports, and trustees should be appointed for the Kiel Canal, while the Dardanelles ought to be free to the commerce of the world. Stalin asked whether this would apply to Russian commerce, and we assured him that it would.

Stalin then asked what could be done for Russia in the Far East. I replied that Russia had Vladivostok, but he pointed out that the port was ice-bound, and also depended on the Straits of Tsushima. At present the only exit that the Russians had was Murmansk. I answered that I wished to meet the Russian grievance, because the government of the world must be entrusted to satisfied nations, who wished nothing more for themselves than what they had. If the world-government were in the hands of hungry nations there would always be danger. But none of us had any reason to seek for anything more. The peace would be kept by peoples who lived in their own way and were not ambitious. Our power placed us above the rest. We were like rich men dwelling at peace within their habitations.

* * *

After a brief interval the third plenary session began as before in the Russian Embassy at four o'clock. There was a full attendance and we numbered nearly thirty.

The President said he was very happy to inform the Conference that agreement had been reached on the main military problems.

Sir Alan Brooke said that, after sitting in combined session, the United States and British Chiefs of Staff had recommended us to launch 'Overlord' in May, 'in conjunction with a supporting operation against the South of France, on the largest scale permitted by the landing-craft available at that time.'

I then emphasised the need for the combined United States and British Staffs to keep in closest touch with the Soviet military authorities, so that all operations on the Eastern as well as the Western and Mediterranean Fronts were concerted. By this means the three Great Powers would close in on the wild beast so that he was engaged on all sides at the same moment. Very detailed Staff work would be necessary to launch 'Overlord', which was the biggest combined operation ever planned.

Stalin said that he understood the importance of the decision taken by the Staffs and the difficulties inherent in carrying it out. The danger period for 'Overlord' would be at the time of deployment from the landings. At this point the Germans might transfer troops from the east in order to create the maximum difficulties for 'Overlord'. In order to prevent any movement from the east of any considerable German forces he undertook to organise a large-scale Russian offensive in May.*

The President remarked on the importance of the timing of operations in all theatres. Now that the three Staffs had got together he hoped they would keep together. He had already informed Marshal Stalin that the next step was to appoint the Commander for 'Overlord'. After consultation with his own Staffs and with me, it should be possible to make a decision

---

* The main Russian attack began on June 23.

within three or four days. Now that the main military decisions had been taken, it seemed right for the British and American Staffs to return to Cairo as soon as possible to work out the details. To this Stalin and I agreed.

I added that now that the supreme decisions had been taken every effort must be bent to find the ways and means to get more landing-craft. With five months still to go before the launching of 'Overlord', and with all the resources of America and Great Britain at our disposal, it should be possible to do this. If 'Overlord' was to be done it must be done with smashing force, and I hoped that the Staffs would find ways and means of increasing the initial assault forces.

I asked if there would be any difficulty in the three Staffs concerting cover plans. Stalin explained that the Russians had made considerable use of deception by means of dummy tanks, aircraft, and airfields. Radio deception had also proved effective. He was entirely agreeable to the Staffs collaborating with the object of devising joint cover and deception schemes. 'In wartime,' I said, 'truth is so precious that she should always be attended by a bodyguard of lies.' Stalin and his comrades greatly appreciated this remark when it was translated, and upon this note our formal conference ended gaily.

I then suggested that the Staffs should draft a short communiqué to cover the military talks for submission to the President, Marshal Stalin, and myself. The note to be sounded was brevity, mystery, and a foretaste of impending doom for Germany. The following communiqué was therefore framed and agreed to by all:

> ... Our Military Staffs have joined in our round table discussions, and we have concerted our plans for the destruction of the German forces. We have reached complete agreement as to the scope and timing of the operations which will be undertaken from the east, west and south.

* * *

Hitherto we had assembled for our conferences or meals in the Soviet Embassy. I had claimed however that I should be the host at the third dinner, which should be held in the British Legation. This could not well be disputed. Great Britain and I myself both came first alphabetically, and in seniority I was four or five years older than Roosevelt or Stalin. We were by centuries the longest established of the three Governments ; I might have added, but did not, that we had been the longest in the war; and, finally, November 30 was my birthday. These arguments, particularly the last one, were conclusive, and all preparations were made by our Minister for a dinner of nearly forty persons, including not only the political and military chiefs, but some of their higher staffs. The Soviet Political Police, the N.K.V.D., insisted on searching the British Legation from top to bottom, looking behind every door and under every cushion, before Stalin appeared; and about fifty armed Russian policemen, under their own general, posted themselves near all the doors and windows. The American Security men were also much in evidence. Everything however passed off agreeably. Stalin, arriving under heavy guard, was in the best of tempers, and the President, from his wheeled chair, beamed on us all in pleasure and goodwill.

This was a memorable occasion in my life. On my right sat the President of the United States, on my left the master of Russia. Together we controlled a large preponderance of the naval and three-quarters of all the airforces in the world, and could direct armies of nearly twenty millions of men, engaged in the most terrible of wars that had yet occurred in human history. I could not help rejoicing at the long way we had come on the road to victory since the summer of 1940, when we had been alone, and, apart from the Navy and the Air, practically un-armed, against the triumphant and unbroken might of Germany and Italy, with almost all Europe and its resources in their grasp. Mr. Roosevelt gave me for a birthday present a beautiful Persian porcelain vase, which, although it was broken into fragments on the homeward journey, has been marvellously reconstructed and is one of my treasures.

During dinner I had a most pleasant conversation with both my august guests. Stalin repeated the question he had posed at the Conference, 'Who will command "Overlord"?' I said that the President had not yet finally made up his mind, but that I was almost certain it would be General Marshall, who sat opposite us at no great distance, and that was how it had stood hitherto. He was evidently very pleased at this. He then spoke about General Brooke. He thought that he did not like the Russians. He had been very abrupt and rough with them at our first Moscow meeting in August 1942. I reassured him, remarking that military men were apt to be blunt and hard-cut when dealing with war problems with their professional colleagues.

Stalin said that he liked them all the better for that. He gazed at Brooke intently across the room.

When the time came I proposed the health of our illustrious guests, and the President proposed my health and wished me many happy returns of the day. He was followed by Stalin, who spoke in a similar strain.

*   *   *

Many informal toasts were then proposed, according to the Russian custom, which is certainly very well suited to banquets of this kind. Hopkins made a speech couched in a happy vein, in the course of which he said that he had made 'a very long and thorough study of the British Constitution, which is unwritten, and of the War Cabinet, whose authority and composition are not specifically defined'. As the result of this study, he said, 'I have learnt that the provisions of the British Constitution and the powers of the War Cabinet are just whatever Winston Churchill wants them to be at any given moment.' This caused general laughter. The reader of these volumes will know how little foundation there was in this jocular assertion. It is true that I received a measure of loyal support in the direction of the war from Parliament and my Cabinet colleagues which may well be unprecedented, and that there were very few large issues upon which I was overruled; but it was with some pride that I reminded my two great comrades on more than one occasion that I was the only one of our trinity who could at any moment be dismissed from power by the vote of a House of Commons freely elected on universal franchise, or could be controlled from day to day by the opinion of a War Cabinet representing all parties in the State. The President's term of office was fixed, and his powers not only as President but as Commander-in-Chief were almost absolute under the American Constitution. Stalin appeared to be, and at this moment certainly was, all-powerful in Russia. They could order; I had to convince and persuade. I was glad that this should be so. The process was laborious, but I had no reason to complain of the way it worked.

*   *   *

As the dinner proceeded there were many speeches, and most of the principal figures, including Molotov and General Marshall, made their contribution. But the speech which stands out in my memory came from General Brooke. I quote the account he was good enough to write for me.

'Half-way through the dinner,' he says, 'the President very kindly proposed my health, referring to the time when my father had visited his father at Hyde Park. Just as he was finishing, and I was thinking what an easy time I should have replying to such kind words, Stalin got up and said he would finish the toast. He then proceeded to imply that I had failed to show real feelings of friendship towards the Red Army, that I was lacking in a true appreciation of its fine qualities, and that he hoped in future I should be able to show greater comradeship towards the soldiers of the Red Army!

'I was very much surprised by these accusations, as I could not think what they were based on. I had however seen enough of Stalin by then to know that if I sat down under these insults I should lose any respect he might ever have had for me, and that he would continue such attacks in the future.

'I therefore rose to thank the President most profusely for his very kind expressions, and then turned to Stalin in approximately the following words:

'"Now, Marshal, may I deal with your toast. I am surprised that you should have found it necessary to raise accusations against me that are entirely unfounded. You will remember that this morning while we were discussing cover plans Mr. Churchill said that 'in war truth must have an escort of lies'. You will also remember that you yourself told us that in all your great offensives your real intentions were always kept concealed from the outer world. You told us that all your dummy tanks and dummy aeroplanes were always massed on those fronts that were of an immediate interest, while your true intentions were covered by a cloak of complete secrecy.

'"Well, Marshal, you have been misled by dummy tanks and dummy aeroplanes, and you have failed to observe those feelings of true friendship which I have for the Red Army, nor have you seen the feelings of genuine comradeship which I bear towards all its members."'

As this was translated by Pavlov, sentence by sentence, to Stalin I watched his expression carefully. It was inscrutable. But at the end he turned to me and said with evident relish, 'I like that man. He rings true. I must have a talk with him afterwards.'

At length we moved into the ante-chamber, and here everyone moved about in changing groups. I felt that there was a greater sense of solidarity and good-comradeship than we had ever reached before in the Grand Alliance. I had not invited Randolph and Sarah to the dinner, though they came in while my birthday toast was being proposed, but now Stalin singled them out and greeted them most warmly, and of course the President knew them well.

As I moved around I saw Stalin in a small circle face to face with 'Brookie', as I call him. The General's account continues:

'As we walked out of the room the Prime Minister told me that he had felt somewhat nervous as to what I should say next when I had referred to "truth" and "lies". He comforted me however by telling me that my reply to the toast had had the right effect on Stalin. I therefore decided to return to the attack in the ante-room. I went up to Stalin and told him how surprised I was, and grieved, that he should have found it necessary to raise such accusations against me in his toast. He replied at once through Pavlov, "The best friendships are those founded on misunderstandings," and he shook me warmly by the hand.'

It seemed to me that all the clouds had passed away, and in fact Stalin's confidence in my friend was established on a foundation of respect and goodwill which was never shaken while we all worked together.

It must have been after two in the morning when we finally separated. The Marshal resigned himself to his escort and departed, and the President was conveyed to his quarters in the Soviet Embassy. I went to bed tired out but content, feeling sure that nothing but good had been done. It certainly was a happy birthday for me.

CHAPTER 5

Teheran: Conclusions

*Conversation at Luncheon, December 1 – How to Gain Turkey –
The Russian Share of Italian Ships – The Frontiers of Poland
– The 'Curzon Line' and the Line of the Oder – A Frank Talk –
Finland – 'No Annexations and No Indemnities' – Final Accord –
The Question of Germany – Partition? – President Roosevelt's
Suggestion – I Unfold a Personal View – Marshal Stalin's
Standpoint – More About Poland – Broad Agreement on
Military Policy – Political Aspects Remote and Speculative –
Deep Fear of German Might at this War Climax – The Present
Partition: 'It Cannot Last.'*

Several of our gravest political issues stood out before and after
the main decision on strategy had been reached. The Three
lunched together again at the President's table in the Soviet
Embassy on December 1. In addition on this occasion Molotov,
Hopkins, Eden, Clark Kerr, and Harriman were present. The
question of inducing Turkey to enter the war was our first topic.

Hopkins asked what support we should have to give Turkey
if she came in. Roosevelt said that Inönü would ask what we
could do. Until the landing-craft situation had been studied we
should be careful in making promises. I said that we had seventeen British squadrons in Egypt which were not under the
Anglo-American command, and Air Marshal Tedder had three
more squadrons which we could spare. They were chiefly fighters
and could be used to protect Turkey. In addition we had three
regiments of anti-aircraft guns. This was all we had promised.
We had not promised Turkey any troops. She had fifty divisions
equipped, and there was no need to send any troops.

Stalin said that if Turkey entered the war she would make
part of her territory available. I agreed, and said Ploesti would
be vulnerable. We British were not offering Turkey anything
that was not ours to give, and we were only giving three squadrons from the Central Mediterranean to make up the number
from seventeen to twenty. Perhaps the Americans could add a
few bomber squadrons. We had said that we would only give
air protection. We had no army available. The landing-craft

required in March for taking Rhodes could be sandwiched in between Italy and 'Overlord'. The President hoped this could be done, but said that casualties among landing-craft were very heavy and we should want all we could get for 'Overlord'. I replied that I saw no difficulty. We had made no offers to Turkey, nor did I know if Inönü would accept any. The President would be in Cairo and could see what his Staffs would have to say. We British could only offer our twenty squadrons. The Turks did not need any army ; they needed air protection. In addition, Inönü might not come to Cairo.

'He might fall ill,' interjected Stalin.

I said that if he refused to come and the President had to leave I proposed to go in a cruiser and see him in Adana. Inönü would come there. Landing-craft were the bottle-neck for all our operations. Some might be forthcoming from the Indian Ocean or the Pacific, or more could be built. If this could not be done we should have to give up something, but it was agreed that 'Overlord' was not to suffer.

Roosevelt then said that my suggestion that landing-craft should be provided from the Pacific was impossible. Distances were too great, and every day the Americans were proceeding north in the Gilbert and Marshall Islands to attack Japanese supply lines. They needed all the landing-craft they had.

Hopkins asked how many landing-craft would be needed for taking Rhodes. I replied that there was no commitment to Turkey about Rhodes or any other island, and there was no commitment in landing-craft. Roosevelt said that if he were Inönü he would ask for Crete and other islands to be taken.

I said: 'What I want is air bases in the region of Smyrna and Badrun. Those airfields have been constructed by us. When we get them and put in squadrons we can drive the Germans out of the air. It pays us anyhow to lose one aircraft for every German machine shot down. We must starve out the German garrisons on the islands. If Turkey takes an active part the islands will fall of themselves. It would not be necessary in that case to attack even Rhodes. The islands have to be supplied by Germany, and if we have air cover from Turkey our destroyers can cut down German convoys, which they cannot do at present because Germany commands the air. Turkish bases will give us continued pressure against the Germans, and that will be a preparation for "Overlord".'

Stalin agreed, and the President consented to go forward on

the basis of twenty squadrons and some bombers, but no amphibious operations.

I then summed up. We were offering Turkey only limited air protection and anti-aircraft guns, but the winter was approaching and Germany would not invade Turkey. We would continue to supply her with arms. There was the priceless opportunity for Turkey of accepting the Soviet invitation to sit beside us at the Peace Conference. There was the assurance that if Bulgaria attacked Turkey because the latter had declared war on Germany the Soviet Union would retaliate on Bulgaria, a thing which had never happened before. Then there was the offer of association with the victorious Powers and our good offices and friendship.

'What measures,' asked Stalin, 'does Mr. Churchill expect from the Soviet Union in case Turkey declares war on Germany, as a result of which Bulgaria attacks Turkey and the Soviet declares war on Bulgaria?'

I said I was not asking for anything specific, but as the Soviet armies advanced through Odessa they would create a great effect among the population in Bulgaria. The Turkish Army had rifles, brave infantry, fairly good artillery, but no A.A. guns, no aircraft, and very few tanks. We had established military schools, but they were not attended regularly. The Turks were not quick to learn. Their Army was brave, but not modern. Twenty-five million pounds had been spent on weapons, mainly American, and we had shipped them.

Stalin said it was possible Turkey would not have to fight. They would give us their air bases; that might be the course of events, and it would be good.

The President then asked Mr. Eden to tell us what the Turks had said in Cairo. Mr. Eden said he had asked the Turkish Foreign Minister to give us air bases and told him that Germany would not attack Turkey. The Foreign Minister had refused, saying that Germany would react against Turkish provocation. Turkey would rather come in by agreement than be brought in indirectly as a result of such action as had been suggested.

I observed that when we asked the Turks to strain their neutrality by giving us their air bases they replied, 'Oh, no, we cannot play a passive *rôle*,' but if we asked them to start war in earnest they answered, 'Oh, no, we are not sufficiently armed.' I proposed, if necessary, to try other methods. If Turkey refused she would forfeit her chance to sit at the Peace Conference. She would be treated like other neutrals. We would say that Great Britain had no further interest in her affairs and we would stop the supply of arms.

Mr. Eden said he would like to get quite clear in his mind the demands that were to be made on Turkey. Was it understood that Turkey should go to war with Germany and no one else? If as a result the Germans made Bulgaria join them in a war against Turkey would the Soviet Government go to war with Bulgaria? Stalin agreed on both points. I said that, for myself, I would be satisfied with strained neutrality from Turkey. There was thus a very great measure of agreement on the limited steps for which I asked in order to win the great prize of bringing Turkey into the war, and it was settled that President Inönü should be invited to come to Cairo and talk it all over with me and the President. Although I felt how deeply Turkish minds had been affected by our failure to attack Rhodes, by the loss of Cos and Leros, and the consequent German command of the air in the Ægean, I left the subject, having got all I had thought it right to ask, and with fair hopes that it would not be insufficient.

*   *   *

Molotov now asked whether the Soviet Government could not be given an answer about the Italian ships. Roosevelt's reply was very simple. A large number of merchant ships and a smaller number of warships could be used by the three nations during the war, and could then be distributed by title. It would be best until then that those should use these ships who could use them best. Molotov said that Russia would be able to make good use of them. I asked where the Soviet Government would like them delivered. Stalin said in the Black Sea, and, if this were not possible, then in the North. If Turkey did not come into the war the Black Sea would be impossible, but use could be made of them in the North.

I said that this was a very small thing after all the efforts that Russia was making or had made. We only asked for a little time to handle the matter with the Italians. I said I should like to see the ships go to the Black Sea, and that perhaps I might at the same time send some of His Majesty's ships with them. The President and I needed time to arrange the matter with the Italians, who were already helping with some of their smaller ships in patrol work, and some Italian submarines were carrying important supplies. There must be no mutiny in the Italian Fleet

and no scuttling of ships. A couple of months should be enough
for me and the President to arrange with the Italians. The ships
could pass under Russian orders by that date, after refitting. I
went on to say that I should like to put four or five British submarines into the Black Sea. This was one of the things which
might be asked of Turkey if she accepted only 'strained neutrality'. But we would abide by Marshal Stalin's wishes. We had
no ambitions in the Black Sea.

Stalin replied that he would be grateful for any help.

*   *   *

After an interval, when luncheon was over, we moved into
another room, and took our seats at a conference table. Our
discussions continued all through the afternoon. Poland was the
next important subject.

The President began by saying that he hoped the Polish and
Soviet Governments would resume relations, so that any decision taken could be accepted by the Polish Government. But
he admitted there were difficulties. Stalin asked with what
Government he would have to negotiate. The Polish Government and their friends in Poland were in contact with the Germans. They killed the Partisans. Neither the President nor I
could have any idea of what was now going on there.

I said that the Polish question was important for us in the
United Kingdom, because we had declared war on Germany for
invading Poland. Although Great Britain had been unprepared
the German attack on Poland had launched us into the war. I
reverted to my illustration of the three matches—Germany,
Poland, and the Soviet Union. One of the main objects of the
Allies was to achieve the security of the Soviet western frontier,
and so to prevent an attack by Germany in the future. Here I
reminded Stalin of his mention of the line of the Oder in the
West.

Stalin, interrupting, said that previously there had been no
mention of re-establishing relations with the Polish Government,
but only of determining Poland's frontiers. To-day the matter
had been put quite differently. Russia, even more than other
States, was interested in good relations with Poland, because for
her it was a question of the security of her frontiers. Russia was
in favour of the reconstruction, development, and expansion of
Poland mainly at the expense of Germany. But he separated
Poland from the Polish Government in exile. He had broken off

relations with the Polish Government in exile, not on account of caprice, but because it had joined with Hitler in slanderous propaganda against Russia. What guarantee was there that this would not happen again? He would like to have a guarantee that the Polish Government in exile would not kill Partisans, but, on the contrary, would urge the Poles to fight the Germans and not concern themselves with any machinations. He would welcome any Polish Government which would take such active measures, and he would be glad to renew relations with them. But he was by no means sure that the Polish Government in exile was ever likely to become the kind of Government it ought to be.

Here I said that it would be a great help if round that very table we could learn what were the Russian ideas about the frontiers. I should then put the matter before the Poles and say frankly if I thought the conditions fair. His Majesty's Government, for whom alone I spoke, would like to be able to tell the Poles that the plan was a good one and the best that they were likely to get and that His Majesty's Government would not argue against it at the peace table. Then we could get on with the President's idea of resuming relations. What we wanted was a strong and independent Poland, friendly to Russia.

Stalin said that that was true, but that the Poles could not be allowed to seize the Ukraine and White Russian territory. That was not fair. According to the 1939 frontier, the soil of the Ukraine and White Russia was returned to the Ukraine and to White Russia. Soviet Russia adhered to the frontiers of 1939, for they appeared to be ethnologically the right ones.

Eden asked if this meant the Ribbentrop–Molotov Line.

'Call it whatever you like,' said Stalin.

Molotov remarked that it was generally called the Curzon Line.

'No,' said Eden, 'there are important differences.'

Molotov said there were none.

I then produced a map and showed the Curzon Line and the 1939 line, and indicated also the line of the Oder. Eden said that the south end of the Curzon Line had never been defined in terms.

At this point the meeting broke into groups. There was a general gathering round my map and round a map which was produced by the Americans, and it was difficult for the interpreters to take notes.

Eden suggested that the Curzon Line was intended to pass to the east of Lvov.

Stalin replied that the line on my map had not been drawn right. Lvov should be left on the Russian side and the line should go westwards towards Przemysl. Molotov would get a map of the Curzon Line and a description of it. He said that he did not want any Polish population, and that if he found any district inhabited by Poles he would gladly give it up.

I suggested that the value of the German land was much greater than the Pripet Marshes. It was industrial and it would make a much better Poland. We should like to be able to say to the Poles that the Russians were right, and to tell the Poles that they must agree that they had had a fair deal. If the Poles did not accept we could not help it. Here I made it clear that I was speaking for the British alone, adding that the President had many Poles in the United States who were his fellow-citizens.

Stalin said again that if it were proved to him that any district were Polish he would not claim it, and here he made some shadowing on the map west of the Curzon Line and south of Vilna, which he admitted to be mainly Polish.

At this point the meeting again separated into groups, and there was a prolonged study of the Oder Line on a map. When this came to an end I said that I liked the picture, and that I would say to the Poles that if they did not accept it they would be foolish, and I would remind them that but for the Red Army they would have been utterly destroyed. I would point out to them that they had been given a fine place to live in, more than three hundred miles each way.

Stalin said that it would indeed be a large, industrial State.

'And friendly to Russia,' I interjected.

Stalin replied that Russia wanted a friendly Poland.

I then, runs the record, said to Mr. Eden, with some emphasis, that I was not going to break my heart about this cession of part of Germany to Poland or about Lvov. Eden said that if Marshal Stalin would take the Curzon and Oder Lines as a basis on which to argue that might provide a beginning.

At this point Molotov produced the Russian version of the Curzon Line, and the text of a wireless telegram from Lord Curzon giving all the place-names. I asked whether Molotov would object to the Poles getting the Oppeln district. He said he did not think so.

I said that the Poles would be wise to take our advice. I was not prepared to make a great squawk about Lvov. Turning to Marshal Stalin, I added that I did not think we were very far apart in principle. Roosevelt asked Stalin whether he thought a transfer of population on a voluntary basis would be possible. The Marshal said that probably it would be.

On this we left the Polish discussion.

* * *

The President next asked Stalin whether he was ready to discuss Finland. Could the United States Government do anything to help to get Finland out of the war?

Stalin said that recently the Swedish Vice-Minister for Foreign Affairs had told Madame Kollontay (the Soviet Ambassadress) that the Finns were afraid that Russia wanted to turn Finland into a Russian province. The Soviet Government had replied that they had no wish to make Finland a Russian province unless the Finns forced them to do so. Madame Kollontay had then been instructed to tell the Finns that the Soviet Government would have no objection to receiving a Finnish delegation in Moscow ; but they wished the Finns to state their views about dropping out of the war. In Teheran he had just received the gist of the Finnish reply, which was conveyed to him through M. Boheman. The reply did not make any mention of Finland's desire to dissociate herself from Germany. It raised the question of frontiers. The Finns suggested that as a basis of discussion the 1939 frontier should be adopted, with some corrections in favour of the Soviet Union. Stalin believed that the Finns were not really anxious to conduct serious negotiations. Their conditions were unacceptable, and the Finns well knew it. The Finns still hoped for a German victory ; and some of them at any rate had a strong belief that the Germans were going to win.

Roosevelt asked if it would help if the United States Government advised the Finns to go to Moscow. Stalin replied they were ready enough to go to Moscow, but it would not do much good if they went with their present programme.

I said that in the days of the Russo-Finnish War I had been sympathetic to Finland, but I had turned against her when she came into the war against the Soviets. Russia must have security for Leningrad and its approaches. The position of the Soviet Union as a permanent naval and air Power in the Baltic must be assured. But people in the United Kingdom would be unhappy if the Finns were incorporated in the Soviet Union against their will. I had therefore been glad to hear what

Marshal Stalin had said. I did not think it useful to ask for indemnities. The Finns might cut down a few trees, but that would not do much good.

Stalin said that he did not want money, but within, say, five or eight years the Finns would be well able to make good the damage they had done to Russia by supplying her with paper, wood, and many other things. He thought the Finns should be given a lesson, and he was determined to get compensation.

I said I imagined that the harm the Finns did to Russia by their improper attack far exceeded what a poor country like Finland could supply. I added, 'There is still ringing in my ears the famous slogan, "No annexations and no indemnities." Perhaps Marshal Stalin will not be pleased with me for saying that.'

Stalin, with a broad grin, replied, 'I have told you that I am becoming a Conservative.'

I then asked what it was he wanted. We had 'Overlord' coming. I should like to have Sweden with us in the war and Finland out of the war by the spring. Stalin said that would be good.

The conversation then turned to territorial detail—Viborg ('Nothing doing about Viborg,' said Stalin), the Karelian Isthmus, Hangö. 'If the cession of Hangö presents a difficulty,' said Stalin, 'I am willing to take Petsamo instead.' 'A fair exchange,' said Roosevelt.

I said the British wanted two things: first, that Russia should be satisfied with her frontiers; second, that the Finns should be free and independent and live as well as they could in those very uncomfortable regions. But we did not want to put any pressure on Russia. Stalin said that, after all, allies could squeeze each other if they wanted to from time to time. But let the Finns live. It would be all right so long as half the damage they had done was made good. Roosevelt asked whether it would be any use if the Finns were to go to Moscow without any conditions. Stalin said that if there were no assurances that an agreement would be concluded, then an expedition to Moscow would help Germany, who would make capital out of any failure, and also the aggressive elements in Finland, who would say that the Russians did not really want peace.

I said that would be a lie, and that we would all say so loudly. 'All right,' said Stalin, 'let them come if you insist.'

Roosevelt said that the present Finnish leaders were pro-German; if there were others we might get somewhere. Stalin thought it would be better to have others, but he did not object even to Ryti. Anyone, even the devil, might come. He was not afraid of devils.

I said I hoped Marshal Stalin would handle the question of Finland with due regard to the possibility of Sweden coming into the war in time for our general offensive in May.

Stalin agreed, but said that he could not diverge from several conditions:

(1) Restoration of the 1940 treaty.
(2) Hangö or Petsamo. (Here he added that Hangö was leased to the Soviet Union, but he would propose to take Petsamo.)
(3) Compensation in kind as to 50 per cent. for damage. Quantities could be discussed later.
(4) A breach with Germany.
(5) The expulsion of all Germans.
(6) Demobilisation.

I replied about compensation that it was easy enough to do damage, but very hard to repair it, and that it was bad for any one country to fall into tribute to another. I said, 'Experience shows that large indemnities do not work.' Stalin proposed to occupy part of Finland if the Finns did not pay, but if they did pay the Russians would withdraw within the year.

'I have not yet,' I said, 'been elected a Soviet commissar, but if I were I would advise against this. There are much bigger things to think about.' We were behind the Russians and ready to help them at every turn, but we must think of the May battle. President Roosevelt said that he was ready to stand behind all that had been said (against large indemnities).

*   *   *

Stalin now asked, 'Are there any other questions?' The President replied, 'There is the question of Germany.' Stalin said that he would like to see Germany split up. The President agreed, but Stalin suggested that I would object.

I said I did not object in principle. Roosevelt said that, so that there could be some discussion, he and his advisers had had a shot at a plan some three months before. This involved the dividing of Germany into five parts. Stalin, with a grin, suggested that I was not listening because I was not inclined to see Germany split up. I said that I considered that the root of the evil lay in Prussia, in the Prussian Army and the General Staff.

Roosevelt then explained his plan for splitting Germany into five parts:

(1) Prussia.
(2) Hanover and the north-west part of Germany.
(3) Saxony and the Leipzig area.
(4) Hesse-Darmstadt, Hesse-Cassel, and the section south of the Rhine.
(5) Bavaria, Baden, and Württemberg.

These five sections would be self-governing, but there were two more that would be governed by the United Nations:

(1) Kiel and its canal and Hamburg.
(2) The Ruhr and the Saar.

These would be under the control of the United Nations as trustees. He was only throwing this out as an idea which might be talked over.

'If,' I said, 'I might use the American idiom, I would say that the President has "said a mouthful". Mr. Roosevelt's plan is a new one to me. In my opinion there are two things, one destructive and the other constructive. I have two clear ideas in mind. First the isolation of Prussia. What is to be done to Prussia after that is only secondary. Then I would like to detach Bavaria, Württemberg, the Palatinate, Saxony, and Baden. Whereas I would treat Prussia sternly, I would make things easier for the second group, which I should like to see work in with what I would call a Danubian Confederation. The people of those parts of Germany are not the most ferocious, and I should like to see them live tolerably, and in a generation they would feel differently. South Germans are not going to start another war, and we would have to make it worth their while to forget Prussia. I do not much mind whether there are one or two groups.'

I asked Marshal Stalin whether he would be prepared to go into action on this front. Stalin said he would, but he preferred a plan for the partition of Germany—something like the President's plan, which was more likely to weaken Germany. When one had to deal with large masses of German troops one found them all fighting like devils, as the British and American Armies would soon learn. The Austrians by themselves were different, and he described the way they surrendered. All Germans were the same. It was the Prussian officers that provided the cement.

But fundamentally there was no difference between North Germans and South Germans, for all Germans fought like fierce beasts. We should be careful not to include the Austrians in any kind of combination. Austria had existed independently, and could do so again. So also must Hungary exist independently. After breaking up Germany it would be most unwise to create new combinations, Danubian or otherwise.

President Roosevelt agreed warmly. There was no difference between Germans. The Bavarians had no officer class; otherwise they were exactly like the Prussians, as the American troops had already discovered.

I said that if Germany were divided into a number of parts as suggested by the President, and these parts were not attached to other combinations, they would reunite. It was not a question of dividing Germany so much as giving a life to the cut-off bits and making them content not to be dependent on the Greater Reich. Even if this were achieved for fifty years that would be a lot.

Stalin said that a Danubian combination would not be able to live, and the Germans would take advantage of this by putting flesh on something that was only a skeleton and thus creating a new great State. He asked whether Hungary and Roumania would be members of any such combination. He then reiterated the advantages which it would present to Germany in the future. It was far better to break up and scatter the German tribes. Of course they would want to unite, no matter how much they were split up. They would always want to reunite. In this he saw great danger, which would have to be neutralised by various economic measures, and in the long run by force if necessary. That was the only way to keep the peace. But if we were to make a large combination with Germans in it trouble was bound to come. We had to see to it that they were kept separate, and that Hungary and Germany were not coupled. There were no measures possible to exclude a movement towards reunion. Germans would always want to reunite and to take their revenge. It would be necessary to keep ourselves strong enough to beat them if they ever let loose another war.

I asked Stalin if he contemplated a Europe of little States, all disjointed, with no larger units at all.

He replied that he was speaking of Germany, not Europe. Poland and France were large States. Roumania and Bulgaria were small States. But Germany should at all costs be broken up so that she could not reunite. The President pointed out that his plan was a way of doing this. I said that I must make it clear that we could now only take a preliminary survey of a vast historical problem. Stalin said that it was certainly very preliminary.

* * *

I then brought the discussion back to Poland. I said I did not ask for any agreement, nor was I convinced on the matter myself, but I would rather like to get something down on paper. I then produced the following formula: 'It is thought in principle that the home of the Polish State and nation should be between the so-called Curzon Line and the line of the Oder,* including for Poland East Prussia (as defined) and Oppeln ; but the actual tracing of the frontier line requires careful study, and possibly disentanglement of population at some points.' Why not a formula on which I could say something like this to the Poles: 'I do not know if the Russians would approve, but I think that I might get it for you. You see, you are being well looked after.' I added that we should never get the Poles to say that they were satisfied. Nothing would satisfy the Poles.

Stalin then said that the Russians would like to have the warm-water port of Königsberg, and he sketched a possible line on the map. This would put Russia on the neck of Germany. If he got this he would be ready enough to agree to my formula about Poland. I asked what about Lvov. Stalin said he would accept the Curzon Line.

* * *

The same evening Roosevelt, Stalin, and I initialled the following document, which sets forth the military conclusions of our Triple Conference.

The Conference:

(1) Agreed that the Partisans in Yugoslavia should be supported by supplies and equipment to the greatest possible extent, and also by Commando operations.

(2) Agreed that, from the military point of view, it was most desirable that Turkey should come into the war on the side of the Allies before the end of the year.

(3) Took note of Marshal Stalin's statement that if Tur-

* No question as to whether it should be the Eastern or Western Neisse had yet arisen.

key found herself at war with Germany, and as a result Bulgaria declared war on Turkey or attacked her, the Soviet would immediately be at war with Bulgaria. The Conference further took note that this fact would be explicitly stated in the forthcoming negotiations to bring Turkey into the war.

(4) Took note that Operation 'Overlord' would be launched during May 1944, in conjunction with an operation against Southern France. The latter operation would be undertaken in as great a strength as availability of landing-craft permitted. The Conference further took note of Marshal Stalin's statement that the Soviet forces would launch an offensive at about the same time with the object of preventing the German forces from transferring from the Eastern to the Western Front.

(5) Agreed that the military Staffs of the three Powers should henceforward keep in close touch with each other in regard to the impending operations in Europe. In particular it was agreed that a cover plan to mystify and mislead the enemy as regards these operations should be concerted between the Staffs concerned.

* * *

Thus our long and hard discussions at Teheran reached their end. The military conclusions governed in the main the future of the war. The cross-Channel invasion was fixed for May, subject naturally to tides and the moon. It was to be aided by a renewed major Russian offensive. At first sight I liked the proposed descent upon the French southern shore by part of the Allied Armies in Italy. The project had not been examined in detail, but the fact that both the Americans and the Russians favoured it made it easier to secure the landing-craft necessary for the success of our Italian campaign and the capture of Rome, without which it would have been a failure. I was of course more attracted by the President's alternative suggestion of a right-handed move from Italy by Istria and Trieste, with ultimate designs for reaching Vienna through the Ljubljana Gap. All this lay five or six months ahead. There would be plenty of time to make a final choice as the general war shaped itself, if only the life of our armies in Italy was not paralysed by depriving them of their modest requirements in landing-craft. Many amphibious or semi-amphibious schemes were open. I expected that the seaborne operations in the Bay of Bengal would be abandoned, and this, as the next chapter will show, proved correct. I was glad to feel that several important options were still preserved. Our strong efforts were to be renewed to bring Turkey into the war, with all that might accompany this in the Ægean, and follow from it in the Black Sea. In this we were to be disappointed. Surveying the whole military scene, as we separated in an atmosphere of friendship and unity of immediate purpose, I personally was well content.

*   *   *

The political aspects were at once more remote and speculative. Obviously they depended upon the results of the great battles yet to be fought, and after that upon the mood of each of the Allies when victory was gained. It would not have been right at Teheran for the Western democracies to found their plans upon suspicions of the Russian attitude in the hour of triumph and when all her dangers were removed. Stalin's promise to enter the war against Japan as soon as Hitler was overthrown and his armies defeated was of the highest importance. The hope of the future lay in the most speedy ending of the war and the establishment of a World Instrument to prevent another war, founded upon the combined strength of the three Great Powers, whose leaders had joined hands in friendship around the table.

We had procured a mitigation for Finland, which on the whole is operative to-day. The frontiers of the new Poland had been broadly outlined both in the east and in the west. The Curzon Line, subject to interpretation in the east, and the line of the Oder, in the west, seemed to afford a true and lasting home for the Polish nation after all its sufferings. At the time the question between the Eastern and Western Neisse, which flow together to form the Oder river, had not arisen. When in July 1945 it arose in a violent form and under totally different conditions at the Potsdam Conference I at once declared that Great Britain adhered only to the eastern tributary. And this is still our position.

*   *   *

The supreme question of the treatment to be accorded to Germany by the victors could at this milestone only be the subject of 'a preliminary survey of a vast political problem', and, as Stalin described it, 'certainly very preliminary'. It must be remembered that we were in the midst of a fearful struggle with the mighty Nazi Power. All the hazards of war lay around us, and all its passions of comradeship among Allies, of retribution upon the common foe, dominated our minds. The President's tentative projects for the partition of Germany into five self-governing states and two territories, of vital consequence, under the United Nations, were of course far more acceptable to Marshal Stalin than the proposal which I made for the isolation of Prussia and the constitution of a Danubian Confederation, or of a South Germany and also a Danubian Confederation. This was only my personal view. But I do not at all repent having put it forward in the circumstances which lay about us at Teheran.

We all deeply feared the might of a united Germany. Prussia had a great history of her own. It would be possible, I thought, to make a stern but honourable peace with her, and at the same time to recreate in modern forms what had been in general outline the Austro-Hungarian Empire, of which it has been well said, 'If it did not exist it would have to be invented.' Here would be a great area in which not only peace but friendship might reign at a far earlier date than in any other solution. Thus a United Europe might be formed in which all the victors and vanquished might find a sure foundation for the life and freedom of all their tormented millions.

I do not feel any break in the continuity of my thought in this immense sphere. But vast and disastrous changes have fallen upon us in the realm of fact. The Polish frontiers exist only in name, and Poland lies quivering in the Russian-Communist grip. Germany has indeed been partitioned, but only by a hideous division into zones of military occupation. About this tragedy it can only be said IT CANNOT LAST.

CHAPTER 6

Cairo again. The High Command

Anglo-American Discussions in Cairo – The Andaman Islands Plan – No Agreement on This at Our First Plenary Meeting, December 4 – The President Decides to Abandon the Plan – Our Joint Telegram to Premier Stalin, December 6 – Question about the Number of Troops Asked for by Mountbatten – Staff Discussion on the Strategy to be Pursued against Japan – Our Conference with the Turks at Cairo – Outline Plan for Aiding Turkey – The Turks Will not Commit Themselves – President Roosevelt Appoints General Eisenhower to Command 'Overlord' – The President and I Visit the Sphinx.

On December 2 I got back to Cairo from Teheran, and was once more installed in the villa near the Pyramids. The President arrived the same evening, and we resumed our intimate discussions on the whole scene of the war and on the results of our talks with Stalin. Meanwhile the Combined Chiefs of Staff, who had refreshed themselves by a visit to Jerusalem on their way back from Teheran, were to carry forward their discussions on all their great business the next day. Admiral Mountbatten had returned to India, whence he had submitted the revised plan he had been instructed to make for an amphibious attack on the Andaman Islands (Operation 'Buccaneer'). This would absorb the vitally needed landing-craft already sent to him from the Mediterranean. I wished to make a final attempt to win the Americans to the alternative enterprise against Rhodes.

The next evening I dined again with the President. Eden was with me. We remained at the table until after midnight, still discussing our points of difference. I shared the views of our Chiefs of Staff, who were much worried by the promise which the President had made to Generalissimo Chiang Kai-shek before Teheran to launch an early attack across the Bay of Bengal. This would have swept away my hopes and plans for taking Rhodes, on which I believed the entry of Turkey into the war largely depended. But Mr. Roosevelt's heart was set upon it. When our Chiefs of Staff raised it in the military conferences the United States Staffs simply declined to discuss the matter.

The President, they said, had taken his decision and they had no choice but to obey.

On the afternoon of December 4 we held our first plenary meeting since Teheran, but made little headway. The President began by saying that he must leave on December 6, and that all reports should be ready for the final agreement of both parties by the evening of Sunday, December 5. Apart from the question of the entry of Turkey into the war, the only outstanding point seemed to be the comparatively small one of the use to be made of a score of landing-craft and their equipment. It was unthinkable that one could be beaten by a petty item like that, and he felt bound to say that the detail *must* be disposed of.

I said that I did not wish to leave the Conference in any doubt that the British delegation viewed our early dispersal with great apprehension. There were still many questions of first-class importance to be settled. Two decisive events had taken place in the last few days. In the first place, Marshal Stalin had voluntarily proclaimed that the Soviet would declare war on Japan the moment Germany was defeated. This would give us better bases than we could ever find in China, and made it all the more important that we should concentrate on making 'Overlord' a success. It would be necessary for the Staffs to examine how this new fact would affect operations in the Pacific and South-East Asia.

The second event of first-class importance was the decision to cross the Channel during May. I myself would have preferred a July date, but I was determined nevertheless to do all in my power to make a May date a complete success. It was a task transcending all others. A million Americans were to be thrown in eventually, and five or six hundred thousand British. Terrific battles were to be expected, on a scale far greater than anything that we had experienced before. In order to give 'Overlord' the greatest chance of success, it was thought necessary that the descent on the Riviera ('Anvil') should be as strong as possible. It seemed to me that the crisis for the invading armies would come at about the thirtieth day, and it was essential that every possible step should be taken by action elsewhere to prevent the Germans from concentrating a superior force against our beachheads. As soon as the 'Overlord' and 'Anvil' forces got into the same zone they would come under the same commander.

The President, summing up the discussion, asked whether he

was correct in thinking that there was general agreement on the following points:

(a) Nothing should be done to hinder 'Overlord'.
(b) Nothing should be done to hinder 'Anvil'.
(c) By hook or by crook we should scrape up sufficient landing-craft to operate in the Eastern Mediterranean if Turkey came into the war.
(d) Admiral Mountbatten should be told to go ahead and do his best [in the Bay of Bengal] with what had already been allocated to him.

On this last point I suggested that it might be necessary to withdraw resources from Mountbatten in order to strengthen 'Overlord' and 'Anvil'. The President said that he could not agree with this. We had a moral obligation to do something for China, and he would not be prepared to forgo the amphibious operation except for some very good and readily apparent reason. I replied that this 'very good reason' might be provided by our supreme adventure in France. At present the 'Overlord' assault was only on a three-division basis, whereas we had put nine divisions ashore in Sicily on the first day. The main operation was at present on a very narrow margin.

Reverting to the Riviera attack, I expressed the view that it should be planned on the basis of an assault force of at least two divisions. This would provide enough landing-craft to do the outflanking operations in Italy, and also, if Turkey came into the war soon, to capture Rhodes. I then pointed out that operations in South-East Asia must be judged in their relation to the predominating importance of 'Overlord'. I said that I was surprised at the demands for taking the Andamans which had reached me from Admiral Mountbatten. In the face of Marshal Stalin's promise that Russia would come into the war operations in the South-East Asia Command had lost a good deal of their value, while, on the other hand, their cost had been put up to a prohibitive extent.

The discussion continued on whether or not to persist in the Andamans project. The President resisted the British wish to drop it. No conclusion was reached, except that the Chiefs of Staff were directed to go into details.

*　　*　　*

On December 5 we met again, and the report of the Combined Staffs on operations in the European theatre was read out by the President and agreed. Everything was now narrowed down to the Far Eastern operation. Rhodes had receded in the picture, and I concentrated on getting the landing-craft for 'Anvil' and the Mediterranean. A new factor had presented itself. The estimates of the South-East Asia Command of the force needed to storm the Andamans had been startling. The President said that 14,000 should be sufficient. Anyhow, the 50,000 men proposed certainly broke the back of the Andamans expedition so far as this meeting was concerned. It was agreed for the moment that Mountbatten should be asked what amphibious operations he could undertake on a smaller scale, on the assumption that most of the landing-craft and assault shipping were withdrawn from South-East Asia during the next few weeks. Thus we parted, leaving Mr. Roosevelt much distressed.

Before anything further could be done the deadlock in Cairo was broken. In the afternoon the President, in consultation with his advisers, decided to abandon the Andaman Islands plan. He sent me a laconic private message: ' "Buccaneer" is off.' General Ismay reminds me that when I told him the welcome news cryptically on the telephone that the President had changed his mind and was so informing Chiang Kai-shek I said, 'He is a better man that ruleth his spirit than he that taketh a city.' We all met together at 7.30 p.m. the next evening at the Kirk villa to go over the final report of the Conference. The Southern France assault operation was formally approved, and the President read out his signal to Generalissimo Chiang Kai-shek, informing him of the decision to abandon the Andamans plan.

* * *

I now worked out with the President a joint summary of our decisions to be sent to Stalin.

Prime Minister and President Roosevelt to   6 Dec 43
Premier Stalin

In the Cairo Conference just concluded we have arrived at following decisions as to the conduct of war in 1944 against Germany additional to the agreement reached by the three of us at Teheran.

The bomber offensive against Germany, with the objective of destroying German air combat strength, the German military, industrial, and economic system, and preparing the way

for a cross-Channel operation, will be given the highest
strategical priority.

We have reduced the scale of operations scheduled for
March in the Bay of Bengal to permit the reinforcement of
amphibious craft for the operation against Southern France.

We have ordered the utmost endeavours to increase the
production of landing-craft in U.K. and the U.S.A. for the
reinforcement of 'Overlord', and further orders have been
issued to divert certain landing-craft from the Pacific for the
same purpose.

* * *

In informing the South-East Asia Command of our decisions
I did not conceal from Mountbatten the shock which the estimates of his advisers which he had endorsed had been to me.

Prime Minister to Admiral Mountbatten (*Delhi*)   9 Dec 43

You will have seen the President's telegram to the Generalissimo about the abandonment of 'Buccaneer', with which, as
you know, I am in entire agreement. This arises from the
decision at Teheran to concentrate everything on 'Overlord'
and a simultaneous operation against the South of France.

Everyone here has been unpleasantly affected by your request to use 50,000 British and Imperial troops, of which
33,700 are combatant, against 5,000 Japanese. I was astounded
to hear of such a requirement, and I cannot feel sure you are
getting competent military advice. The Americans have been
taking their islands on the basis of two and a half to one, and
that your generals should ask for six and a half to one has
produced a very bad impression. Even the detailed figures
with which I have been furnished do not remove it.

I hope that preparations will now go forward for Sumatra
after the monsoon. However, while such standards as those
you have accepted for the Andamans prevail there is not
much hope of making any form of amphibious war.

Mountbatten replied that the United States in their recent
landings had deployed a superiority of troops varying from between three to one to over six to one. The larger figure applied
when cover from shore-based aircraft was not possible. For
taking the Andamans he would have carrier-borne and not
shore-based aircraft, and their effort was likely to be expended
after four days. It was therefore essential to capture the Andamans airfield within that time. The resources already allotted to
him would enable him to carry the 50,000 men proposed. Of

these however only 9,000 could be landed by the first two waves. He did not therefore feel he was asking for an undue superiority in order to ensure quick success. He cited the American landing at Munda, where with an even higher ratio of superiority only very slow progress had been made.

I remained unconvinced. But the following post-war comment from the War Office should be printed in order that the point at issue may be fairly presented.

Operation 'Buccaneer', an assault on the Andaman Islands, involved transporting our forces 1,000 miles from the nearest base, and the force included all troops required for the development of facilities, the building of airfield and strips, and for work in the docks. It was estimated that 16,000 would be non-fighting troops, and included in the balance of 'fighting' troops were all headquarters, engineers, and anti-aircraft units. The enemy was considered to have air superiority in the area. Admittedly the 'teeth' part of the force outnumbered the estimated Japanese garrison by about four to one, but this was not much greater than what was at that time accepted as a desirable preponderance for an assault landing. It cannot be overlooked that we had been uniformly unsuccessful against the Japanese for the previous twelve months. Lord Mountbatten undoubtedly wished to make his first assault a success, if only for the sake of theatre morale.

* * *

The Combined Chiefs of Staff also discussed among themselves the British share in the strategy to be pursued against Japan, and presented their recommendations to the President and me in their final report of the Cairo Conference. In summary, they proposed that the main effort of the South-East Asia Command should be in Burma. After the defeat of Germany an Army and air contingent, with air resources all based on Australia, should be sent to co-operate with General MacArthur. The British effort by sea should be mainly in the Pacific, and not in the Bay of Bengal. The British Chiefs of Staff, like myself, recoiled from the idea of a strenuous and wasteful campaign in North Burma for the sake of building a road to China of doubtful value. On the other hand, they accepted the fact that Admiral Mountabatten could not carry out any large-scale amphibious operations until six months after a German collapse. The plan of reinforcing the Pacific could be begun much sooner. They therefore endorsed the American view. In their final report both Staffs stated that they 'had agreed in principle as a basis for further investigation and preparation' the overall plan for the defeat of Japan. This plan contemplated the dispatch of a detachment of the British Fleet which was provisionally scheduled to become active in the Pacific in June 1944. The President and I both initialled this document, but in the pressure of more urgent business and of the President's imperative need to return to the United States no occasion was found when we could discuss these long-term schemes either with our own advisers or between ourselves. We however felt sure there would be time to review the whole position later.

* * *

One of the main purposes of our Cairo meeting had been to resume talks with the Turkish leaders. I had telegraphed President Inönü on December 1 from Teheran suggesting that he should join the President and myself in Cairo. It was arranged that Vyshinsky should also be present. These conversations arose out of the exchange of views between Mr. Eden and the Turkish Foreign Minister in Cairo at the beginning of November on the former's journey home from Moscow. The Turks now came again to Cairo on December 4, and the following evening I entertained the Turkish President to dinner. My guest displayed great caution, and in subsequent meetings showed to what extent his advisers were still impressed by the German military machine. I pressed the case hard. With Italy out of the war the advantages of Turkey's entry were manifestly increased and her risks lessened.

On December 6 I drafted a memorandum to the British Chiefs of Staff setting forth in detail the policy and action which would be necessary if, after all, Turkey came in on our side.

Prime Minister to General Ismay, for C.O.S. 6 Dec 43
Committee

OPERATION 'SATURN'

After the Cairo Conference the Turkish Government will state that their policy is unchanged, and use all precautionary measures to allay enemy suspicions.

2. Nevertheless it is necessary that the preparation and protection of the Turkish airfields should proceed at full speed without a day's delay, and that all necessary personnel, in mufti, and materials should be sent in. A period of six or seven weeks should suffice for this, the British squadrons being

ready to fly in to the airfields at any time after February 1, the exact date to be fixed in consultation with the Turkish Government and in relation to the move of the enemy. A margin of a fortnight may be allowed for this, during which time further supplies and personnel will be introduced at full speed.

3. In the lull following the expected capture of Rome in January it is desirable that three groups of medium bombers should be placed under the command of the A.O.C.-in-C. Middle East and posted in Cyrenaica for 'softening' action against enemy airfields and shipping and to cover the fly-in of the British fighter squadrons. The action of these bombers can begin irrespective of any decision taken about the fly-in. But if the enemy are quiescent it would be better to reserve their action to cover the fly-in and the events immediately following it. The details of the employment and timing of the movement of this force should be worked out by the Commander-in-Chief.

4. By February 15 the fly-in should be completed, and from that moment onwards a very considerable degree of protection against air attack will have been secured to Turkey.

5. Once established in the airfields the British squadrons, in consultation with the Turkish Government, will begin their operations in the Ægean, being supported at the same time by the medium bomber groups from Cyrenaica. Under this air cover British naval forces in the Levant, strengthened as may be necessary, will attack enemy shipping and convoys engaged in supplying the islands.

6. All preparations should meanwhile be made for Rhodes. For this purpose a first-class British division should be used for the assault, a lower category division being held ready to garrison the island, thereby setting free the British division for further operations in Italy. Rhodes of course depends upon the landing-craft being available. This operation should take place before the end of February, all landing-craft thereafter being prepared for 'Anvil'.

7. What action should be expected from the enemy? Evidently it is the Allied interest to delay this as long as possible. Therefore the Turkish Government should continue to the last moment in relations with Germany and Bulgaria, and should reply diplomatically to any protest they may make, while continuing their preparations. If Bulgaria adopts a threatening attitude to Turkey she should be notified by the Russians that if she delivers an attack at Germany's orders the Russian Soviet Union will immediately declare war on Bulgaria. It is for consideration whether the Bulgarians should not also be told that for every ton of bombs dropped by the

Germans or by them upon Constantinople or Smyrna two or three tons will be dropped on Sofia. Should the Russian armies be continuing their victorious advance in South Russia and should the Anglo-American armies prosper in the Battle of Rome it seems most unlikely that Bulgaria will attempt to invade Turkey. She may however withdraw her nine divisions from Greece and Yugoslavia and make a concentration opposite the Turkish front in Thrace.

8. Meanwhile it is also possible that, under the increasing pressure of events, Bulgaria will endeavour to make a separate peace with the three Great Allies. It is not suggested that Turkey should declare war at any stage ; she should continue her protective re-equipment and await the enemy's actions.

9. Meanwhile, as soon as the sea passage from Egypt to Turkey has been opened by the British and naval domination of the Ægean achieved every effort will be made to pass supplies and support into Smyrna, and if possible through the Dardanelles, so that the further equipment of the Turkish Army and the feeding of Constantinople can proceed as fast as possible.

10. After the fly-in of the British squadrons has been completed the Turkish Government should facilitate the secret passage into the Black Sea of six or eight British submarines, together with the necessary stores. As no depot ship can be made available base facilities should, if possible, be arranged at Ismet. These submarines should suffice to take a heavy toll of any Roumanian and German evacuations from the Crimea, and also assist any Russian descent on the Roumanian shore which the Roumanian political attitude might render possible. Such a movement would however be dependent on Russian wishes.

The Turks departed to report to their Parliament, and it was agreed that in the meantime British specialists should be assembled to implement the first stages of Operation 'Saturn'. And there the matter rested.

*   *   *

In all our many talks at Cairo the President never referred to the vital and urgent issue of the command of 'Overlord', and I was under the impression that our original arrangement and agreement held good. But on the day before his departure from Cairo he told me his final decision. We were driving in his motor-car from Cairo to the Pyramids. He then said, almost casually, that he could not spare General Marshall, whose great influence at the head of military affairs and of the war direction, under the President, was invaluable, and indispensable to the successful conduct of the war. He therefore proposed to nominate Eisenhower to 'Overlord', and asked me for my opinion. I said it was for him to decide, but that we had also the warmest regard for General Eisenhower, and would trust our fortunes to his direction with hearty goodwill.

Up to this time I had thought Eisenhower was to go to Washington as Military Chief of Staff, while Marshall commanded 'Overlord'. Eisenhower had heard of this too, and was very unhappy at the prospect of leaving the Mediterranean for Washington. Now it was all settled: Eisenhower for 'Overlord', Marshall to stay at Washington, and a British commander for the Mediterranean.

The full story of the President's long delay and hesitations and of his final decision is referred to by Mr. Hopkins' biographer, who says that Roosevelt made the decision on Sunday, December 5, 'against the almost impassioned advice of Hopkins and Stimson, against the known preference of both Stalin and Churchill, against his own proclaimed inclination'. Then Mr. Sherwood quotes the following extract from a note which he had from General Marshall after the war. 'If I recall,' said Marshall, 'the President stated, in completing our conversation, "I feel I could not sleep at night with you out of the country." '* There can be little doubt that the President felt that the command only of 'Overlord' was not sufficient to justify General Marshall's departure from Washington.

*   *   *

At last our labours were finished. I gave a dinner at the villa to the Combined Chiefs of Staff, Mr. Eden, Mr. Casey, and one or two others. I remember being struck by the optimism which prevailed in high Service circles. The idea was mooted that Hitler would not be strong enough to face the spring campaign, and might collapse even before 'Overlord' was launched in the summer. I was so much impressed by the current of opinion that I asked everybody to give his view in succession round the table. All the professional authorities were inclined to think that the German collapse was imminent. The three politicians present took the opposite view. Of course, on these vast matters on which so many lives depend there is always a great deal of

* Sherwood, *Roosevelt and Hopkins*, pp. 802–3.

guesswork. So much is unknown and immeasurable. Who can tell how weak the enemy may be behind his flaming fronts and brazen mask? At what moment will his will-power break? At what moment will he be beaten down?

*　　*　　*

The President had found no time for sightseeing, but I could not bear his leaving without seeing the Sphinx. One day after tea I said, 'You must come now.' We motored there forthwith, and examined this wonder of the world from every angle. Roosevelt and I gazed at her for some minutes in silence as the evening shadows fell. She told us nothing and maintained her inscrutable smile. There was no use waiting longer.

On December 7 I bade farewell to my great friend when he flew off from the airfield beyond the Pyramids.

CHAPTER 7

In Carthage Ruins

ANZIO

Our Air Journey to Tunis – I Have Pneumonia – Choice of Commanders for 'Overlord' and in the Mediterranean – The President Agrees with the Appointments – My Wife Arrives from England – A Climax of the War – How to Break the Deadlock in Italy – The Genesis of 'Anzio' – The British Chiefs of Staff Agree to the Operation – The Problem of Landing-craft – Our Conference on Christmas Day – Anxieties at Home – I Report to the President.

I had not been at all well during this journey and Conference. Soon after I started I had a temperature. After several days this was succeeded by a cold and sore throat, which made me keep to my bed most of the time I was in Malta. I arrived voiceless at Teheran, but this did not last long, and I was able to carry on sufficiently. All these symptoms had disappeared when I got back to Cairo. As the Conference drew to its close I became conscious of being very tired. For instance, I noticed that I no longer dried myself after my bath, but lay on the bed wrapped in my towel till I dried naturally.

A little after midnight on December 11 I and my personal party left in our York machine for Tunis. I had planned to spend one night there at General Eisenhower's villa, and to fly next day to Alexander's and then Montgomery's headquarters in Italy, where the weather was reported to be absolutely vile and all advances were fitful.

Morning saw us over the Tunis airfields. We were directed by a signal not to land where we had been told, and were shifted to another field some forty miles away. We all got out, and they began to unload the luggage. It would be an hour before motor-cars could come, and then a long drive. As I sat on my official boxes near the machines I certainly did feel completely worn out. Now however came a telephone message from General Eisenhower, who was waiting at the first airfield, that we had been wrongly transferred and that landing was quite possible there. So we scrambled back into our York, and in ten minutes were with him, quite close to his villa. Ike, always the soul of hospitality, had waited two hours with imperturbable good-humour. I got into his car, and after we had driven for a little while I said, 'I am afraid I shall have to stay with you longer than I had planned. I am completely at the end of my tether, and I cannot go on to the front until I have recovered some strength.'

All that day I slept, and the next day came fever and symptoms at the base of my lung which were adjudged to portend pneumonia. So here I was at this pregnant moment on the broad of my back amid the ruins of ancient Carthage.

* * *

› When the X-ray photographs showed that there was a shadow on one of my lungs I found that everything had been diagnosed and foreseen by Lord Moran. Dr. Bedford and other high medical authorities in the Mediterranean and excellent nurses arrived from all quarters as if by magic. The admirable M and B, from which I did not suffer any inconvenience, was used at the earliest moment, and after a week's fever the intruders were repulsed. Although Lord Moran records that he judged that the issue was at one time in doubt, I did not share his view. I did not feel so ill in this attack as I had the previous February. The M and B, which I also called Moran and Bedford, did the work most effectively. There is no doubt that pneumonia is a very different illness from what it was before this marvellous drug was discovered. I did not at any time relinquish my part in the direction of affairs, and there was not the slightest delay in giving the decisions which were required from me.

Prime Minister to Foreign Secretary   13 Dec 43
    I am caught amid these ancient ruins with a temperature and must wait till I am normal. Future movements uncertain.
    Angora must be left under no illusions that failure to comply when request is made on February 15 is the virtual end of the alliance, and that making impossible demands is only another way of saying no.
    You should ask the Staffs to report upon the possibilities of the Germans being able to gather enough forces for a further separate invasion of Turkey. I believe this to be absolute rubbish.

Prime Minister to President Roosevelt 15 Dec 43

Am stranded amid the ruins of Carthage, where you stayed, with fever which has ripened into pneumonia. All your people are doing everything possible, but I do not pretend I am enjoying myself. I hope soon to send you some of the suggestions for the new commands. I hope you had a pleasant voyage and are fit. Love to Harry.

President Roosevelt to Prime Minister 17 Dec 43

I am distressed about the pneumonia, and both Harry and I plead with you to be good and throw it off rapidly. I have just left the *Iowa* and am on my way up the Potomac. The Bible says you must do just what Moran orders, but at this moment I cannot put my finger on the verse and the chapter. ... Nothing further seems to be imminent, so do what Sarah says, and give her my love and take it easy.

* * *

It now fell to me, as British Minister of Defence responsible to the War Cabinet, to propose a British Supreme Commander for the Mediterranean. This post we confided to General Wilson, it being also settled that General Alexander should command the whole campaign in Italy, as he had done under General Eisenhower. It was also arranged that General Devers, of the U.S. Army, should become General Wilson's Deputy in the Mediterranean, and Air Chief Marshal Tedder General Eisenhower's Deputy in 'Overlord', and that General Montgomery should actually command the whole cross-Channel invasion force until such time as the Supreme Commander could transfer his headquarters to France and assume the direct operational control. All this was carried out with the utmost smoothness in perfect agreement by the President and by me, with Cabinet approval, and worked in good comradeship and friendship by all concerned.

I should add that when in November 1944 General Alexander was nominated to succeed General Wilson as Supreme Commander in the Mediterranean I myself proposed, on behalf of His Majesty's Government, that United States General Mark Clark should take command under him of the whole of the forces in Italy, three-quarters of which were British, Imperial, or British-controlled. This he did with marked distinction and success.

The operative telegrams were:

Prime Minister to President Roosevelt   18 Dec 43

Thank you so much for your telegram. I have hearkened unto the voice of Moran and made good progress, but I am fixed here for another week.

2. Since our last talk on the subject I have given much thought to the remodelling of the commands, and have had discussions with Eisenhower, Alexander, and Tedder. I have also consulted my colleagues at home, and have to-day had a long conversation with the C.I.G.S. on his return from a visit to Italy. As a result I am able to place before you the following proposals, which, if you approve them, will, I am satisfied, be generally accepted.

3. I had always thought that Alexander would succeed Eisenhower, but am convinced by the arguments of the C.I.G.S., Eisenhower, and others that it would be impossible for him or Montgomery to act as Supreme Commander and at the same time fight the battles which will take place in Italy after the conquest of Rome. Alexander himself quite saw this.

4. I therefore propose General Wilson as Supreme Commander, *vice* Eisenhower. Under him will be:

(*a*) General Commanding, Algiers: a United States officer. We have heard that it might be convenient to you to transfer General Devers from his present post.

(*b*) Commander-in-Chief of the Armies in Italy: Alexander.

(*c*) General in charge of Operation 'Anvil': Clark. We understand that this was what you and General Marshall had in mind. If so, we concur.

(*d*) A British major-general in charge of the Yugoslav assistance measures, Tito, Greeks, etc.

(*e*) Commander-in-Chief Mid-East, for operational purposes within the Mediterranean theatre, and also in charge of the Turkish operations: Paget (now commanding British Home Forces).

5. The Air Officer Commanding-in-Chief should be an American, appointed by you. Arnold when passing through here spoke of Brereton or Eaker. We would agree to either, but we should miss the latter from the bombing and 'Overlord' build-up. Sholto Douglas will be Deputy Air Officer Commanding-in-Chief, and also Commander-in-Chief of all the R.A.F. in the Mediterranean theatre.

6. Political assistance will be provided for the Supreme Commander:

(*a*) by Messrs. Murphy and Macmillan, who work hand-in-hand;

(*b*) from the French angle by Duff Cooper and Wilson;

(c) from the Middle Eastern area by the Minister of State or his successor.

7. Bedell Smith will accompany Eisenhower after a few weeks and become his Chief of Staff in England, being replaced here by a British Chief of Staff. We leave it to you to decide whether you would like to have a Deputy Supreme Commander, who would of course be an American.

8. You will understand that I have given most careful consideration to the appointment of Sir Henry Maitland Wilson, and I am satisfied that for the great co-ordination task which will be entrusted to him he has all the qualifications and the necessary vigour. This is also the opinion of the C.I.G.S. When I mentioned this idea to you at Cairo you seemed to like it.

9. Turning to the 'Overlord' theatre, I propose to you that Tedder shall be Eisenhower's Deputy Supreme Commander, on account of the great part the air will play in this operation, and this is most agreeable to Eisenhower. The War Cabinet desires that Montgomery should command the first expeditionary group of armies. I feel the Cabinet are right, as Montgomery is a public hero and will give confidence among our people, not unshared by yours.

10. I beg most earnestly that I may soon have your reply on these proposals, or at least upon the key ones, as the Commander of 'Overlord' is urgently required, and I should like to arrange for Wilson to take over from Eisenhower at an early date, and to come to him even sooner in order to settle the many consequential details.

President Roosevelt to Prime Minister   20 Dec 43

I am agreeable to an announcement on January 1 of selection of Eisenhower to command 'Overlord', Tedder to be Eisenhower's Deputy Supreme Commander, Wilson to relieve Eisenhower as Supreme Commander Mediterranean (this change to be made when Eisenhower reports that conditions in Italy justify the change), Eaker to command Allied Air Force Mediterranean.

2. I prefer to delay announcement of changes in subordinate commands until after the first of the year, because I want to have opportunity to discuss it with Marshall, who will return to Washington in a few days.

3. I am delighted that you are really so much better, and I wish I could be with you at Marrakesh. I hope you have sent for your brushes.

*   *   *

The days passed in much discomfort. Fever flickered in and out. I lived on my theme of the war, and it was like being transported out of oneself. The doctors tried to keep the work away from my bedside, but I defied them. They all kept on saying, 'Don't work, don't worry,' to such an extent that I decided to read a novel. I had long ago read Jane Austen's *Sense and Sensibility*, and now I thought I would have *Pride and Prejudice*. Sarah read it to me beautifully from the foot of the bed. I had always thought it would be better than its rival. What calm lives they had, those people! No worries about the French Revolution, or the crashing struggle of the Napoleonic wars. Only manners controlling natural passion so far as they could, together with cultured explanations of any mischances. All this seemed to go very well with M and B.

One morning Sarah was absent from her chair at the foot of my bed, and I was about to ask for my box of telegrams in the prohibited hours when in she walked with her mother. I had no idea that my wife was flying out from England to join me. She had hurried to the airport to fly in a two-engined Dakota. The weather was bad, but Lord Beaverbrook was vigilant. He got to the airport first, and stopped her flight until a four-engined plane could be procured. (I always think it better to have four engines when flying long distances across the sea.) Now she had arrived after a very rough journey in an unheated plane in midwinter. Jock Colville had escorted her, and was a welcome addition to my hard-pressed personal staff, through whom so much business was being directed. 'My love to Clemmie,' cabled the President. 'I feel relieved that she is with you as your superior officer.'

*　　　*　　　*

As I lay prostrate I felt we were at one of the climaxes of the war. The mounting of 'Overlord' was the greatest event and duty in the world. But must we sabotage everything we could have in Italy, where the main strength overseas of our country was involved? Were we to leave it a stagnant pool from which we had drawn every fish we wanted? As I saw the problem, the campaign in Italy, in which a million or more of our British, British-controlled, and Allied troops were engaged. was the faithful and indispensable comrade and counterpart to the main cross-Channel operation. Here the American clear-cut, logical, large-scale, mass production style of thought was formidable.

In life people have first to be taught 'Concentrate on essentials'. This is no doubt the first step out of confusion and fatuity ; but it is only the first step. The second stage in war is a general harmony of war effort by making everything fit together, and every scrap of fighting strength play its full part all the time. I was sure that a vigorous campaign in Italy during the first half of 1944 would be the greatest help to the supreme operation of crossing the Channel, on which all minds were set and all engagements made. But every item which any Staff officer could claim as 'essential' or 'vital', to use these hard-worked words, had to be argued out as if it carried with it the success or failure of our main purpose. Twenty or a dozen vehicle landing-craft had to be fought for as if the major issue turned upon them.

The case seemed to me brutally simple. All the ships we had would be used to carry to England everything the United States could produce in arms and men. Surely the enormous forces we could not possibly move by sea from the Italian theatre should play their part. Either they would gain Italy easily and immediately bite upon the German inner front, or they would draw large German forces from the front which we were to attack across the Channel in the last days of May, or the early days of June, as the moon and the tides prescribed.

*   *   *

The deadlock to which our armies in Italy had been brought by the stubborn German resistance on the eighty-mile front from sea to sea had already led General Eisenhower to contemplate an amphibious flanking attack. He had planned to land with one division south of the Tiber and make a dart for Rome, in conjunction with an attack by the main armies. The arrest of these armies and the distance of the landing point from them made everyone feel that more than one division was required. I had of course always been a partisan of the 'end run', as the Americans call it, or 'cat-claw', which was my term. I had never succeeded in getting this manœuvre open to sea-power included in any of our Desert advances. In Sicily however General Patton had twice used the command of the sea flank as he advanced along the northern coast of the island with great effect. Both at Carthage and at Marrakesh I was near enough to the scene of action to convene meetings of all the chief commanders.

There was a great deal of professional support. Eisenhower

was already committed in principle, though his new appointment to the command of 'Overlord' now gave him a different sense of values and a new horizon. Alexander, Deputy Supreme Commander and commanding the armies in Italy, thought the operation right and necessary; Bedell Smith was ardent and helpful in every direction. This was also true of Admiral John Cunningham, who held all the naval cards, and of Air Marshal Tedder. I had therefore a powerful array of Mediterranean authorities. Moreover, I felt sure the British Chiefs of Staff would like the plan, and that with their agreement I could obtain the approval of the War Cabinet. When you cannot give orders hard and lengthy toils must be faced.

'Overlord' in May was sacrosanct. We had pledged ourselves at Teheran only a month before. Nothing could be considered which prevented our keeping our supreme engagement. In this case troops, air-power, and sea-power presented no obstacles. All turned upon L.S.T.s (Landing-ships, Tanks). This included 'Landing-ships, Vehicles', because landing tanks was only a small proportion of their indispensable work. A lengthy correspondence conducted in cipher between me and Whitehall and Washington arose. The military student may some day be interested to read the details of this tense and clear-cut argument, of which only a skeleton is here printed. The L.S.T.s must, in the name of 'Overlord', be in England at certain dates. These dates had been calculated with extreme precision, and of course with all the margins for accident which, at every stage, enter into military planning, and would make almost all action impossible if they were not controlled from the top. Everyone claims his margin at every stage, and the sum of the margins is usually 'No'.

I began my effort on December 19, when the C.I.G.S arrived at Carthage to see me on his way home from Montgomery's headquarters in Italy. We had hoped to go there together, but my illness had prevented me. We had a full discussion, and I found that General Brooke had by a separate route of thought arrived at the same conclusion as I had. We agreed on the policy, and also that while I should deal with the commanders on the spot he would do his best to overcome all difficulties at home. General Brooke then left by air for London. I telegraphed:

Prime Minister to Chiefs of Staff　　　　　　　　　19 Dec 43
　I am anxiously awaiting a full list of all landing-craft of all

types in the Mediterranean now, showing their condition and employment, and especially whether it is true that a large number are absorbed in purely supply work to the prevention of their amphibious duties. There is no doubt that the stagnation of the whole campaign on the Italian front is becoming scandalous. The C.I.G.S.'s visit confirmed my worst forebodings. The total neglect to provide amphibious action on the Adriatic side and the failure to strike any similar blow on the west have been disastrous.

None of the landing-craft in the Mediterranean have been put to the slightest use [for assault purposes] for three months, neither coming home in preparation for 'Overlord', nor for the Ægean islands, nor in the Italian battle. There are few instances, even in this war, of such valuable forces being so completely wasted.

The Chiefs of Staff had evidently been thinking on the same lines, and, after hearing General Brooke's account, replied on the 22nd:

We are in full agreement with you that the present stagnation cannot be allowed to continue. For every reason it is essential that something should be done to speed things up. The solution, as you say, clearly lies in making use of our amphibious power to strike round on the enemy's flank and open up the way for a rapid advance on Rome.

After the L.S.T.s are withdrawn for 'Overlord' on January 15 General Eisenhower should have at his disposal an amphibious lift sufficient for a little more than one division, and he has a plan to make a landing behind the enemy just south of Rome. The weakness of this plan is that the assault in that strength on the coast cannot be launched until the Fifth Army is within supporting distance of the force to be landed. If the available lift could be increased however a stronger force could be landed without waiting for the main army to arrive within immediate supporting distance. Such a landing moreover would have a more far-reaching effect on the whole progress of the campaign, and would be much more likely to open the way for a rapid advanve. We think the aim should be to provide a lift for at least two divisions.

We have telegraphed to the Commander-in-Chief Mediterranean for the information you ask for on landing-craft. We have every hope that it will be possible to make some economy in this direction, but we must look farther afield if we are to give General Eisenhower the two-divisional lift.

A possible source of supply is the craft already on their way back from South-East Asia to the Mediterranean. ... A small number of craft have also been left in South-East Asia.

After explaining that the new plan would involve giving up both the capture of Rhodes and also a minor amphibious operation on the Arakan coast of Burma, they ended:

> If you approve the above line of thought we propose to take the matter up with the Combined Chiefs of Staff with a view to action being taken on these lines at once.

*   *   *

This led to a hard scrutiny of our resources. Some landing-craft for the cancelled operation against the Andamans were on their way to the Mediterranean across the Indian Ocean. Others were due to return home for 'Overlord'. All were in extreme demand.

I had been reluctant to agree to the abandonment of the attack on Rhodes we had talked of to President Inönü. A far greater effort must be made with the Turks, as well as to expedite the operation and the subsequent return of landing-craft for 'Anvil' (the assault on Southern France). By December 23 however I was becoming resigned to Turkish neutrality, and I replied from Carthage:

> You will observe that whereas you are thinking of a decision in Italy Ike is looking forward to 'Anvil', which is now very much part of his main interest. I recognise that if the Turks will not play we may have to sacrifice the Ægean policy especially if it is marked up so high and so slow. I hope however that this decision will not be taken till after full exploration of the whole scene. I hope to see Eisenhower to-day, and Alexander is visiting me. Thereafter I shall ask Jumbo [General Wilson] to come here on his way home. I wish to keep all the issues open for the next three or four days. Supposing Turkey jibs and Rhodes is shut out, we must have the big Rome amphibious operation, and also have some clearing up on the Dalmatian coast, especially Argostoli and Corfu. In no case can we sacrifice Rome for the Riviera. We must have both.

Meanwhile I had had a long talk with Alexander. He demurred to the suggestion that he was not very keen on the Anzio landing. He wanted a two-division lift, and the problem was how this could be supplied. Bedell Smith, who had also arrived thought he could make up pretty nearly a two-division lift provided that airborne troops were counted as well. If this were supplied and decision taken on the morrow or the next day Alexander could strike in the last week of January. The question was, how to find the landing-craft. When I asked Bedell Smith why we should not delay the 'Overlord' L.S.T.s, etc., till February 15 he replied he just could not bear asking for a third extension. I had no such compunction.

There were 104 L.S.T.s in the Mediterranean, but most of them were due to return home for 'Overlord'. By the middle of January we should only have thirty-six, with another fifteen arriving from the Indian Ocean about that time. To carry two divisions it was said we needed eighty-eight. No more could arrive till April. The only solution was to hold most of those in the Mediterranean for another three weeks. There were good hopes that this could be done without injury to 'Overlord' or to the landing on the Riviera.

*   *   *

On the 24th the Chiefs of Staff sent me a detailed statement of their ideas, and a draft which they proposed to send to their Washington colleagues. They favoured the plan, but feared we should never win American consent.

Their conclusions were:

> We ask the Combined Chiefs of Staff to agree:
>
> (*a*) That the remainder of the Andamans assault shipping and craft should be ordered to the Mediterranean.
>
> (*b*) That such resources as can reach the Central Mediterranean in time should be employed by the Supreme Allied Commander Mediterranean Theatre for the launching of a two-divisional amphibious assault designed to enable Rome to be captured and the armies to advance to the Pisa–Rimini line, and that instructions to this effect should be issued forthwith. There will be sufficient time for the subsequent withdrawal of these resources for the South of France attack.
>
> (*c*) That our negotiations with Turkey should continue on the present basis, but that amphibious operations in the Ægean should be ruled out.
>
> (*d*) That Admiral Mountbatten should be informed of these decisions, and instructed to make his final recommendations for operations to be carried out in his theatre with the resources remaining to him.

*   *   *

I had with me at this tense period from my Defence Office only General Hollis, but he proved a tower of strength. I was also greatly aided by Captain Power, R.N., who was Admiral John Cunningham's Deputy Chief of Staff (Plans). He cleared away a mass of argument which obstructed the decision. He said in his able paper, which the Admiral fully approved:

> The L.S.T.s now in the Mediterranean are thoroughly trained. They have all taken part in at least two assault operations, and have done a great deal of additional work on ferrying, continually loading and unloading over beaches, yards, or quays. They are well manned and accustomed to steaming and manœuvring in close company. They should require no further naval training prior to 'Overlord', except that they are unaccustomed to problems of tide and the technique of beaching and unbeaching in tidal waters. Being good seamen however, they should require but very brief instruction and training before they master the new problem. ... Mediterranean experience shows that there is no need to marry the L.S.T.s and the troops concerned until eleven days before calling for the operation—three days for initial loading, six days for rehearsal, two days for reloading. ...
>
> I should estimate that seven days' allowance for tide training would be more than adequate for these well-trained ships
>
> Total training allowance should therefore be approximately three weeks. . . . They therefore have ample time before 'Overlord', except that they cannot all refit at once.

*   *   *

As a result of detailed discussion with the assembled commanders I sent home the following proposals after midnight on the 24th:

Prime Minister to Chiefs of Staff and   25 Dec 43
First Sea Lord   (12.30 a.m.)
    I have had talks to-night with General Wilson and General Alexander and Air Chief Marshal Tedder and their staffs about Anzio.
    We are all agreed that it must be carried out on sufficient scale to ensure success, namely, at least a two-divisional assault. Target date will be about January 20. Assumption is that Rhodes is not on. We feel strongly that the only right course is to delay for not more than one month departure from Mediterranean of all British L.S.T.s now due to leave in January and on February 1 (totalling fifty-six L.S.T.s). The

fifteen L.S.T.s from the Bay of Bengal would not arrive in time for Anzio, but would play their part in repayment of 'Overlord' a little later. . . .

I wish Chiefs of Staff to give earliest attention to the paper prepared at my request by Captain Power. This sets out the economies in time which might be effected in the preparation of L.S.T.s for 'Overlord'. All present to-night considered that Captain Power's paper showed a firm grasp of the situation, and his proposals should be capable of achievement. . . .

The Chiefs of Staff were not at first convinced. They mentioned various points of detail ; and details were decisive. They also 'earnestly hoped' I would agree to their draft note explaining the situation to the Combined Chiefs of Staff. I was sure that we must be agreed among ourselves on all essentials first, and I replied as follows:

Prime Minister to Chiefs of Staff   26 Dec 43

I have been into the facts most thoroughly with the Admiral and with General Gale and their staffs. There is not the slightest chance of mounting Anzio on a two-division basis unless the whole fifty-six L.S.T.s are held back another three weeks—*i.e.*, until February 5. They know a good deal about training for assault landings in the Mediterranean. Pray let me know the argument as between three weeks and a month, and let me know exactly each day's employment prescribed for vessels on return. . . . You are expected to organise dockyards so as to refit twenty-five a month.

The success of Anzio depends on the strength of the initial landing. If this is two full divisions plus paratroops it should be decisive, as it cuts the communications of the whole of the enemy forces facing the Fifth Army. The enemy must therefore annihilate the landing force by withdrawals from the Fifth Army front or immediately retreat. Nothing less than two divisions will serve. Weather uncertainties make it necessary to put them ashore with at least four days' supplies. It is not intended to maintain these divisions for long over the beaches, but rather to bring the battle to a climax in a week or ten days. . . .

It is no use your telegraphing to the Combined Chiefs of Staff until we are in agreement on the one vital matter, namely, the delay of three weeks in the return of the fifty-six L.S.T.s. On this depends the success or ruin of our Italian campaign.

The Chiefs of Staff gave many solid reasons for their anxieties in their reply of December 27, and added, We feel we should not conceal from you the difficulty we expect with the United States Chiefs of Staff if we tell them frankly the true position as we see it.'

*   *   *

All the morning of Christmas Day our conference at Carthage continued. Eisenhower, Alexander, Bedell Smith, General Wilson, Tedder, Admiral John Cunningham, and other high officers were present. The only one not there was General Mark Clark, of the Fifth Army. This was an oversight which I regret, as it was to his army that the operation was eventually entrusted and he ought to have had the background in his mind. We were all agreed that nothing less than a two-division lift would suffice. At this time I contemplated an assault by two British divisions from the Eighth Army, in which Montgomery was about to be succeeded by General Leese. I thought the amphibious operation involved potential mortal risks to the landed forces, and I preferred to run them with British troops, because it was to Britain that I was responsible. Moreover, the striking force would then have been homogeneous instead of half and half.

Everything turned on landing-craft, which held for some weeks all our strategy in the tightest ligature. What with the rigid date prescribed for 'Overlord' and the movement, repair, and refitting of less than a hundred of these small vessels, all plans were in a strait-jacket. The telegrams which passed show how we escaped, though mauled, from this predicament. But I must also admit that I was so much occupied in fighting for the principle that I did not succeed in getting, and indeed did not dare to demand, the necessary weight and volume for the 'cat-claw'. Actually there were enough L.S.T.s for the operation as planned, and in my opinion, if the extravagant demands of the military machine had been reduced, we could, without prejudice to any other pledge or commitment, have flung ashore south of the Tiber a still larger force with full mobility. However, the issue was fought out in terms of routine Army requirements and the exact dates when L.S.T.s could be free for 'Overlord', making of course all allowances for their return home in winter Biscay weather, and with the time-margins for their refits stated at their maximum. If I had asked for a three-division lift I should not have got anything. How often in life must one be content with what one can get! Still, it would be better to do it right.

*   *   *

The brute fact of delaying the return to England of the fifty-six L.S.T.s for three weeks had to be faced. Against this towered up the date of 'Overlord'—MAY. The reader will note in the following telegram the first appearance of JUNE 6.

Prime Minister to Chiefs of Staff   26 Dec 43

I am proceeding entirely on the basis of keeping to the May 'Overlord'. I am sure this can be done and problem solved by persevering energetically. I may however say in strictest secrecy that both Eisenhower and Montgomery have expressed themselves entirely dissatisfied with what they have heard of the present plan for 'Overlord', and I gather they will demand a far larger first flight. I should think it very likely that when they have examined the plan they will propose a delay. Our contract is 'during May', but I do not know whether if responsible commanders required the June moon around June 6, and could show much better prospects then, the extra week might not have to be conceded. Preliminary air bombardment would begin anyhow in May.

Beware therefore that we do not sacrifice our vital task in Italy in order to achieve a date which anyhow may be postponed on other and larger grounds. Eisenhower even spoke of telegraphing himself to Stalin, once he had assumed effective command and was master of the problem, demanding a reasonable measure of delay. I did not lend myself to this at all, as I am fighting the case on the Teheran [agreement] line. All the more do I expect you to help me. Be careful this is kept to yourselves and the three War Cabinet Ministers on Defence Committee, Mr. Attlee, Mr. Eden, and Mr. Lyttelton.

At the close of this decisive Christmas Day conference at Carthage I sent the following to the President, and a similar telegram home. I was careful to state the root fact bluntly.

25 Dec 43

I held a conference to-day with Eisenhower, and all his high officers. Report as follows:

General Alexander is prepared to execute the landing at Anzio about January 20 if he can get a lift of two divisions. This should decide the Battle of Rome, and possibly achieve the destruction of a substantial part of enemy's army. To strike with less than two divisions would be to court disaster, having regard to the positions likely to be achieved by that date by Fifth and Eighth Armies.

For this purpose eighty-eight L.S.T.s are required. These can only be obtained by delaying the return home of fifty-six

L.S.T.s due to leave the Mediterranean from January 15 onward, sending them home by convoys starting February 5. Nothing less than this will suffice. The fifteen L.S.T.s from India cannot arrive in time, though they would be invaluable to replace casualties and for the building up of 'Anvil'.

By various expedients it is believed that the lost three weeks can be recovered and the existing prescribed build-up for 'Overlord' maintained.

Having kept these fifty-six L.S.T.s in the Mediterranean so long, it would seem irrational to remove them for the very week when they can render decisive service. What, also, could be more dangerous than to let the Italian battle stagnate and fester on for another three months? We cannot afford to go forward leaving a vast half-finished job behind us. It therefore seemed to those present that every effort should be made to bring off Anzio on a two-division basis around January 20, and orders have been issued to General Alexander to prepare accordingly. If this opportunity is not grasped we must expect the ruin of the Mediterranean campaign of 1944. I earnestly hope therefore that you may agree to the three weeks' delay in return of the fifty-six landing-craft, and that all the authorities will be instructed to make sure that the May 'Overlord' is not prejudiced thereby.

I recognise with regret that Rhodes and the Ægean policy must be side-tracked in these higher interests, and it may well be that 'Pigstick' [the attack on the Arakan, west of Burma] will require to be moderated into 'Pigstuck' in order to build up three divisions for the landing in the South of France. This has been most painful to me, but I could not face the Italian stalemate and disaster which will otherwise ensue.

It was at this point, while all hung in suspense, that I flew from Carthage to Marrakesh, bearing my burdens with me.

CHAPTER 8

At Marrakesh

CONVALESCENCE

By Air to Marrakesh – Joyful News: The President's Telegram of December 28 – June 3 versus May 5 as the Date for 'Overlord' – The American Parachute Regiment – Montgomery's Visit – New Year Correspondence with the President – Conferences at Marrakesh on the Anzio Expedition, January 7 and 8 – Generals Eisenhower and Montgomery Incline to the Moon Period of June 3 for 'Overlord' – The President's View – The Polish Question Again – Visit of President Beneš – A Tribute to Beneš – Friendly Contacts with General de Gaulle – Russia's Share in the Italian Fleet – A Compromise – Home Before Anzio.

Lord Moran thought it possible for me to leave Carthage after Christmas, but insisted that I must have three weeks' convalescence somewhere. And where could be better than the lovely villa at Marrakesh, where the President and I had stayed after Casablanca a year before? All plans had been made during the past few days. I was to be the guest of the United States Army at Marrakesh. It was also thought that I had been long enough at Carthage to be located. Small vessels had ceaselessly to patrol the bay in front of the villa in case some U-boat turned up for a surprise raid. There might also be a long-range air attack. I had my own protection in a battalion of the Coldstream Guards. I was too ill, or too busy, to be consulted about all this, but I saw in my beloved Marrakesh a haven where I could regain my strength. Tedder had planned out the flight with great care. The doctors did not want me to fly above six thousand feet, and he had arranged our route through the Atlas Mountains on this basis. I was delighted when the morning of December 27 came and I dressed for the first time again in my uniform. As I was leaving the door a telegram was put in my hand, giving the fateful news of the sinking of the *Scharnhorst*.* I stopped to dictate the following telegram to Stalin:

* See Book 9, Chapter 15.

Prime Minister to Premier Stalin   27 Dec 43
   The Arctic convoys to Russia have brought us luck.
Yesterday enemy attempted to intercept with battle-cruiser
Scharnhorst. Commander-in-Chief Admiral Fraser with the
Duke of York (35,000-ton battleship) cut off *Scharnhorst*'s
retreat, and after an action sunk her.
   2. Am much better, and off to the south for convales-
cence.

A very cordial reply to this was received a few days later,
ending, 'I shake your hand firmly.'
   Outside the villa a magnificent guard of the Coldstream was
drawn up. I had not realised how much I had been weakened
by my illness. I found it quite a difficulty to walk along the
ranks and climb into the motor-car. The flight at six thousand
feet had been planned on the weather forecast that the skies
would be clear. However, as we sailed on and the uplands of
Tunisia began to rise about us I saw a lot of large fleecy and
presently blackish clouds gathering around, and after a couple
of hours we were more often in mist than in sunlight. I have
always had a great objection to what are called 'stuffed clouds'
—*i.e.,* clouds with mountains inside them—and flying an intricate route through the various valleys before us in order to keep
under six thousand feet seemed to me an unfair proposition for
the others in the plane. I therefore sent for the pilot and told
him to fly at least two thousand feet above the highest mountain
within a hundred miles of his route. Lord Moran agreed. Oxygen
was brought by a skilled adminstrator, specially provided for
the journey.* We sailed up into the blue. I got along all right, and
we made a perfect landing at about four o'clock on the Marrakesh airfield. Our second plane, which had adhered strictly to
its instructions, had a very severe and dangerous flight through
the various gorges and passes, many of which were traversed
with only fleeting glimpses of the towering mountains. At this
low height the weather was by no means good. The plane
arrived safely an hour behind us with one of its doors blown off
and nearly everybody very sick. I was sorry indeed they should
have been put to so much discomfort and risk on my account.
They could have flown it all out comfortably under blue skies
at twelve or even eleven thousand feet.
   Nothing could exceed the comfort, and even luxury, of my
new abode, or the kindness of everyone concerned. But one

* Air Commodore Kelly, Principal Medical Officer of the Royal Air Force in North
Africa, who rightly insisted on travelling in the aircraft for this purpose.

thing rose above all others in my mind—what answer would the President give to my telegram? When I thought of the dull, dead-weight resistance, taking no account of timing and proportion, that I had encountered about all Mediterranean projects I awaited the answer with deep anxiety. What I asked for was a hazardous enterprise on the Italian coast, and a possible delay of three weeks from May 1—four if the moon phase was to be observed—in the date of the Channel crossing. I had gained the agreement of the commanders on the spot. The British Chiefs of Staff had always agreed in principle, and were now satisfied in detail. But what would the Americans say to a four weeks' postponement of 'Overlord'? However, when one is thoroughly tired out the blessing of sleep is not usually denied.

*   *   *

It was with joy, not, I confess, unmingled with surprise, that the next day I received the following:

President Roosevelt to Prime Minister   28 Dec 43
It is agreed to delay the departure of fifty-six L.S.T.s scheduled for 'Overlord' for mounting Anzio on January 20, and on the basis that 'Overlord' remains the paramount operation and will be carried out on the date agreed to at Cairo and Teheran. All possible expedients should be undertaken to overcome probable effect on 'Overlord' preparation, to which end the other twelve L.S.T.s for 'Overlord' should depart as now scheduled and the fifteen L.S.T.s *ex* Andamans arriving in Mediterranean on January 14 should proceed directly to United Kingdon. I agree that Rhodes and the Ægean must be sidetracked and that we cannot give further consideration to launching Rhodes prior to 'Anvil' [Riviera]. In view of the Soviet-British-American agreement reached in Teheran I cannot agree without Stalin's approval to any use of forces or equipment elsewhere that might delay or hazard the success of 'Overlord' or 'Anvil'.

I replied:

Prime Minister to President Roosevelt   28 Dec 43
I thank God for this fine decision, which engages us once again in wholehearted unity upon a great enterprise.

I have heard from the British Chiefs of Staff that the Admiralty can conform to the conditions provided the releases are made from the Anzio plan of the number which are agreed upon. The Chiefs of Staff will be telegraphing to-day in full detail to the Combined Chiefs of Staff. Meanwhile here the word is 'Full steam ahead'.

After travelling quite unaffected at 13,000 feet I arrived yesterday at our villa, where I am indeed in the lap of luxury, thanks to overflowing American hospitality. Max [Beaverbrook] has just flown in from London. I propose to stay here in the sunshine till I am quite strong again.

Great efforts had indeed been made by the Staffs at home, and especially by the Admiralty, to accomplish the 'cat-claw', and I hastened to congratulate them. General Alexander had asked for eighty-eight landing-craft; they promised him all but one. The President's telegram was a marvel. I was sure that I owed it not only to his goodwill, but to Marshall's balance of mind, to Eisenhower's loyalty to the show he was about to quit, and to Bedell Smith's active, knowledgeable, fact-armed diplomacy.

On the same day Alexander sent us his plan. After conferring with General Mark Clark and General Brian Robertson, Chief Administrative Officer and son of the C.I.G.S. of the First World War, he had decided to use an American and a British division. Armour, paratroops, and Commandos would be on a fifty-fifty basis, and the whole would be under an American corps commander. The attack would go in about January 20. Ten days beforehand he would launch a big offensive against Cassino to draw off the German reserves. The forward plunge of the main armies would follow. I was well content. So far so good.

*   *   *

I had however another small margin on which to draw. I wired to the Chiefs of Staff:

I am fighting the issue [of the date of 'Overlord'] entirely on the Teheran basis. This assumed May 20 rather than May 5, which is an altogether new date. Our contract with Stalin would be fulfilled by any date up to May 31. It seems to me from what I have heard from Eisenhower that June 3, which is the corresponding moon phase, would be perfectly permissible, especially if it were asked for by the commanders now nominated for the operation. There is no need to discuss such matters now, but here is something to veer and haul on.

Pray let me have the alternative build-up comparing May 5 with June 3. I repeat this is not to be considered as anything in the nature of a decision for delay, and is not to go to anyone outside our circle.

The Chiefs of Staff replied:

To fulfil the conditions of the plan made by existing commanders the 'Overlord' assault should take place about May 5. However, this date cannot be regarded as final, and even if delays occur in the return and refitting programme of the L.S.T.s so that all have not joined their assault forces by April 13, this should not rule out a May date for the 'Overlord' assault.

The arrangements proposed certainly do not preclude the achievement of a May assault, but the programme is tightly stretched. No violation of the agreement reached at Teheran is however involved, and we do not think it necessary at this stage to consult the Russians.

I commented on this as follows:

30 Dec 43

Our contract would be fulfilled by May 31. In my opinion it would be a *bona fide* execution of it if we fixed June 3, which is the corresponding moon phase to May 5, for the actual assault. It is however better to work to May 5, and thus have a month to spare.

* * *

Now a new point of importance arose.

Prime Minister to Field-Marshal Dill, Washington   3 Jan 44

Alexander signals as follows:

'Clark is planning Anzio, and the usual difficulties are coming to light. For example, it appears that we shall not be able to keep the 504th American Parachute Regiment, and Eisenhower is reluctant to press for their retention. The British Parachute Brigade is in the line and engaged. I have nothing immediately available to relieve them with, and we cannot afford the delay in getting them out and across to the Naples area. Further, they are not operationally experienced and badly need training.'

2. Eisenhower is now with Marshall. Will you appeal to them to let this 504th American Regiment do this one fine and critical job before they come home for 'Overlord'? It is so rarely that opportunities for decisive air action by paratroops present themselves, and it seems improvident to take them from the decisive point just when they might render exemplary and outstanding service. They can be sent home immediately afterwards in time for 'Overlord', observing that we have already [at home] about double as many parachute

and airborne troops for 'Overlord' as there are transport aircraft to lift. Let me know what happens.

General Marshall agreed. We shall see later how this sacrifice was wasted.

* * *

I had asked Montgomery to visit me on his way home from Italy to take up his new command in 'Overlord'. I had offered him this task so full of hazard. Of course in the absence of special reasons a general should accept any duty to which he is called by national authority. At the same time nothing in the unwritten law obliges enthusiasm. In the Grenadier Guards, with whom I once had the honour to serve, all orders are received with the one word 'Sir'. However, all kinds of inflections may be given to this monosyllable. I was gratified and also relieved to find that Montgomery was delighted and eager for what I had always regarded as a majestic, inevitable, but terrible task. When he arrived at Marrakesh we had a two hours' drive out to our picnic at the foot of the Atlas. I had given him early in the morning the plan prepared over so many months by General Morgan and the Anglo-American Joint Staffs in London. After he had read it in summary he said at once, 'This will not do. I must have more in the initial punch.' After considerable argument a whole set of arrangements was made in consequence of his opinion, and proved right. Evidently he was a firm believer in the operation, and I was very pleased at this.

The ladies had now come up, and we all lunched by the side of a dazzling stream in fresh air and brilliant sunshine. It was indeed an oasis in the vast desert of human conflict through which we had to toil. Presently I pushed forward into the mountains and our cars zigzagged slowly up the road to a viewpoint which I knew. But the General would have none of this. He got out of the car and walked straight up the hill, 'to keep himself in training,' as he put it. I warned him not to waste his vigour, considering what was coming. I emphasised the truths that energy of mind does not depend on energy of body ; that energy should be exercised and not exhausted ; that athletics are one thing and strategy another. These admonitions were in vain. The General was in the highest spirits ; he leaped about the rocks like an antelope, and I felt a strong reassurance that all would be well.

* * *

The New Year opened for me in agreeable correspondence with the President.

Prime Minister (Marrakesh) to President Roosevelt
30 Dec 43

I have now received from my brother Jack full accounts of the Christmas tree at Chequers.* All my grandchildren were there, and a number of other children, and a good time was had by all. Winant, who was present, has promised to write to you about it. Thank you so much for sending me this token. I have also to thank you for the wonderful map case which has arrived from you for me, and which I am longing to see. We are indeed in comfort at this beautiful villa, and I am making good progress. The sun is shining to-day, but nothing did me the same good as your telegram showing how easily our minds work together on the grimly simple issues of this vast war. Alexander reports he has arranged satisfactory plans with Clark for Anzio. He is using the British 1st and the American 3rd Divisions, with paratroops and armour. I am glad of this. It is fitting that we should share equally in suffering, risk, and honour.

I received on the same day congratulations on my recovery from Franco and Tito. So what?

Sarah thanks you for your message and sends her love.

Unhappily the President was himself laid up with influenza.

President Roosevelt to Prime Minister
31 Dec 43

I am in bed for two or three days with a mild case of the 'flu, which, in a mild form, has become epidemic throughout the country.

I am delighted that you are safely at the villa. I suggest that on New Year's Day you invite the two gentlemen who congratulated you, then lock them in the top of the tower where we saw the sunset, and tell them you will stay at the bottom to see whether the black or the red throws the other one over the battlements.

Prime Minister to President Roosevelt
1 Jan 44

I am so sorry about your influenza. I earnestly hope you will defer to Dr. McIntyre's advice and show that attitude of submission to the medical faculty which you have so sedulously enjoined on me.

The villa is perfect. The doctors want me to stay here for

---

* Mr. Roosevelt grew Christmas trees at Hyde Park, and prided himself on this. He had sent me one.

the next three weeks. The weather is bright, though cool. The cook is a marvel. We go for picnics to the mountains. Last night Eisenhower was with us on his way to you, and I had long talks with him. Montgomery is here now on his way to England. I think we have a fine team, and they certainly mean to pull together.

I have not yet been able to arrange the contest in the tower. The Red is in better training than the Black.

Accept all my best wishes for a New Year which will not only be marked by triumph but will open wider doors to our future work together.

Clemmie and Sarah also send their salutations.

*   *   *

Although the main issue about the landing-craft for Anzio had been settled many details of their employment raised serious discussion.

General Alexander to Prime Minister   4 Jan 44

I have just returned from conference with General Clark on my way back from Tunis, and certain factors have come to light which are causing me grave concern, and I must therefore ask for your help and assistance. The facts are these. The removal of all but six of the L.S.T.s after the initial landing will not allow us to put the two divisions ashore complete with their essential fighting vehicles. ... My experience of combined operations is that the initial assault to get ashore can be effected, but the success of the operation depends on whether the full fighting strength of the expedition can be concentrated in time to withstand the inevitable counter-attack. For Anzio two divisions are the minimum force to put ashore in face of likely German resistance. Yet we are willing to accept this if the two divisions can be concentrated on land in strength and in time. ... We are willing to accept any risks to achieve our object, but if the two divisions get sealed off by the Germans we obviously cannot leave them there without any support when there will be L.S.T.s somewhere in the Mediterranean sufficient for that purpose. ... Clark and I are confident that we have a great chance of pulling off something big if given the means with which to do it. The means required are fourteen L.S.T.s for maintenance until such time as the Anzio force and the Fifth Army join hands, and a further ten L.S.T.s for a period of fifteen days from the landing to build up the two divisions in guns, tanks, and other supporting arms to a strength sufficient to fight on level terms with the Germans. Even if this does interfere with preparations for 'Anvil' to some extent, surely the prize is worth it.

I therefore summoned the authorities concerned to Marrakesh, and held two conferences on January 7 and 8, attended by Lord Beaverbrook, General Wilson, Admiral John Cunningham, General Alexander, General Devers, General Bedell Smith, and others. Captain Power had just returned from London after clearing up many intricate points about the landing-craft with the Chiefs of Staff, and now, with the full support of his admiral, rendered us similar services. I was able to report to the President on the 8th as follows:

A unanimous agreement for action as proposed was reached by the responsible officers of both countries and of all Services as a result of our two conferences. Everyone is in good heart and the resources seem sufficient. Every aspect was thrashed out in full detail by sub-committees in the interval between the two conferences. ... Intention is to land a corps of two divisions for the assault, and to follow up with a mobile striking force based on the elements of a third division to cut enemy's communications.

It should be possible to do this, barring accident, without conflicting with requirements of 'Overlord' or 'Anvil', and still have sufficiency of landing-craft to maintain the force up till the end of February, weather permitting and God being with us.

General Wilson, who to-day assumes duty as Supreme Allied Commander-in-Chief Mediterranean, has issued instructions to subordinate commanders to give effect to the above. He is also informing Combined Chiefs of Staff.

All these calculations were based upon the May (or X) date being maintained for 'Overlord', though I myself had always thought that the moon period of June 3 (Y date) would probably be found most suitable, and I was glad to learn from General Eisenhower on his passage through Marrakesh that he was inclining towards this solution, which gave him and Montgomery more time to arrange for the larger forces it was now proposed to use in the first descent. I had telegraphed to the President setting out the whole question, and reminding him of our talks and agreements at Teheran.

Prime Minister to President Roosevelt   6 Jan 44
Bedell Smith and Devers came through here morning of

5th. Bedell told me that he and Montgomery are convinced that it is better to put in a much heavier and broader 'Over lord' than to expand the landing on the Riviera above ou pre-Teheran conception, and that he is putting this to Eisen hower and your Chiefs of Staff. I have always expected tha when the commanders took the matter into their hands the would make alterations in the plans, which nevertheless hav proved invaluable as a basis for future decisions. As you know I have always hoped that the initial assault at 'Overlord' could be with heavier forces than we have hitherto mentioned.

It also seems to me, from what I heard, very probable tha the June moon will be the earliest practicable date. I do no see why we should resist this if the commanders feel the have a better chance then. At Teheran the Chiefs of Staff' recommendation was June 1 or one day earlier, which yo and I agreed to express more agreeably as 'during May'. I conversation with Uncle Joe we never mentioned such a dat as May 5, or even May 8, but always spoke to him [of] aroun the 20th. Neither did we at any time dwell upon the exac phase of the operation which should fall on any particula day. If now the June date is accepted as final I do not fee that we shall in any way have broken faith with him. Th operation will anyhow begin in May with feints and softenin bombardments, and I do not think U.J. is the kind of man t be unreasonable over forty-eight hours.

On the other hand, the ground will be drier for U.J.' great operations by June. We shall make a much heavie attack, and with much better chances of success. I am makin you suggestions through Leathers for running another Arcti convoy, for which we can provide the escorts if you ca provide the ships and cargoes, we having practically finishe our quotas.

I do not think it necessary to make any communication t U.J. at the present time, but in a few weeks, after Eisenhowe has presented his final conclusions to us, we should no doub tell him all the story in all its strength, including any modifi cation of 'Anvil', with the authority of the responsible com manders behind our statement.

The President answered this important telegram, the facts o which were not in dispute between us, a week later. He had by then also received full reports of the conclusions of our meeting about the Anzio operation, which were all on the basis that th earlier date could be maintained for 'Overlord' if desired.

President Roosevelt to Prime Minister   14 Jan 4
    It is my understanding that in Teheran Uncle J. was give

a promise that 'Overlord' would be launched during May and supported by strongest practicable landing in the South of France at about the same time, and that he agreed to plan for simultaneous Russian attack on Eastern Front.

I do not believe that we should make any decision now to defer the operations, certainly not until the responsible commanders, Eisenhower and Wilson, have had full opportunity to explore all possibilities and make factual reports. In the meantime no communication should be sent to Uncle J. on this subject.

I think the psychology of bringing this thing up at this time would be very bad, in view of the fact that it is only a little over a month since the three of us agreed on the statement in Teheran.

'I am very glad,' I replied, on the 16th, 'to see that we are in complete agreement.'

*　　*　　*

Physical weakness oppressed me at Marrakesh following my illness at Carthage. All my painting tackle had been sent out, but I could not face it. I could hardly walk at all. Even tottering from the motor-car to a picnic luncheon in lovely weather amid the foothills of the Atlas was limited to eighty or a hundred yards. I passed eighteen hours out of the twenty-four prone. I never remember such extreme fatigue and weakness in body. On the other hand, every temptation, inducement, exhortation, and to some extent compulsion, to relax and lie down presented itself in the most seductive form. The Taylor villa was a perfect haven, lacking nothing that comfort could require or luxury suggest. I was utterly tired out, and here was the most attractive bed of repose, not only offered by gracious hosts, but enjoined by Lord Moran, the President, and the War Cabinet. However, events continued to offer irresistible distraction.

*　　*　　*

The Polish question, which had played so great a part at Teheran, had led me to cable Eden from Carthage.

Prime Minister to Foreign Secretary　　　　　20 Dec 43

I think you should now open the Polish frontiers question with the Poles, stating it is at my personal wish, and that I would have done it myself but for my temporary incapacitation. You should show them the formula and the rough line on the map on the eastern side, and the line of the Oder, including the Oppeln district, on the west. This gives them a magnificent piece of country three or four hundred miles across each way, and with over 250 miles of seaboard, even on the basis that they do not begin till west of Königsberg. The Poles should understand of course that these are only very broad, tentative suggestions, but that they would be most unwise to let them fall to the ground. Even if they do not get Lvov, I should still advise their acceptance, and that they put themselves in the hands of British and American friends to try to turn this plan into reality. You should put it to them that by taking over and holding firmly the present German territories up to the Oder they will be rendering a service to Europe as a whole by making the basis of a friendly policy towards Russia and close association with Czechoslovakia. This would give a chance for the rebirth of the Polish nation brighter than any yet seen.

Once we know that they will accept and endorse these proposals we will address ourselves to the Russians and endeavour to make matters firm and precise. On the other hand, if they cast it all aside I do not see how His Majesty's Government can press for anything more for them. The Russian armies may in a few months be crossing the frontiers of pre-war Poland, and it seems of the utmost consequence to have friendly recognition by Russia of the Polish Government and a broad understanding of the post-war frontiers settlement agreed before then. I shall be most interested to hear what their reaction is.

*   *   *

President Beneš was now on his way from Moscow to London. As these Books show, I had had a long contact with him. It will be remembered that he had played perhaps a decisive part in warning Stalin of the pro-German conspiracy against him in 1936.* At any rate, his relations with the Soviets were of the most friendly and intimate character. I asked him to look in on me at Marrakesh on his way back. His profound knowledge of the Eastern European scene made his views on Poland and on what the Russians would do for Poland most important. For twenty years or more Beneš, as Foreign Secretary or President of Czechoslovakia, had been the faithful ally of France and friend of the Western Powers, while at the same time maintaining a unique association with Stalin. When France and Britain sacrificed Czechoslovakia, and later when, on the eve of the war, Ribbentrop made his agreement with Molotov, Beneš was a very

* See Book 1, Chapter 18.

lonely man. But then, after a lengthy interval, came Hitler's attack on Russia, and all Beneš's common stock with the Soviets came again into full validity. Russia might well have fought Germany about Czechoslovakia in 1938. Anyhow, both were now under the same cruel lash.

It was very pleasant to me to talk in the sunshine and amid the flowers of my Marrakesh abode to this old political associate and mature European statesman, whom I had first met in 1918, in company with the great Masaryk, the founder of his country and the father of a son who died faithfully in her cause. Beneš was of course at this time optimistic.

I gave the following account of our talk to the President.

6 Jan 44

Beneš has been here, and is very hopeful about the Russian situation. He may be most useful in trying to make the Poles see reason and in reconciling them to the Russians, whose confidence he has long possessed. He brought a new map with pencil marks by U.J. showing the eastern frontier from Königsberg to the Curzon Line, giving the Poles Lomza and Bialystok regions in the north, but not Lemberg [Lvov] at the southern end. For their western frontier he offers the line of the Oder, including the major part of Oppeln. This gives the Poles a fine place to live in, more than 300 miles square, and with 250 miles of seaboard on the Baltic. As soon as I get home I shall go all out with the Polish Government to close with this or something like it, and, having closed, they must proclaim themselves as ready to accept the duty of guarding the bulwark of the Oder against further German aggression upon Russia, and also they must back the settlement to the limit. This will be their duty to the Powers of Europe, who will twice have rescued them. If I can get this tidied up early in February a visit from them to you would clinch matters.

The Russians are quite agreeable to Beneš having his old pre-Munich frontier back, with a slight military adjustment along the northern crests of the mountains and a little territory to the eastward linking them with Russia.

As this was the last time I ever saw President Beneš I will record my tribute to him. In all his thought and aims he consistently sustained the main principles on which Western civilisation is founded, and was ever true to the cause of his native land, over which he presided for more than twenty years. He was a master of administration and diplomacy. He knew how to endure with patience and fortitude long periods of adverse fortune. Where he failed—and it cost him and his country much —was in not taking violent decisions at the supreme moment. He was too experienced a diplomatist, too astute a year-to-year politician, to realise the moment and to stake all on victory or death. Had he told his cannons to fire at Munich time the Second World War would have begun under conditions far less favourable to Hitler, who needed many months to make his army and his armour.

* * *

In spite of the tension with General de Gaulle about Peyrouton, Boisson, and Flandin, all of whom had been arrested by the Free French authorities in December, I determined to make an effort to renew friendly relations with him before returning home. On New Year's Day I asked him to dine and sleep at the villa on January 3. 'This,' I said, 'would give us an opportunity of long-needed talks. My wife is with me here, and if Madame de Gaulle would care to accompany you it would give us both much pleasure.' The General evidently thought the notice too short. I ought to have known that he would not sleep anywhere in North Africa but in a French official residence. He pleaded the pressure of his other engagements. So I let it alone. However, having learnt later that he would arrive in Marrakesh on January 12, I invited him to luncheon that day, and he accepted. Mr. Duff Cooper and Lady Diana, Lord Beaverbrook, Mr. Nairn the Consul and his wife, were also our guests. The General arrived in the best of humour, greeted Mrs. Churchill in English, and spoke it throughout the meal. To make things equal I spoke French.

After luncheon the ladies went off to visit the bazaars, and de Gaulle and I and the other men settled down in the garden for a long talk. I had a lot of awkward subjects to deal with, and I thought my speaking French would add a lighter touch to them. Mr. Nairn, who made a few notes afterwards, records, 'I heard Mr. Churchill say to Mr. Duff Cooper in English in a very audible whisper, "I'm doing rather well, aren't I? Now that the General speaks English so well he understands my French perfectly." Then everyone, General de Gaulle setting the example, burst out laughing. The Prime Minister continued in French, but the supersensitive General was completely disarmed and ready to accept Mr. Churchill's comments in a friendly and helpful spirit.'

The comments were numerous and serious. Why was he pursuing this vendetta against the French notabilities who had fallen into his power? Did he not realise how much difficulty he made for himself in the United States? How angry the President was with him? How much we all depended on American aid and goodwill? Why should he complicate his own task by this and all sorts of other needless friction? Why should he always try to offend these powerful Governments, without whose help he could not live? Upon a smaller point, why had he driven General Georges, whom I had specially brought from France to make things easier, off the Committee? At this de Gaulle said he had offered General Georges the Chancellorship of the Legion of Honour. I asked what reply he had received. 'I received no reply,' he answered. I said I was not surprised. Had he the Chancellorship to bestow? But all ended pleasantly, and the General proposed that I should attend a review he would hold in my honour the next morning, which I agreed to do. And accordingly de Gaulle and I stood on a small platform while quite a large array of French and Moroccan troops marched past for an hour amid the cheers of the inhabitants of the Marrakesh oasis.

*   *   *

Another question arising out of Teheran raised considerable difficulty. We have seen how Stalin had asked for a share in the Italian Fleet, and the President was under the impression that he himself had mentioned in conversation one-third. The British Chiefs of Staff did not like this, and had always spoken to their Russian colleagues on a different basis. The President was worried about his personal remark 'one-third', and set the whole position out to me with great frankness.

President Roosevelt to Prime Minister   9 Jan 44
     As I told you, Harriman requested information on the action we were taking to carry out our commitments to turn over Italian ships to the Soviet by February 1 so that he could discuss the matter with Molotov if he were queried. I told him it was my intention to allocate one-third of the captured Italian ships to the Soviet war effort, beginning February 1, as rapidly as they could be made available.

Harriman then reminded me that Stalin's request at Teheran was a reiteration of the Soviet request originally made at Moscow in October [namely, for one battleship, one cruiser, eight destroyers, and four submarines for North Russia, and 40,000 tons of merchant shipping for the Black Sea], and that no mention was made at Moscow or Teheran of the Russians getting additional ships up to one-third of those captured. Accordingly, Harriman regarded my cable of December 21 as being for his information, and he has not discussed the question of one-third with Molotov.

Harriman also emphasised the very great importance of fulfilling our pledge to yield these ships. For us to fail or to delay would, in his opinion, only arouse suspicion in Stalin and in his associates as to the firmness of other commitments made at Teheran.

On the other hand, the Chiefs of Staff have raised numerous objections to the transfer, based on probably effects that this course would have on pending operations. They fear a loss of Italian naval and military co-operation, and the scuttling or sabotage of valuable ships which we need for 'Anvil' and 'Overlord'. They foresee no material benefit to the Russian war effort at this time, since the warships are presently quite unsuited for Northern waters and the Black Sea is closed to merchant vessels.

The very wise provisions of the modified agreement [negotiated by Admiral Cunningham] give the United Nations the right to make disposition of any or all Italian ships as they may think fit. It is of importance that we should acquire and maintain the confidence of our Ally, and I feel that every practicable effort should be made to arrive at a solution whereby the Italian ships requested by the Soviet be turned over to them, beginning about February 1.

Do you believe it wise to present to Uncle J. the possible effect on 'Overlord-Anvil' as expressed by our Staffs, and suggest a delay in assigning Italian ships to him until after the launching of 'Overlord-Anvil'? I am particularly desirous of having an expression of your opinion in view of the present British command of the Mediterranean theatre and in order that we may reach a complete agreement as to the action to be taken. It is patently impracticable for either of us to act singly in this matter, but I think you will agree that we must not go back on what we told Uncle J.

This message was not entirely clear. I agreed to the ships mentioned in our agreement of October, but not to the more general terms of 'one-third'. I therefore replied:

Prime Minister to President Roosevelt   9 Jan 44
I entirely agree with you that we must not break faith with Stalin about the ships. I have been for a week in correspondence with Anthony on the subject, and hope to submit a proposal to you for a joint communication from you and me in a day or two.

I was myself in full accord with the Chiefs of Staff on both sides of the Atlantic. I felt that the immediate transfer of these Italian warships, which had so resolutely made their way to Malta and placed themselves in our hands, might have most damaging results to Italian co-operation with the Allies. Throughout the year 1943 my aim had been not only to make Italy surrender, but to bring her in on our side, with all that that meant to the progress of the war and to the future settlement of Europe. I was therefore prepared to press the War Cabinet and the Admiralty to make a substantial British sacrifice and to supply a number of British ships to the Russians, instead of breaking Italian hearts at this moment, so pregnant, as it seemed to me, with consequences for the future. Various messages passed between us, and I was very glad indeed to find how closely my colleagues at home and the Chiefs of Staff agreed. One could not expect the United States, with the whole burden of war in the Pacific weighing upon them, to make any large contribution. We, on the other hand, had certainly at this time an ample margin of naval power, both in the Mediterranean and, now that the *Scharnhorst* was at the bottom, in home and Arctic waters as well. As soon as I had reached an agreement with my friends at home I sent the following proposals to the President:

Prime Minister to President Roosevelt   16 Jan 44
My recollection is clear that nothing was said at Teheran about 'one-third', but that a promise was made to meet the Russian claim put forward at Moscow to have transferred to them one battleship, one cruiser, eight destroyers, four submarines, and 40,000 tons of merchant shipping.
2. On the other hand, the main difficulties raised by the Chiefs of Staff are solid, and I think it very likely that once Stalin is convinced of our intentions and our good faith he will leave us to handle the matter in the smoothest and swiftest way possible.

T—s.w.w.–10—E

3. I suggest therefore that we now signal him jointly to the following effect.

'(i) ... The Combined Chiefs of Staff ... think it would be dangerous to our triple interests actually to carry out any transfer or to say anything about it to the Italians at present. Nevertheless if after full consideration you desire us to proceed we will make a secret approach to Badoglio with a view to concluding the necessary arrangements. ... These would have to be on the lines that Italian ships selected should be sailed to a suitable Allied port, where they would be collected by Russian crews, who would sail them into Russian Northern ports, which are the only ones now open where any refitting necessary could be undertaken.

'(ii) We are however very conscious of the dangers of this course, and have therefore decided to propose the following alternative:

'The British battleship *Royal Sovereign* has recently completed refit in the United States. She is fitted with Radar for all types of armament. Great Britain has also a cruiser available. His Majesty's Government are willing, for their part, that these vessels should be taken over during February at British ports by Soviet crews and sailed to North Russian ports. You could then make such alterations as you find necessary for Arctic conditions. These vessels would be temporarily transferred on loan to the Soviet Government, and would fly the Soviet flag until, without prejudice to the military operations, the necessary transfer of Italian vessels could be arranged.

'If events should take a favourable turn with Turks and the Straits become open the vessels would be ready to operate if desired in the Black Sea. We hope you will very carefully consider this alternative, which we think is in every way superior to first proposal.'

4. If you could find the cruiser instead of our having to do so we should be relieved. We cannot do anything about the eight destroyers, but perhaps you may be able to supply this need. Otherwise we must say we have absolutely not got them until after 'Overlord' and 'Anvil'. As to the 40,000 tons of merchant shipping, I should think that with your great supply and vastly improved sinkings you might supply these, but we should be willing to share fifty-fifty.

5. I hope, my dear friend, you will consider all these possibilities and let me know how you feel. In my opinion Stalin will be moved in a favourable manner by this handsome proposal. At any rate, it shows our faith and our goodwill. I doubt whether, having this alternative before him, he will

press for the premature raising of the Italian problem, but we shall have done the right thing.

*　　　*　　　*

This alternative was accepted by the President. The Americans undertook themselves to furnish a cruiser, and the whole matter was presented to Stalin substantially in the form I suggested in a joint telegram from the President and me on January 23. Stalin's reply, when it came later, was as follows:

Premier Stalin to Prime Minister and President   29 Jan 44
Roosevelt

I received on January 23 both your joint messages, signed by you, Mr. Prime Minister, and you, Mr. President, regarding the question of the handing over of Italian shipping for the use of the Soviet Union.

I must say that, after your joint affirmative reply at Teheran to the question which I raised of the handing over to the Soviet Union of Italian shipping by the end of January 1944, I considered this question settled, and the thought never entered my mind of the possibility of any kind of reconsideration of this decision, which was taken and agreed between the three of us. All the more so since, as we agreed at the time, this question was to be completely settled with the Italians. Now I see that this is not so, and that nothing has even been mentioned to the Italians on the subject.

In order however not to complicate this question, which is of such great importance for our common struggle against Germany, the Soviet Government is prepared to accept your proposal regarding the dispatch from British ports to the U.S.S.R. of the battleship *Royal Sovereign* and one cruiser, and regarding the temporary use of these vessels by the Naval High Command of the U.S.S.R. until such time as the appropriate Italian shipping is made available to the Soviet Union. Similarly, we shall be prepared to accept from the U.S.A. and Great Britain 40,000 tons of merchant shipping, which will also be used by us until such time as a similar tonnage of Italian shipping is handed over to us. It is important that there should be no delays now regarding the matter, and that all the shipping indicated should be handed over to us during the month of February.

In your reply however there is no mention of the handing over to the Soviet Union of eight Italian destroyers and four submarines, to the handing over of which to the Soviet Union at the end of January you, Mr. Prime Minister, and you, Mr. President, agreed in Teheran. Meanwhile, for the Soviet

Union this very question of destroyers and submarines, without which the handing over of one battleship and one cruiser has no significance, is of capital importance. You understand yourselves that a cruiser and a battleship are powerless without escorting destroyers. Since the whole of Italy's Fleet is under your control, to carry out the decision which was taken at Teheran to hand over for the use of the Soviet Union eight destroyers and four submarines out of that Fleet should present no difficulties. I am agreeable [literally, 'I agree'] that, instead of Italian destroyers and submarines, a similar number of American or British destroyers and submarines should be handed over to the Soviet Union for our use. Moreover, the question of the handing over of destroyers and submarines cannot be postponed, but must be settled at one and the same time with the handing over of the battleship and cruiser, as was definitely agreed between us at Teheran.

Eventually the matter was settled as I hoped, although there was a good deal of correspondence, not all of a pleasant character, about it with our Soviet Ally. The *Royal Sovereign* and the American cruiser were handed over as proposed. There was an inevitable delay about the destroyers till after the 'Overlord' operation was complete. The Admiralty sweetened this pill by lending Russia four of our modern submarines. As is well known, the Soviets after the war faithfully returned the ships, and arrangements were made to transfer vessels from the Italian Fleet in a manner acceptable to all concerned.

*　　*　　*

Much as I should have liked, and much as I was pressed, to recuperate for another fortnight in this delectable asylum, I determined to be at home before the shock of Anzio occurred. On January 14 therefore we all flew in beautiful weather to Gibraltar, where the *King George V* awaited me. I arrived early in the afternoon, and repaired again to the Convent.* General Wilson, who had assumed his duties as Supreme Commander in the Mediterranean, and Admiral John Cunningham, the Naval Commander-in-Chief, had both arrived by air from Algiers, and we had an anxious but hopeful talk about the momentous operation for which we were all working. On the 15th I joined the rest of my party, who were already on board the *King George V*. She made her way out of Algeciras Bay wide into the Atlantic,

* See Book 8, Chapter 22.

and thence to Plymouth. After a restful voyage we were welcomed by the War Cabinet and Chiefs of Staff, who really
seemed quite glad to see me back. I had been more than two
months away from England, and they had been through a lot
of worry on account both of my illness and my activities. It was
indeed a homecoming, and I felt deeply grateful to all these
trusty friends and fellow-workers.

CHAPTER 9

Marshal Tito and Yugoslavia

Mihailović and Tito – Importance of the Balkan Struggle – The Deakin and Maclean Missions – Growth of Partisan Strength after the Italian Surrender – My Telegram to Roosevelt of October 23, 1943 – Bitter Quarrels between Mihailović and Tito – Three New Factors in Our Policy – Randolph Joins Maclean – Difficult Position of King Peter – My Letter to Tito of January 8, 1944 – His Reply – Further Correspondence – We Withdraw Our Liaison Officers from Mihailović – My Account To Parliament of February 22, 1944 – King Peter Dismisses the Purić Government.

The reader must now go back to a fierce and sombre tale, which the main narrative has outstripped. Yugoslavia since Hitler's invasion and conquest in April 1941 had been the scene of fearful events. The spirited boy King took refuge in England with such of Prince Paul's ministers and other members of the Government as had defied the German assault. In the mountains there began again the fierce guerrilla with which the Serbs had resisted the Turks for centuries. General Mihailović was its first and foremost champion, and round him rallied the surviving *élite* of Yugoslavia. In the vortex of world affairs their struggle was hardly noticeable. It belongs to the 'unestimated sum of human pain'. Mihailović suffered as a guerrilla leader from the fact that many of his followers were well-known people with relations and friends in Serbia, and property and recognisable connections elsewhere. The Germans pursued a policy of murderous blackmail. They retaliated for guerrilla activities by shooting batches of four or five hundred selected people in Belgrade. Under this pressure Mihailović drifted gradually into a posture where some of his commanders made accommodations with the German and Italian troops to be left alone in certain mountain areas in return for doing little or nothing against the enemy. Those who have triumphantly withstood such strains may brand his name, but history, more discriminating, should not erase it from the scroll of Serbian patriots. By the autumn of 1941 Serbian resistance to the German terror had become only a shadow. The national struggle could only be sustained by the innate valour of the common people. This however was not lacking.

A wild and furious war for existence against the Germans broke into flame among the Partisans. Among these Tito stood forth, pre-eminent and soon dominant. Tito, as he called himself, was a Soviet-trained Communist who, until Russia was invaded by Hitler, and after Yugoslavia had been assailed, had fomented political strikes along the Dalmatian coast, in accordance with the general Comintern policy. But once he united in his breast and brain his Communist doctrine with his burning ardour for his native land in her extreme torment he became a leader, with adherents who had little to lose but their lives, who were ready to die, and if to die to kill. This confronted the Germans with a problem which could not be solved by the mass executions of notables or persons of substance. They found themselves confronted by desperate men who had to be hunted down in their lairs. The Partisans under Tito wrested weapons from German hands. They grew rapidly in numbers. No reprisals, however bloody, upon hostages or villages deterred them. For them it was death or freedom. Soon they began to inflict heavy injury upon the Germans and became masters of wide regions.

It was inevitable that the Partisan movement should also come into savage quarrels with their fellow-countrymen who were resisting half-heartedly or making bargains for immunity with the common foe. The Partisans deliberately violated any agreements made with the enemy by the Cetniks—as the followers of General Mihailović were called. The Germans then shot Cetnik hostages, and in revenge Cetniks gave the Germans information about the Partisans. All this happened sporadically and uncontrollably in these wild mountain regions. It was a tragedy within a tragedy.

*   *   *

I had followed these events amid other preoccupations so far as was possible. Except for a trickle of supplies dropped from aircraft, we were not able to help. Our headquarters in the Middle East was responsible for all operations in this theatre, and maintained a system of agents and liaison officers with the followers of Mihailović. When in the summer of 1943 we broke into Sicily and Italy, the Balkans, and especially Yugoslavia, never left my thoughts. Up to this point our missions had only gone to the bands under Mihailović, who represented the official resistance to the Germans and the Yugoslav Government in Cairo. In May 1943 we took a new departure. It was decided to send small parties of British officers and N.C.O.s to establish contact with the Yugoslav Partisans, in spite of the fact that cruel strife was proceeding between them and the Cetniks, and that Tito was waging war as a Communist not only against the German invaders but against the Serbian monarchy and Mihailović. At the end of that month Captain Deakin, an Oxford don who had helped me for five years before the war in my literary work, was dropped by parachute to set up a mission with Tito. Other British missions followed, and by June much evidence had accumulated. The Chiefs of Staff reported on June 6: 'It is clear from information available to the War Office that the Cetniks are hopelessly compromised in their relations with the Axis in Herzegovina and Montenegro. During the recent fighting in the latter area it has been the well-organised Partisans rather than the Cetniks who have been holding down the Axis forces.'

Towards the end of the month my attention was drawn to the question of obtaining the best results from local resistance to the Axis in Yugoslavia. Having called for full information, I presided at a Chiefs of Staff conference at Downing Street on June 23. In the course of the discussion I emphasised the very great value of giving all possible support to the Yugoslav anti-Axis movement, which was containing about thirty-three Axis divisions in that area. This matter was of such importance that I directed that the small number of additional aircraft required to increase our aid must be provided, if necessary at the expense of the bombing of Germany and of the U-boat war.

On July 7, the eve of our landing in Sicily, I drew General Alexander's attention to these possibilities.

Prime Minister to General Alexander   7 July 43
    I presume you have read about the recent heavy fighting in Yugoslavia and the widespread sabotage and guerrilla beginning in Greece. Albania also should be a fertile field. All this has grown up with no more aid from Britain than the dropping of a few bundles by parachute. If we can get hold of the mouth of the Adriatic so as to be able to run even a few ships into Dalmatian or Greek ports the whole of the Western Balkans might flare up, with far-reaching results. All this is however hunting in the next field.

A fortnight later I elaborated my thought on the essential

connection between the Italian and Balkan theatres in the following important telegram:

Prime Minister to General Alexander   22 July 43
    I am going with the Staffs to meet the President before August 15 in Canada. Thus we shall all be on the spot at the time when Sicily may very likely be cleaned up. . . .
    I am sending you by an officer a full account which I have had prepared of the marvellous resistance put up by the so-called Partisan followers of Tito in Bosnia and the powerful cold-blooded manœuvres of Mihailović in Serbia. Besides this there are the resistances of the guerrillas in Albania and recently in Greece. The Germans have not only been reinforcing the Balkan peninsula with divisions, but they have been continually improving the quality and mobility of these divisions and have been stiffening up the local Italians. The enemy cannot spare these forces, and if Italy collapses the Germans could not bear the weight themselves. Great prizes lie in the Balkan direction.
    No objective can compete with the capture of Rome, which in its turn gives a stage later all the advantages hoped for from the Balkan liberation. . . . The fall of Italy, the effect upon the other German satellites, and the subsequent utter loneliness of Germany may conceivably produce decisive results in Europe, especially in view of the vast strength evinced by the Russian armies.
    This message is sent to give you my whole mind, which is, I believe, in full harmony with the Chiefs of Staff.

*   *   *

Before leaving for Quebec I decided to pave the way for further action in the Balkans by appointing a senior officer to lead a larger mission to the Partisans in the field, and with authority to make direct recommendations to me about our future action towards them.

Prime Minister to Foreign Secretary   28 July 43
    Mr. Fitzroy Maclean, M.P., is a man of daring character, with Paliamentary status and Foreign Office training. He is to go to Yugoslavia and work with Tito. The idea is that a brigadier should be sent out to take command later on. In my view we should plump for Maclean and make him the head of any mission now contemplated, and give him a good military staff officer under his authority. What we want is a daring Ambassador-leader with these hardy and hunted guerrillas.

This mission landed in Yugoslavia by parachute in September 1943, to find the situation revolutionised. The news of the Italian surrender had reached Yugoslavia only with the official broadcast announcements. But, in spite of complete absence of any warning by us, Tito took quick and fruitful action. Within a few weeks six Italian divisions had been disarmed by the Partisan forces, and another two went over to fight with them against the Germans. With Italian equipment the Yugoslavs were now able to arm 80,000 more men, and to occupy for the moment most of the Adriatic coastline. There was now a good chance of strengthening our general position in the Adriatic in relation to the Italian front. The Yugoslav Partisan army, now totalling 200,000 men, although fighting primarily as guerrillas, was now engaged in widespread action against the Germans, who continued their violent reprisals with increasing fury.

One effect of this increased activity in Yugoslavia was to exacerbate the conflict between Tito and Mihailović. Tito's growing military strength raised in an increasingly acute form the ultimate position of the Yugoslav monarchy and the exiled Government. Till the end of the war sincere and prolonged efforts were made both in London and within Yugoslavia to reach a working compromise between both sides. I had hoped that the Russians would use their good offices in this matter. When Mr. Eden went to Moscow in October 1943 the subject of Yugoslavia was placed on the Conference agenda. At the meeting of October 23 he made a frank and fair statement of our attitude in the hope of securing a common Allied policy towards Yugoslavia, but the Russians displayed no wish either to pool information or to discuss a plan of action.

Even after many weeks I saw little prospect of any working arrangement between the hostile factions in Yugoslavia.

Former Naval Person to President Roosevelt   23 Oct 43
    In spite of the vexatious broils between the followers of Tito and Mihailović in Yugoslavia and those that have broken out between the two sets of Greek guerrillas, the situation in the Balkan peninsula is grievous for the enemy. . . . We British have about eighty separate missions under General Wilson's control working with Partisans and Patriot bands scattered over these immense mountainous regions, 900 miles by about 300 miles in extent. Some of our officers there of brigadier's rank are very capable, and have in numerous cases been there for two years. . . .

The fighting is of the most cruel and bloody character, with merciless reprisals and executions of hostages by the Huns. But the enemy also is suffering heavily, and is now consuming not less than twenty-five German and eight Bulgarian divisions in the theatre, without being able to control more than key points and with increasing difficulty in maintaining railway traffic. We hope soon to compose the Greek quarrels, but the differences between Tito's Partisans and Mihailović's Serbs are very deep-seated.

My gloomy forecast proved true. At the end of November Tito summoned a political congress of his movement at Jajce, in Bosnia, and not only set up a Provisional Government, 'with sole authority to represent the Yugoslav nation,' but also formally deprived the Royal Yugoslav Government in Cairo of all its rights. The King was forbidden to return to the country until after the liberation. The Partisans had established themselves without question as the leading elements of resistance in Yugoslavia, particularly since the Italian surrender. But it was important that no irrevocable political decisions about the future *régime* in Yugoslavia should be made in the atmosphere of occupation, civil war, and *émigré* politics. The tragic figure of Mihailović had become the major obstacle. We had to maintain close military contact with the Partisans, and therefore to persuade the King to dismiss Mihailović from his post as Minister of War. Early in December we withdrew official support from Mihailović and recalled the British missions operating in his territory.

*　　　*　　　*

Yugoslav affairs were considered at the Teheran Conference against this background. Although it was decided by the three Allied Powers to give the maximum support to the Partisans, the *rôle* of Yugoslavia in the war was dismissed by Stalin as of minor importance, and the Russians even disputed our figures of the number of Axis divisions in the Balkans. The Soviet Government however agreed to send a Russian mission to Tito as a result of Mr. Eden's initiative. They also wished to keep contact with Mihailović.

On my return from Teheran to Cairo I saw King Peter, and told him about the strength and significance of the Partisan movement and that it might be necessary for him to dismiss Mihailović from his Cabinet. The only hope which the King possessed of returning to his country would be, with our mediation, to reach some provisional arrangement with Tito without delay and before the Partisans further extended their hold upon the country. The Russians too professed their willingness to work for some kind of compromise. On December 21 the Soviet Ambassador handed the following message to Mr. Eden:

> The Soviet Government is aware that at the present time very strained relations exist between Marshal Tito and the National Committee of Liberation of Yugoslavia on the one hand and King Peter and his Government on the other. Mutual attacks and hard accusations on both sides, especially those which have recently taken place, have led to open hostilities, which hamper the cause of the struggle for the liberation of Yugoslavia. The Soviet Government shares the view of the British Government that in the interests of the fight of the Yugoslavian people against the German invaders it is necessary to make efforts to find a basis for collaboration between the two sides. The Soviet Government sees the great difficulties standing in the way of the realisation of this task, but it is ready to do everything possible to find a compromise between the two sides, with the purpose of uniting all the forces of the Yugoslavian people in the interests of the common struggle of the Allies.

I received almost unanimous advice as to what course to pursue in this disagreeable situation. Officers who had served with Tito and the commanders of missions to Mihailović presented similar pictures. The British Ambassador to the Royal Yugoslav Government, Mr. Stevenson, was equally convinced. He telegraphed to the Foreign Office on December 25: 'Our policy must be based on three new factors: The Partisans will be the rulers of Yugoslavia. They are of such value to us militarily that we must back them to the full, subordinating political considerations to military. It is extremely doubtful whether we can any longer regard the monarchy as a unifying element in Yugoslavia.'

* * *

This crisis in Yugoslav affairs pressed on me as I lay ill at Marrakesh. Maclean, who had been with me in Cairo, was now due to return to Yugoslavia. He was anxious to have my son with him, and it was arranged that Randolph should join the mission by parachute.

Prime Minister to Foreign Secretary   29 Dec 43

Randolph, who is now waiting for a drop into Yugoslavia, left behind the following note for me, dated 25th instant. It seems to me sound, and to represent to a large extent your point of view and mine. He will be going in a few days.

'1. Three weeks ago in Cairo Stevenson made no attempt to resist the arguments of Maclean and Deakin that the condition precedent for any useful political action in Yugoslavia was the repudiation of General Mihailović. Despite the polemics indulged in by both sides, this is as true to-day as it was three weeks ago, though perhaps, owing to the procrastination of the King, we shall only gain a military and not a political advantage.

'2. Maclean stressed in Cairo that no *quid pro quo* could be obtained for the King by the dismissal of Mihailović, but that this gesture might create an atmosphere in which the King's fortunes could be advanced. This position has been prejudiced, but is still true, with limitations, to-day.

'3. Two things are surely therefore required:

(i) The immediate repudiation of Mihailović by His Majesty's Government and if possible by King Peter.

(ii) The immediate return to Tito's headquarters of Maclean to try (*a*) to obtain the maximum military advantage from the situation, and (*b*) to explore what advantage may be gained for the King from the new situation that will be created upon the dismissal of Mihailović.'

I added my own views, and a draft reply to Tito.

Prime Minister to Foreign Secretary   30 Dec 43

There is no possibility now of getting Tito to accept King Peter as a *quid pro quo* for repudiating Mihailović. Once Mihailović is gone the King's chances will be greatly improved and we can plead his case at Tito's headquarters. I thought we were all agreed in Cairo to advise Peter to dismiss Mihailović before the end of the year. Everything Deakin and Maclean said and all the reports received show that he had been in active collaboration with the Germans. We shall never bring the parties together till he has been disowned not only by us, but by the King.

Pray let me know whether I shall send the following message, or whether I shall merely give a friendly acknowledgment, in which latter case I fear we shall have lost a good opportunity of my establishing a personal relationship with this important man.

I do not wish to hawk this private message around to the United States and Stalin, with the inevitable delays involved.

Unless you disagree I propose to send it, as a letter, by air courier to Maclean at Bari, who will deliver it. He and Randolph will be dropping in a few days. Let me know also the form in which you will repudiate Mihailović, and invite the King to do so. It is, in my opinion, Peter's only chance.

And on January 2:

I have been convinced by the arguments of men I know and trust that Mihailović is a millstone tied round the neck of the little King, and he has no chance till he gets rid of him.

The Foreign Secretary agreed, and I now wrote to Tito, who had sent me congratulations on my recovery:

AFRICA: *January* 8, 1944

I thank you very much for your kind message about my health from yourself and the heroic Patriot and Partisan army of Yugoslavia. From Major Deakin, who is a friend of mine, I learnt all about your valiant efforts. It is my most earnest desire to give you all aid in human power by sea supplies, by air support, and by Commandos helping you in the island fighting. Brigadier Maclean is also a friend of mine, and a colleague in the House of Commons. With him at your headquarters will soon be serving my son, Major Randolph Churchill, who is also a Member of Parliament.

One supreme object stands before us, namely, to cleanse the soil of Europe from the filthy Nazi-Fascist taint. You may be sure that we British have no desire to dictate the future government of Yugoslavia. At the same time we hope that all will pull together as much as possible for the defeat of the common foe, and afterwards settle the form of government in accordance with the will of the people.

I am resolved that the British Government shall give no further military support to Mihailović and will only give help to you, and we should be glad if the Royal Yugoslavian Government would dismiss him from their councils. King Peter the Second however escaped as a boy from the treacherous clutches of the Regent Prince Paul, and came to us as the representative of Yugoslavia and as a young prince in distress. It would not be chivalrous or honourable for Great Britain to cast him aside. Nor can we ask him to cut all his existing contacts with his country. I hope therefore that you will understand we shall in any case remain in official relations with him, while at the same time giving you all possible military support. I hope also that there may be an end to polemics on either side, for these only help the Germans.

You may be sure I shall work in the closest contact with my

friends Marshal Stalin and President Roosevelt; and I earnestly hope that the Military Mission which the Soviet Government are sending to your headquarters will work in similar harmony with the Anglo-American Mission under Brigadier Maclean. Please correspond with me through Brigadier Maclean, and let me know of anything you think I can do to help, for I will certainly try my best.

Looking forward to the end of your sufferings and to the liberation of all Europe from tyranny . . .

It took nearly a month to get an answer.

Marshal Tito to Prime Minister [*received February* 3, 1944]
Your Excellency,

Your message brought by Brigadier Maclean is valuable proof that our people have in their superhuman struggle for freedom and independence a true friend and Ally at their side who deeply comprehends our needs and our aspirations. For me personally your message is an honour, for it expresses your high acknowledgment of our struggle and the efforts of our National Liberation Army. I thank you heartily for your photographs from the Teheran Conference, with your dedication. Your Excellency may be sure that we will endeavour to keep your friendship, won in a most difficult hour of our people's history, and which is extremely dear to us. The devastation of the country, and the people exhausted with suffering, need, and will need in future, the help of our great Allies not only during the war but also in peace to enable us to heal the terrible wounds inflicted on us by the ignoble Fascist invader. It is our wish to fulfil to the utmost our duty as an Ally in the common military effort against our common enemy. Aid tendered to us by our Allies very much contributes to ease our situation on the battlefield. We also hope, with your help, to obtain heavy armaments (tanks and aircraft), which in the present phase of the war and owing to the present strength of our National Liberation Army is indispensable to us.

2. I quite understand your engagements towards King Peter II and his Government, and I will contrive as far as the interests of our peoples permit to avoid unnecessary politics and not cause inconvenience to our Allies in this matter. I assure you however, Your Excellency, that the internal political situation created in this arduous struggle for liberation is not only a machine for the strivings of individuals or some political group, but it is the irresistible desire of all patriots, of all those who are fighting and long connected with this struggle, and these are the enormous majority of the peoples of

Yugoslavia. Therefore the people have set [themselves] difficult tasks, and we are bound to accomplish them.

3. At the present moment all our efforts turn to one direction, and that is, (1) to assemble all patriotic and honourable elements so as to render our struggle against the invader as efficient as possible ; (2) to create union and brotherhood of the Yugoslav nations, which did not exist before this war, and the absence of which caused the catastrophe in our country ; (3) to create conditions for the establishment of a State in which all nations of Yugoslavia would feel happy, and that is a truly democratic Yugoslavia, a federative Yugoslavia. I am convinced that you understand us, and that we will have your valuable support in these strivings of our people.

Yours very sincerely,

TITO
Marshal of Yugoslavia

I replied at once.

Prime Minister to Marshal Tito (Yugoslavia)   5 Feb 44

I am very glad my letter has reached you safely, and I have received your message with pleasure. I can understand the position of reserve which you adopt towards King Peter. I have for several months past been in favour of advising him to dismiss Mihailović and to face the consequent resignation of all his present advisers. I have been deterred from doing this by the argument that I should thus be advising him to cast away his only adherents. You will understand I feel a personal responsibility towards him. I should be obliged if you would let me know whether his dismissal of Mihailović would pave the way for friendly relations with you and your Movement, and, later on, for his joining you in the field, it being understood that the future question of the monarchy is reserved until Yugoslavia has been entirely liberated. There is no doubt that a working arrangement between you and the King would consolidate many forces, especially Serbian elements, now estranged, and that it would invest your Government and Movement with added authority and provide them with numerous resources. Yugoslavia would then be able to speak with a united voice in the councils of the Allies during this formative period, when so much is in flux. I much hope that you will feel able to give me the answer you can see I want.

2. His Britannic Majesty's Government desire to assemble all patriotic and honourable elements so as to render your struggle against the invader as efficient as possible ; secondly, to create union and brotherhood of the Yugoslav nations ;

The Teheran Conference, November–December, 1943. Mr. Churchill in Persian head-dress

His Majesty King George VI

A flotilla of tank landing craft massed in a North African harbour preparatory to the invasion of Sicily. A marked lack of L.C.T.s was a great limiting factor during the 1943–4 operations

Monte Cassino Monastery, near Naples, was established in A.D. 529 by Benedict. German resistance there became a thorn in the side of the Allied advance to Rome. Here the Monastery is shown before and after the Allied bombing in February, 1944

A 'V2' rocket ready to be fired

Top: The bridges built for the crossing of the Volturno (Italy) were no
strong enough for tanks. Here, a Sherman has found a place shallow
enough to cross unaided. *Bottom:* Mr. Churchill and General Alexande
watch an attack on a German stronghold in Italy

Yugoslav partisans taken prisoner by the Germans

The American Marines in Bougainville, Solomon Islands, take the Army Alsatian 'Caesar', wounded in battle, to a nearby dressing station. The dogs were used to track Japanese troops in the jungle

and, thirdly, to create conditions for a truly democratic and federative Yugoslavia. You will certainly have the support of His Majesty's Government in all this.

3. I have asked the Supreme Allied Commander in the Mediterranean to form immediately an amphibious force of Commandos, supported by air and flotillas, to attack, with your aid, the garrisons which the Germans have left in the islands they have taken along the Dalmatian coast. There is no reason why these garrisons should not be exterminated with forces which will shortly be available. Secondly, we must try to get a through line of communication with you from the sea, even if we have to move it from time to time. This alone will enable tanks and anti-tank guns and other heavy munitions, together with other necessary supplies, to be brought in in the quantities which your armies require. You should talk all this over with Brigadier Maclean, who has my entire confidence and immediate access to me, as well as to the Supreme Commander.

Tito replied:

9 Feb 44

I was obliged to consult the members of the National Committee of Liberation of Yugoslavia and members of the Anti-Fascist Council of National Liberation on the points raised in your messages. The analysis of these points led to the following conclusions:

(1) The Anti-Fascist Council of National Liberation of Yugoslavia, as you know, confirmed at their second session on November 29, 1943, that they firmly stand for the Union of Yugoslav Nations. However, as long as there are two Governments, one in Yugoslavia and the other in Cairo, there can be no complete union. Therefore the Government in Cairo must be suppressed, and with them Draza Mihailović. That Government must account to the Government of A.C.N.L.Y. for having squandered enormous sums of the nation's money.

(2) The National Committee of Liberation of Yugoslavia should be acknowledged by the Allies as the only Government of Yugoslavia, and King Peter II, in support, should submit to the laws of A.C.N.L.Y.

(3) If King Peter accepts all these conditions the Anti-Fascist Council of National Liberation will not refuse to co-operate with him, on condition that the question of the monarchy in Yugoslavia be decided after the liberation of Yugoslavia by the free will of the people.

(4) King Peter II should issue a declaration to the effect

that he has only the interests of his fatherland at heart, which he wishes to be free and organised as the people themselves decide after the war is over by their free will, and until then he will do all in his power to support the arduous struggle of the peoples of Yugoslavia. ...

Prime Minister to Marshal Tito   25 Feb 44

I fully comprehend your difficulties, and I welcome the spirit in which you approach them. I thank you for understanding mine. The first step for us is to withdraw our liaison officers safely from Mihailović. Orders have been issued accordingly, but may take a few weeks to fulfil. Meanwhile, can you not assure me that if King Peter frees himself from Mihailović and other bad advisers he will be invited by you to join his countrymen in the field, provided always that the Yugoslav nations are free to settle their own constitution after the war? If I judge this boy aright, he has no dearer wish than to stand at the side of all those Yugoslavs who are fighting the common foe, but you can understand that I cannot press him to dismiss Mihailović, throw over his Government, and cut off all contact with Serbia before knowing whether he can count on your support and co-operation.

I have suggested to King Peter that he should return to London to discuss these matters with me. I hope therefore that you will on reflection be ready to modify your demands, and thus enable us both to work for the unification of Yugoslavia against the common enemy. Do not hesitate to make me precise and specific requests. If meanwhile I cannot do all you wish, be sure it is not from lack of goodwill to you or your country.

*   *   *

When I was able to explain all this to Parliament on February 22, 1944, I told the following tale:

'Led with great skill, organised on the guerrilla principle, the Partisans were at once elusive and deadly. They were here, they were there, they were everywhere. Large-scale offensives have been launched against them by the Germans, but in every case the Partisans, even when surrounded, have escaped, after inflicting great losses and toil upon the enemy. The Partisan movement soon outstripped in numbers the forces of General Mihailović. Not only Croats and Slovenes, but large numbers of Serbians, joined with Marshal Tito, and he has at this moment more than a quarter of a million men with him, and large quantities of arms taken from the enemy or from the Italians, and these men are organised into a considerable number of divisions and corps.

'The whole movement has taken shape and form, without losing the guerrilla quality without which it could not possibly succeed. Around and within these heroic forces a national and unifying movement has developed. The Communist element had the honour of being the beginners, but as the movement increased in strength and numbers a modifying and unifying process has taken place and national conceptions have supervened. In Marshal Tito the Partisans have found an outstanding leader, glorious in the fight for freedom. Unhappily, perhaps inevitably, these new forces came into collision with those under General Mihailović. Their activities upset his commanders' accommodations with the enemy. He endeavoured to repress them, and many tragic fights took place and bitter feuds sprang up between men of the same race and country, whose misfortunes were due only to the common foe.

'For a long time past I have taken a particular interest in Marshal Tito's movement, and have tried, and am trying, by every available means to bring him help. A young friend of mine, an Oxford don, Captain Deakin, now Lieut.-Colonel Deakin, D.S.O., entered Yugoslavia by parachute nearly a year ago, and was for eight months at Marshal Tito's headquarters. On one occasion both were wounded by the same bomb. They became friends. Certainly it is a bond between people, but a bond which, I trust, we shall not have to institute in our own personal relationships. From Colonel Deakin's reports we derived a lively picture of the whole struggle and its personalities.'

*   *   *

For two months longer the political wrangle over Yugoslav affairs continued in *émigré* circles in London. Each day lost diminished the chances of a balanced arrangement.

Prime Minister to Foreign Secretary   1 Apr 44

I consider that the King should be pressed to the utmost limit to get rid of his present fatal millstone advisers. As you know, I thought this would have been accomplished before the end of last year. I do not know what has been gained by all the spinning out that has gone on. . . . My idea throughout has been that the King should dissociate himself from Mihailović, that he should accept the resignation of the Purić Government or dismiss them, and that it would not do any great harm if he remained without a Government for a few weeks. ... I agree that King Peter should make a suitable declaration. I fear we must leave things at this for the time being.

... I have seen somewhere that three German divisions have been recalled out of Yugoslavia to hold down Hungary, and of course it will be of the greatest importance for Tito's forces to make contact with the Hungarian Partisans and take the fullest possible advantage of the situation now opening to his northward.

All these developments help us and help Tito, but they certainly do not help the King and his bedraggled Government. Unless he acts promptly, as the sense of your minute indicates, his chances of regaining his throne will, in my opinion, be lost. Since we discussed these matters in Cairo we have seen the entry of a grandiose Russian Mission to Tito's headquarters, and there is little doubt that the Russians will drive straight ahead for a Communist Tito-governed Yugoslavia, and will denounce everything done to the contrary as 'undemocratic'.

I hope therefore you will act most promptly now, draft the King a good declaration, make him dismiss Purić and Co. repudiate all contact with Mihailović, and make him form a stop-gap Government not obnoxious to Tito. Thus we may have a forlorn hope of making a bridge between them in the next five or six weeks. We are not justified in withholding military forces that wish or can be induced to fight with the Partisans because of the complexities of Serbian politics.

It was not until nearly the end of May that Mihailović was dismissed, and a moderate politican, Dr. Subašić, the former Governor of Croatia and member of Dr. Maček's Peasant Party was asked to form a new Administration.

Prime Minister to Marshal Tito (Yugoslavia) 17 May 44

This morning, as the result of British advice, King Peter II dismissed M. Purić's Administration, which included General Mihailović as Minister of War. He is now about to form an Administration or found a Council of State under the Ban of Croatia (Dr. Ivan Subašić). This of course has the strong approval of His Britannic Majesty's Government.

We do not know what will happen in the Serbian part of Yugoslavia. Mihailović certainly holds a powerful position locally as Commander-in-Chief, and it does not follow that his ceasing to be Minister of War will rob him of his influence. We cannot predict what he will do. There is also a very large body, amounting perhaps to 200,000, of Serbian peasant proprietary who are anti-German but strongly Serbian, and who naturally hold the views of a peasants' ownership community, contrary to the Karl Marx theory. My object is that these forces may be made to work with you for a united, independent Yugoslavia, which will expel from the soil of Yugoslavia the filthy Hitlerite murderers and invaders till not one remains.

It is of importance to the common cause and to our relations with you that these changes should be given a fair chance to develop in a favourable way to the main object. I should greatly regret it if you were at all in a hurry to denounce them in public. Crucial events impend in Europe. The battle in Italy goes in our favour. General Wilson assures me of his resolve to aid you to the very utmost. I feel therefore that I have a right to ask you to forbear from any utterances adverse to this new event, at least for a few weeks till we can have exchanged telegrams upon it.

Brigadier Maclean, who is with me now, will be with you in less than three weeks, with all the views he has gathered here, and I hope that at the very least you will await his return.

Meanwhile I congratulate you once more upon the number of enemy divisions which you are holding gripped on your various fronts. You will realise, Marshal Tito, that the war will soon come to a very high pitch of intensity, and that British, American, and Russian forces will all hurl themselves on the common foe. You must be at your strongest during this climax. While I cannot guarantee a speedy breakdown of the enemy's power, there is certainly a chance of it.

And on the 24th:

The King has sacked Purić and Co., and I think the Ban of Croatia will rally a certain force round him. My idea is that this Government should lie quiet for a bit and let events flow on their course. This, I think, was rather in accord with your idea in the first telegrams we exchanged. I am keeping the Russians and Americans informed of all that goes on between us.

Give my love to Randolph should he come into your sphere. Maclean will be coming back soon. I wish I could come myself, but I am too old and heavy to jump out on a parachute.

Here then we may leave this scene for others not less convulsive but larger.

CHAPTER 10

The Anzio Stroke

*Bitter Fighting on the Cassino Front – The Anzio Surprise
Landing – The Disastrous Pause – Kesselring's Critical Posi-
tion – Delay at the Beach-head – Renewed Attacks at Cassino
– Frustration at Anzio – My Questions to General Wilson of
February 6 – My Telegram to Field-Marshal Dill, February 8 –
Immense Number of Vehicles in the Beach-head – Disappoint-
ment and Casualties – German Effort to Drive Us into the Sea,
February 16 – The Deadly Battle Won – Kesselring Accepts
Failure, March 1 – I Tell the Story to Parliament, February 22
– Smuts' Message of February 23 – My Reply – Important
German Forces Diverted from France to Italy.*

The first weeks of January were spent in intensive preparations
for Operation 'Shingle', as Anzio was called in our codes, and
preliminary operations by the Fifth Army to draw the enemy's
attention and reserves away from the beach-head. To that end
the Army carried out a series of attacks which, it was hoped,
would take them across the rivers Garigliano and Rapido, while
the French Corps on the right swung round to threaten the high
ground north of Cassino. Fighting was bitter, for the Germans
clearly meant to prevent us from breaking into the Gustav Line,
which, with Cassino as its central feature, was the rearmost position of their deep defensive zone. In these rocky mountains a great
fortified system had been created, with lavish use of concrete
and steel. From their observation posts on the heights the enemy
could direct their guns on all movements in the valleys below.

After preliminary attacks in severe winter weather the Fifth
Army opened their main offensive on January 12, with the
French Corps making a ten-mile advance on the northern flank.
Three days later the IInd U.S. Corps occupied Monte Trocchio,
the last barrier before the river Liri, across which they formed,
but could not retain, a bridgehead. Then the Xth British Corps
crossed the lower Garigliano, and captured Minturno and the outskirts of Castelforte, but were held in their further attempts to
advance northwards. Nor could their right wing take Sant'
Ambrogio.

All this however had the desired effect on the enemy. It distracted their attention from the approaching threat to their vulnerable seaward flank and caused them to bring up three good divisions from reserve to restore the situation. They attacked the Xth British Corps, but failed to throw it back. By the afternoon of the 21st the convoys for Anzio were well out to sea, covered by our aircraft. The weather was well suited to a concealed approach. Our heavy attacks on enemy airfields, and especially at Perugia, the German air reconnaissance base, kept many of their aircraft grounded. General Westphal, who was Kesselring's Chief of Staff, gives a vivid picture of the position at German headquarters during these days.

On January 21 Admiral Canaris, Chief of the German Intelligence, visited Army Group headquarters, where he was pressed to communicate any information he might have about the enemy intentions in regard to a landing. In particular we wanted to know about the positions of aircraft-carriers, battleships, and landing-craft. Canaris was unable to give us any details, but thought that there was no need to fear a new landing in the near future. This was certainly his view. Not only air reconnaissance, but also the German counter-espionage, was almost completely out of action at this time. A few hours after the departure of Canaris the enemy landed at Anzio.*

*   *   *

It was with tense, but I trust suppressed, excitement that I awaited the outcome of this considerable stroke.

To Stalin I telegraphed:

21 Jan 44

We have launched the big attack against the German armies defending Rome which I told you about at Teheran. The weather conditions seem favourable. I hope to have good news for you before long.

Presently I learned that the VIth Corps, under the American General Lucas, had landed on the Anzio beaches at 2 a.m. on the 22nd, the 3rd United States Division south of the town, and the 1st British Division north of it. There was very little opposition and practically no casualties. By midnight 36,000 men and

---

* Westphal, *Heer in Fesseln*, p. 240.

over 3,000 vehicles were ashore. 'We appear,' signalled Alexander, who was on the spot, 'to have got almost complete surprise. I have stressed the importance of strong-hitting mobile patrols being boldly pushed out to gain contact with the enemy, but so far have not received reports of their activities.' I was in full agreement with this, and replied: 'Thank you for all your messages. Am very glad you are pegging out claims rather than digging in beach-heads.'

* * *

But now came disaster, and the ruin in its prime purpose of the enterprise. General Lucas confined himself to occupying his beach-head and having equipment and vehicles brought ashore. General Penney, commanding the British 1st Division, was anxious to push inland. His reserve brigade was however held back with the corps. Minor probing attacks towards Cisterna and Campoleone occupied the 22nd and 23rd. No general attempt to advance was made by the commander of the expedition. By the evening of the 23rd the whole of the two divisions and their attached troops, including two British Commandos, the United States Rangers, and parachutists, had been landed, with masses of impedimenta. The defences of the beach-head were growing, but the opportunity for which great exertions had been made was gone.

Kesselring reacted quickly to his critical situation. The bulk of his reserves were already committed against us on the Cassino front, but he pulled in whatever units were available, and in forty-eight hours the equivalent of about two divisions was assembled to resist our further advance.

The German General Westphal's comments on the way in which this was done are illuminating.

At the moment of the landing south of Rome, apart from certain coastal batteries standing by, there were only two battalions. ... There was nothing else in the neighbourhood which could be thrown against the enemy on that same day. The road to Rome was open. No one could have stopped a bold advance-guard entering the Holy City. The breath-taking situation continued for the first two days after the landing. It was only then that German counter-measures were effective. What was their nature? In December 1943 the [German] Army Group had issued a comprehensive plan of emergency for the whole of Italy. In it was laid down what troops and

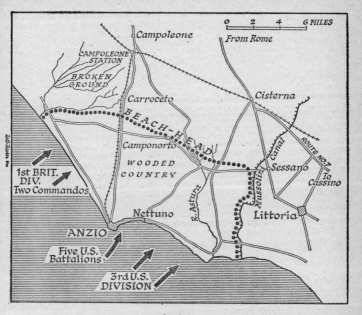

Anzio

columns should move against the possible landing-points, on what roads and at what times, and what tasks they should undertake. It was only necessary to issue the code-word 'Case Richard' to put into effect these prearranged plans. In fact, most of the troops, in spite of icy roads over the Apennines, arrived before schedule. The German High Command helped by sending troops from France, Yugoslavia, and the homeland. . . . The enemy kept surprisingly quiet. They were apparently engaged in building up a bridgehead. It was thus possible to build up a new front opposite them. The command of this sector was taken over by the general headquarters of the Fourteenth Army, up to now based in Northern Italy and under General von Mackensen.*

The threat to his flank did not weaken Kesselring's determination to withstand our assaults at Cassino. The German intentions were made crystal-clear by an order from Hitler captured on the 24th:

* *Heer in Fesseln*, p. 242.

The Gustav Line must be held at all costs for the sake of the political consequences which would follow a completely successful defence. The Fuehrer expects the bitterest struggle for every yard.

He was certainly obeyed.

*   *   *

On the 25th Alexander reported that the beach-head was reasonably secure. The 3rd United States Division was four miles from Cisterna and the British 1st Division two miles from Campoleone, and contact was continuous along the entire front. On the 27th serious news arrived. Neither place had been taken. The Guards Brigade had beaten off a counter-attack of infantry and tanks and had gone forward, but they were still about a mile and a half short of Campoleone, and the Americans were still south of Cisterna. Alexander said that neither he nor General Clark was satisfied with the speed of the advance, and that Clark was going to the beach-head at once. I replied:

Prime Minister to General Alexander   28 Jan 44
I am glad to learn that Clark is going to visit the beach-head. It would be unpleasant if your troops were sealed off there and the main army could not advance up from the south.

This however was exactly what was going to happen.

*   *   *

Meanwhile our attacks on the Germans in the Cassino positions continued. The Xth British Corps having drawn to its front most of the enemy reinforcements, it was decided to attack farther north so as to seize the high ground above Cassino and envelop the position from that side. Good progress was made. The IInd U.S. Corps crossed the river Rapido above Cassino town, with the French Corps on their right keeping abreast of them, and took Monte Castellone and Colle Majola. Thence they attacked southwards against Monastery Hill; but the Germans had reinforced and held on fanatically. By early February the IInd Corps had expended its strength. General Alexander decided that fresh troops would be needed to restore impetus to the assault. He had already ordered a New Zealand Corps to be formed, under General Freyberg, composed of three divisions brought over from the Eighth Army on the

Adriatic. Indeed, that army, which had attempted to pin the enemy on their front by offensive action, had had to send no fewer than five divisions to sustain the heavy fighting on the west coast, and for the next few months had to remain on the defensive.

Further severe battles obviously impended on both fronts, and it was necessary to find more troops. The 3rd Polish Carpathian Division was due to arrive on the main front at the beginning of February. General Wilson had ready the 18th Infantry and the 1st Guards Brigade in North Africa. By January 30 the 1st U.S. Armoured Division had landed at Anzio and the 45th U.S. Division was on its way. All this had to be done over the difficult beaches or through the tiny fishing port. 'The situation as it now stands,' signalled Admiral John Cunningham, 'bears little relation to the lightning thrust by two or three divisions envisaged at Marrakesh, but you may rest assured that no effort will be spared by the Navies to provide the sinews of victory.' This promise, as will be seen, was amply redeemed.

*   *   *

While the fighting at Cassino was at its zenith, on January 30 the VIth Corps at Anzio made its first attack in strength. Some ground was gained, but the 3rd U.S. Division failed to take Cisterna and the 1st British Division Campoleone. More than four divisions were already ashore in the beach-head. But the Germans, despite our air action against their communications, had reinforced quickly and strongly. Elements of eight divisions faced us in positions which they had now had time to fortify. Galling artillery fire harassed the crowded lodgments we had gained, and our shipping lying off the beaches suffered damage from air attacks by night. On February 2 Alexander again visited the battle-front, and sent me a full report. German resistance had increased, and was especially strong opposite the 3rd U.S. Division at Cisterna and the 1st British Division at Campoleone. No further offensive was possible until these points were captured. The 3rd Division had fought hard for Cisterna during the last two or three days. The men were tired and were still about a mile from the town. A brigade of the 1st Division was holding Campoleone railway station, but they were in a very long and narrow salient and were being shot at 'by everything from three sides'. Alexander concluded: 'We shall presently be in a position to carry out a properly co-ordinated thrust in full strength to achieve our object of cutting the enemy's main line of supply, for which I have ordered plans to be prepared.'

Before effect could be given to Alexander's orders the enemy launched a counter-attack on February 3 which drove in the salient of the 1st British Division and was clearly only a prelude to harder things to come. In the words of General Wilson's report, 'the perimeter was sealed off and our forces therein are not capable of advancing.'

I had been much troubled at several features of the Anzio operation, as the following telegrams will show.

Prime Minister to General Wilson (Algiers) and   6 Feb 44
C.-in-C. Mediterranean

I do not want to worry General Alexander in the height of the battle, but I am not at all surprised at the inquiry from the United States Chiefs of Staff. There are three points on which you should touch. First, why was the 504th Regiment of paratroops not used at Anzio as proposed, and why is the existing British Parachute Brigade used as ordinary infantry in the line? Secondly, why was no attempt made to occupy the high ground and at least the towns of Velletri, Campoleone, and Cisterna twelve or twenty-four hours after the unopposed landing? Thirdly, the question asked by the United States Chiefs of Staff: why has there been no heavily mounted aggressive offensive on the main front to coincide with the withdrawal of troops by the Germans to face the landing?

2. In my early telegrams to General Alexander I raised all these points in a suggestive form, and particularly deprecated a continuance of the multiplicity of small attacks in battalion, company, and even platoon strength. I repeat however that I do not wish General Alexander's attention to be diverted from the battle, which is at its height, in order to answer questions or write explanations about the past.

General Wilson replied that the 504th Paratroop Regiment was seaborne and not airborne because of a last-minute decision by General Clark. The British paratroops were employed in the line because of infantry shortage. On my second question he said there was no lack of urging from above, and that both Alexander and Clark went to the beach-head during the first forty-eight hours to hasten the offensive. Though General Lucas had achieved surprise he had failed to take advantage of it. This was due to his 'Salerno complex'—that as a prelude to success the first task was to repel the inevitable enemy counter-attack. He did not feel sure of achieving this before the arrival of the 1st U.S. Armoured Division combat team. The assault, said Wilson, was only geared to function at a slow speed. He also explained the difficulties of forcing the main front on the Rapido river and around Cassino.

General Marshall shared my concern, and I passed this report to Washington with the following comment:

Prime Minister to Field-Marshal Dill   8 Feb 44
(Washington)
You should impart this report to General Marshall at your discretion.
... My comment is that senior commanders should not 'urge', but 'order'.
All this has been a disappointment to me. Nevertheless it is a great advantage that the enemy should come in strength and fight in South Italy, thus being drawn far from other battle-fields. Moreover, we have a great need to keep continually engaging them, and even a battle of attrition is better than standing by and watching the Russians fight. We should also learn a good many lessons about how not to do it which will be valuable in 'Overlord'.

*   *   *

The Admiral had been even better than his word about the landing-craft. I now put a direct question to him.

Prime Minister to Commander-in-Chief Mediterranean
8 Feb 44
Let me know the number of vehicles landed at Anzio by the seventh and fourteenth days respectively. I should be glad, if it were possible without too much trouble or delay, to distinguish trucks, cannon, and tanks.

The reply was both prompt and startling. By the seventh day 12,350 vehicles had been landed, including 356 tanks; by the fourteenth day 21,940 vehicles, including 380 tanks. This represented a total of 315 L.S.T. shipments. It was interesting to notice that, apart from 4,000 trucks which went to and fro in the ships, nearly 18,000 vehicles were landed in the Anzio beach-head by the fourteenth day in order to serve a total force of 70,000 men, including of course the drivers and those who did the repair and maintenance of the vehicles.

I replied on February 10:

Thank you for information.

How many of our men are driving or looking after 18,000 vehicles in this narrow space? We must have a great superiority of chauffeurs. I am shocked that the enemy have more infantry than we. Let me have our latest ration strength in the bridgehead.

Later the same day further reports came in. General Wilson said that the weather had spoilt our air attacks. The 1st British Division was under severe pressure and had had to give ground and Alexander was arranging to relieve it.

All this was a great disappointment at home and in the United States. I did not of course know what orders had been given to General Lucas, but it is a root principle to push out and join issue with the enemy, and it would seem that his judgment was against it from the beginning. As I said at the time, I had hoped that we were hurling a wild cat on to the shore, but all we had got was a stranded whale. The spectacle of 18,000 vehicles accumulated ashore by the fourteenth day for only 70,000 men, or less than four men to a vehicle, including drivers and attendants, though they did not move more than twelve or fourteen miles, was astonishing. We were apparently still stronger than the Germans in fighting power. The ease with which they moved their pieces about on the board and the rapidity with which they adjusted the perilous gaps they had to make on their southern front was most impressive. It all seemed to give us very adverse data for 'Overlord'.

I cabled to Alexander:

... I have a feeling that you may have hesitated to assert your authority because you were dealing so largely with Americans and therefore *urged* an advance instead of *ordering* it. You are however quite entitled to give them orders, and I have it from the highest American authorities that it is their wish that their troops should receive direct orders. They say their Army has been framed more on Prussian lines than on the more smooth British lines, and that American commanders expect to receive positive orders, which they will immediately obey. Do not hesitate therefore to give orders just as you would to our own men. The Americans are very good to work with, and quite prepared to take the rough with the smooth.

Alexander replied on February 11:

The first phase of operations, which started so full of promise, has now just passed, owing to the enemy's ability to concentrate so quickly sufficient force to stabilise what was to him a very serious situation. The battle has now reached the second phase, in which we must now at all costs crush his counter-attacks, and then, with our own forces regrouped, resume offensive to break inland and get astride his communications leading from Rome to the south. This I have every intention of doing. Out of the thirty-five battalions of the VIth Corps casualties are as follows: British, up to February 6, killed, 285; wounded, 1,371; missing, 1,048. American, up to February 9, killed, 597; wounded, 2,506; missing, 1,116. These losses include those of nine Ranger battalions. Total casualties, 6,923. I am very grateful for your kind message at the end of your telegram. I well realise the disappointment to you and all at home. I have every hope and intention of reaching the goal we set out to gain.

* * *

The expected major effort to drive us back into the sea at Anzio opened on February 16, when the enemy employed over four divisions, supported by 450 guns, in a direct thrust southwards from Campoleone. Hitler's special order of the day was read out to the troops before the attack. He demanded that our beach-head 'abscess' be eliminated in three days. The attack fell at an awkward moment, as the 45th U.S. and 56th British Divisions, transferred from the Cassino front, were just relieving our gallant 1st Division, who soon found themselves in full action again. A deep, dangerous wedge was driven into our line, which was forced back here to the original beach-head. The artillery fire, which had embarrassed all the occupants of the beach-head since they landed, reached a new intensity. All hung in the balance. No further retreat was possible. Even a short advance would have given the enemy the power to use not merely their long-range guns in harassing fire upon the landing stages and shipping, but to put down a proper field artillery barrage upon all intakes or departures. I had no illusions about the issue. It was life or death.

But fortune, hitherto baffling, rewarded the desperate valour of the British and American armies. Before Hitler's stipulated three days the German attack was stopped. Then their own salient was counter-attacked in flank and cut out under fire from all our artillery and bombardment by every aircraft we could fly. The fighting was intense, losses on both sides were heavy, but the deadly battle was won.

One more attempt was made by Hitler—for his was the will-power at work—at the end of February. The 3rd U.S. Division, on the eastern flank, was attacked by three German divisions. These were weakened and shaken by their previous failure. The Americans held stubbornly, and the attack was broken in a day, when the Germans had suffered more than 2,500 casualties. On March 1 Kesselring accepted his failure. He had frustrated the Anzio expedition. He could not destroy it. I cabled to the President:

> I must send you my warmest congratulations on the grand fighting of your troops, particularly the United States 3rd Division, in the Anzio beach-head. I am always deeply moved to think of our men fighting side by side in so many fierce battles and of the inspiring additions to our history which these famous episodes will make. Of course I have been very anxious about the beach-head, where we have so little ground to give. The stakes are very high on both sides now, and the suspense is long-drawn. I feel sure we shall win both here and at Cassino.

*　　*　　*

In my report to Parliament on February 22, 1944,* Anzio was presented in its proportion. I told the story as far as was then possible.

'It was certainly no light matter to launch this considerable army upon the seas—40,000 or 50,000 men in the first instance—with all the uncertainty of winter weather and all the unknowable strength of enemy fortifications. The operation itself was a model of combined work. The landing was virtually unopposed. Subsequent events did not however take the course which had been hoped or planned. In the upshot we got a great army ashore, equipped with masses of artillery, tanks, and very many thousands of vehicles, and our troops moving inland came into contact with the enemy.

'The German reactions to this descent have been remarkable. Hitler has apparently resolved to defend Rome with the same obstinacy which he showed at Stalingrad, in Tunisia, and, recently, in the Dnieper Bend. No fewer than seven extra German divisions were brought rapidly down from France, Northern

* See p. 132.

Italy, and Yugoslavia, and a determined attempt has been made to destroy the bridgehead and drive us into the sea. Battles of prolonged and intense fierceness and fury have been fought. At the same time the American and British Fifth Army to the southward is pressing forward with all its strength. Another battle is raging there.

'On broad grounds of strategy, Hitler's decision to send into the south of Italy as many as eighteen divisions, involving, with their maintenance troops, probably something like half a million Germans, and to make a large secondary front in Italy, is not unwelcome to the Allies. We must fight the Germans somewhere, unless we are to stand still and watch the Russians. This wearing battle in Italy occupies troops who could not be employed in other greater operations, and it is an effective prelude to them.'

*   *   *

General Smuts telegraphed to me next day in terms which illustrated so well his breadth of vision.

General Smuts to Prime Minister   23 Feb 44
    Your very effective recital of British war effort will greatly impress world public opinion. It gives vast number of new facts not generally known, which form the proper pendant to Russia's magnificent effort. It will also counterbalance the one-sided impression given by our propaganda of our own ineffectiveness in Burma and at Anzio in comparison with vast sweep of Russian victories. I myself have not followed our strategy in the Anzio beach-head, which I had thought would link up with the Cassino front with the object of breaking resistance of Germans in the mountains in the south. An isolated pocket has now been created, which is unconnected with enemy's main southern front, and which is itself besieged instead of giving relief to the pressure against us in the south.
    The position is once more restored to its right proportions by your emphasis on our vast air effort, which destroyed Germany's war effort at its source and prepares for the coming Western Front in the best possible way. But I would not myself give undue publicity to this front, since it may hold unpleasant surprises for us. The retreat of the German armies in the East is not only due to Russian prowess and our attraction of Luftwaffe from that front, but probably also to the Germans withdrawing large strategic reserves to counter our threat in the West. In a theatre where enemy is fully prepared

for us serious delays, if not setbacks, may be met with, and we may have to face grave disappointments. The German plan may be to halt us effectively in the West, and then hasten back to the East to stop the penetration of Russian armies into Germany, which he must mortally fear. If this is not the German plan, I do not understand their strategy of fighting stubbornly against us for every inch of ground in Italy, while letting Russia achieve such successes on the Eastern Front.

Instead of giving undue publicity to our Western Front, our propaganda should for the present be concentrated on our air offensive against Germany. I do believe that this has had even more far-reaching effects than the Russian land victories.

If any reserves are called for, remember our now well-trained South African 6th Armoured Division, which is in Egypt. They only need some added transport to give a good account of themselves in a suitable theatre.

To this I relied, expressing views which I hold to this day:

Prime Minister to Field-Marshal Smuts   27 Feb 44

Thank you for your telegram. During the Conferences at Carthage and at Marrakesh I was able to clear difficulties out of the way and get this big amphibious operation at Anzio soundly organised. My personal efforts did not extend to the conduct of the battle, which of course I left altogether to the commanders, once they were landed safely at the right place, as they were. In all his talks with me Alexander envisaged that the essence of the battle was the seizure of the Alban Hills with the utmost speed, and to this end I was able to obtain from the United States their 504th Parachute Regiment, although at the time it was under orders to return for 'Overlord'. But at the last moment General Clark cancelled the use of this regiment, and the American General Lucas, a man of fifty-five, who at Salerno had distinguished himself in command of a corps, seems to have had the idea in his mind that at all costs he must be prepared for a counter-attack. As a result, although directly I learnt the landing was successful I sent Alexander injunctions that he should peg out claims rather than consolidate bridgeheads, the whole operation became stagnant. Needless to say, the logistic calculations all turned out to be on the overgenerous side and there were very large margins in hand. No one can deny that this was lucky, seeing that plans originally made for 50,000 men are now comfortably supporting 170,000.

Naturally I am very disappointed at what has appeared to be the frittering away of a brilliant opening in which both

fortune and design had played their part. I do not in any way
however repent of what has been done. As a result the Germans have now transferred into the south of Italy at least
eight more divisions, so that in all there are eighteen south
of Rome. It is vital to the success of 'Overlord' that we keep
away from that theatre and hold elsewhere as many German
divisions as possible, and hard fighting in Italy throughout the
spring will provide for the main operation a perfect prelude
and accompaniment.

We had hoped that a big thrust would be launched northwards from the Cassino front to correspond with the landing.
This was indeed planned, but it did not take place because
apparently it proved immensely difficult to debouch past
Cassino up the Liri valley. Naturally we are striving with
might and main to join up the two forces, and at any moment
the curtain may go up on the next act of the drama. Truscott,
a young American Divisional Commander, whom everyone
speaks of most highly, has now superseded Lucas. My confidence in Alexander remains undiminished.

Here at home all goes fairly well, though the little folk are
more active. However, their chirrupings will be stilled before
long by the thunder of the cannonade.

Most earnestly do I look forward to seeing you, and I
rejoice that you will be at my side in momentous times.

*　　　*　　　*

Such is the story of the struggle of Anzio; a story of high
opportunity and shattered hopes, of skilful inception on
our part and swift recovery by the enemy, of valour shared by
both. We now know that early in January the German High
Command had intended to transfer five of their best divisions
from Italy to North-West Europe. Kesselring protested that in
such an event he could no longer carry out his orders to fight
south of Rome and he would have to withdraw. Just as the
argument was at its height the Anzio landing took place. The
High Command dropped the idea, and instead of the Italian
front contributing forces to North-West Europe the reverse took
place. Hitler was enraged at the failure of his Fourteenth Army
to drive the Allies into the sea. After their offensive of February 16 he ordered a selected group of twenty officers of all arms
and ranks fighting in Italy to report to him personally about
conditions at the front. This was the first and only time that this
happened during the war. 'He would have done much better,'

comments General Westphal, 'to visit the front himself and been convinced of Allied superiority in planes and guns.'

We knew nothing of all these changes of plan at the time, but it proves that the aggressive action of our armies in Italy, and specifically the Anzio stroke, made its full contribution towards the success of 'Overlord'. We shall see later on the part it played in the liberation of Rome.

CHAPTER 11

Italy: Cassino

*Mussolini and Ciano – Marshal Badoglio's Harassed Govern-
ment – Correspondence with President Roosevelt on This –
My Statement on Italian Political Affairs in the House of Com-
mons, February 22 – Bombing of the Monastery at Cassino –
The Weather Brings a Deadlock – Discussion with Roosevelt
on the Italian Political Situation – The Russians Recognise the
Badoglio Government – The Campaign in Italy Drags – Alex-
ander's Convincing Explanation – Anglo-American Argument
about 'Overlord', 'Anvil', and the Italian Campaign – Views of
General Eisenhower and General Wilson – My Telegram to
General Marshall of April 16 on the Military Position – The
Crown Prince Umberto Becomes Lieutenant-Governor of the
Realm – Prelude to the New Allied Offensive.*

The bitterness and confusion of the Italian scene were height-
ened in the New Year. Mussolini's phantom republic came under
mounting pressure from the Germans. The governing circles
around Badoglio in the south were assailed by intrigues in
Italy and despised by public opinion in Britain and the United
States. Mussolini was the first to react.

When he arrived in Munich after his escape he found there
his daughter Edda and her husband, Count Ciano. These two had
fled from Rome at the time of the surrender, and, although
Ciano had voted against his father-in-law at the fateful meeting of the Grand Council, he hoped, thanks to the influence of
his wife, for a reconciliation. During these days in Munich this
in fact happened. This aroused the indignation of Hitler, who
had already placed the Ciano family under house arrest on their
arrival. The reluctance of the Duce to punish the traitors to
Fascism, and particularly Ciano, was perhaps the main reason
why Hitler formed such a low opinion of his colleague at this
critical time.

It was not until the declining strength of the 'Republic of
Salo' had fallen far, and the impatience of its German masters
had sharpened, that Mussolini agreed to let loose a wave of
calculated vengeance. All those leaders of the old Fascist

régime who had voted against him in July and who could be caught in German-occupied Italy were brought to trial at the end of 1943, in the medieval fortress at Verona. Among them was Ciano. Without exception they received the death sentence. In spite of the entreaties and threats of Edda, the Duce could not relent. In January 1944 the group, which included not only Ciano but also the seventy-eight-year-old Marshal de Bono, a colleague in the march on Rome, were taken out to die a traitor's death—to be shot in the back tied to a chair. They all died bravely.

The end of Ciano was in keeping with all the elements of Renaissance tragedy. Mussolini's submission to Hitler's vengeful demands brought him only shame, and the miserable neo-Fascist republic dragged on by Lake Garda—a relic of the Broken Axis.

* * *

In the south Badoglio was continually harassed by the remnants of the opposition to Fascism in its early days, and which had sprung up in political groupings since the previous summer. They not only pressed for a broader Administration in which they would share, but also sought to destroy the monarchy, which they declared to be compromised by prolonged acquiescence in Mussolini's rule. There was growing public support for their activities, both in America and in England. In January a congress of the six Italian parties was held in Bari, and resolutions in this sense were passed.

I therefore telegraphed to the President:

Prime Minister to President Roosevelt   3 Feb 44
I earnestly hope that the existing *régime* in Italy will be allowed to function at least until the great battles now being fought by the soldiers of our two countries have resulted in our capture of Rome. I am sure that a disturbance now of such authority as remains in the Italian State and the attempt to create a new authority out of political groups with no real backing will add greatly to our difficulties. Moreover, these groups, when formed into a Government, in order to win credit from the Italian people, would feel it essential to assert Italian interests in a much stronger form than the King and Badoglio dare to do. I feel it would be a great pity if Badoglio threw in his hand, and our reports show that the Italian Navy might be powerfully affected by action against the

King. Much British and American blood is flowing, and I plead that military considerations should carry weight.

His reply was reassuring.

President Roosevelt to Prime Minister　　　　　11 Feb 44

I have directed the Department of State to take no action toward effecting any change in the existing Government of Italy at the present time, and until our military situation in the Italian campaign is sufficiently improved to warrant risking the disaffection of those Italians who are now assisting the Allied forces.

I think, though, that you and I should regard this only as a temporary reprieve for the two old gentlemen.

I elaborated my view.

Prime Minister to President Roosevelt　　　　　13 Feb 44

I fully agree we should review the whole scene after we are settled in Rome. We have not got there yet, and Lincoln's birthday celebrations remind me about not crossing the Fox River till you get to it.

The present *régime* is the lawful Government of Italy, with whom we have concluded an armistice, in consequence of which the Italian Navy came over, and, with some of the Italian Army and Air Force, are fighting on our side. This Italian Government will obey our directions far more than any other that we may laboriously constitute. On the other hand, it has more power over the Fleet, Army officials, etc., than anything else which can be set up out of the worn-out débris of political parties, none of whom have the slightest title by election or prescription. A new Italian Government will have to make its reputation with the Italian people by standing up to us. They will very likely try to wriggle out of the armistice terms. As for being instrumental in handing over without a mutiny part of the Italian Fleet to Russia, I cannot conceive that they would do so, or that if they did their writ would run with the Italian Navy. I hope therefore that when the time comes we shall consult together. I gave strong support to the State Department over Darlan. They seem rueful about that episode now. Looking back upon it, I consider it was right. Several thousand British and American soldiers are alive to-day because of it, and it got us Dakar at a time when we could ill have spared the large forces needed for its capture. . . .

I have had a letter from Harry. He is an indomitable spirit. I cannot help feeling very anxious about his frail body and another operation. I should always be grateful for any news about him, for I rate him high among the Paladins. I have just heard that his son has been killed in the Marshall Islands battle. As I do not know whether his state of health will have permitted him to receive this news, I am sending him a message through you.

As the President and myself were at one on the main issue, I made a statement on Italian political affairs in my speech of February 22 in the House of Commons.

'The battle in Italy will be hard and long. I am not yet convinced that any other Government can be formed at the present time in Italy which could command the same obedience from the Italian armed forces. Should we succeed in the present battle and enter Rome, as I trust and believe we shall, we shall be free to discuss the whole Italian political situation, and we shall do so with many advantages that we do not possess at the present time. It is from Rome that a more broadly based Italian Government can best be formed. Whether a Government thus formed will be so helpful to the Allies as the present dispensation I cannot tell. It might of course be a Government which would try to make its position good with the Italian people by resisting, as much as it dared, the demands made on them in the interests of the Allied armies. I should be sorry however to see an unsettling change made at a time when the battle is at its climax, swaying to and fro. When you have to hold a hot coffee-pot it is better not to break the handle off until you are sure that you will get another equally convenient and serviceable, or at any rate until there is a dishcloth handy.

'The representatives of the various Italian parties who assembled a fortnight ago at Bari are of course eager to become the Government of Italy. They will have no elective authority, and certainly no constitutional authority, until either the present King abdicates or his successor invites them to take office. It is by no means certain that they would have any effective authority over the Italian armed forces now fighting with us. Italy lies prostrate under her miseries and disasters. Food is scarce ; shipping to bring it is voraciously absorbed by our ever-expanding military operations. I think we have gained this year 12,000,000 tons increase to the Allies, yet the shortage continues, because our great operations absorb every ship as it comes, and the movement of food is difficult.

'It would be a mistake to suppose that the kind of political conditions or forces exist in Italy which work so healthily in unbeaten lands, or in countries which have not been shattered by war or stifled by a long period of Fascist rule. We shall see more clearly how to proceed and have more varied resources at our disposal if and when we are in possession of the capital city. The policy therefore which His Majesty's Government have agreed provisionally with the Government of the United States is to win the battle for Rome and take a new view when we are there.'

*   *   *

The second major attack at Cassino began on February 15 with the bombing of the monastery.* The height on which the monastery stood surveyed the junction of the rivers Rapido and Liri and was the pivot of the whole German defence. It had already proved itself a formidable, strongly defended obstacle. Its steep sides, swept by fire, were crowned by the famous building, which several times in previous wars had been pillaged, destroyed, and rebuilt. There is controversy about whether it should have been destroyed once again. The monastery did not contain German troops, but the enemy fortifications were hardly separate from the building itself. The monastery dominated the whole battlefield, and naturally General Freyberg, the Corps Commander concerned, wished to have it heavily bombarded from the air before he launched the infantry attack. The Army Commander, General Mark Clark, unwillingly sought and obtained permission from General Alexander, who accepted the responsibility. On February 15 therefore, after the monks had been given full warning, over 450 tons of bombs were dropped, and heavy damage was done. The great outer walls and gateway still stood. The result was not good. The Germans had now every excuse for making whatever use they could of the rubble of the ruins, and this gave them even better opportunities for defence than when the building was intact.

It fell to the 4th Indian Division, which had recently relieved the Americans on the ridges north of the monastery, to make the attack. On two successive nights they tried in vain to seize a knoll that lay between their position and Monastery Hill. On the night of February 18 a third attempt was made. The fighting was desperate, and all our men who reached the knoll

* See maps, pp. 244–50.

T—s.w.w.—10—H

were killed. Later that night a brigade by-passed the knoll and moved directly at the monastery, only to encounter a concealed ravine heavily mined and covered by enemy machine-guns at shortest range. Here they lost heavily and were stopped. While this fierce conflict was raging on the heights above them the New Zealand Division succeeded in crossing the river Rapido just below Cassino town; but they were counter-attacked by tanks before their bridgehead was secure and forced back again. The direct attack on Cassino had failed.

At the beginning of March the weather brought about a deadlock. Napoleon's fifth element—mud—bogged down both sides. We could not break the main front at Cassino, and the Germans had equally failed to drive us into the sea at Anzio. In numbers there was little to choose between the combatants. By now we had twenty divisions in Italy, but both Americans and French had had very heavy losses. The enemy had eighteen or nineteen divisions south of Rome, and five more in Northern Italy, but they too were tired and worn.

There could be no hope now of a break-out from the Anzio beach-head and no prospect of an early link-up between our two separated forces until the Cassino front was broken. The prime need therefore was to make the beach-head really firm, to relieve and reinforce the troops, and to pack in stores to withstand a virtual siege and nourish a subsequent sortie. Time was short, since many of the landing-craft had to leave for 'Overlord' in the middle of the month. Their move had so far been rightly postponed, but no further delay was possible. The Navies put all their strength into the effort, with admirable results. The previous average daily tonnage landed had been 3,000; in the first ten days of March this was more than doubled. I followed this process with attention.

On March 12 I asked, 'What is the ration strength in the bridgehead at present? How many vehicles have been landed there from the beginning? How many days' reserve supplies of food and ammunition have been built up, and what is the basis of this calculation?'

General Alexander replied that the ration strength was 90,200 United States and 35,500 British. Nearly 25,000 vehicles of all kinds had been landed. He gave full details of the supplies of food, ammunition, and petrol. The margins were not large, but improving.

A few days later Vesuvius was in violent eruption. For several days traffic from the Naples airfields was partially interrupted, but the work in the ports went on. On March 24 a report to the Naval Commander-in-Chief stated: 'The Naples group of ports is now discharging at the rate of twelve million tons a year, while Vesuvius is estimated to be doing thirty millions a day. We can but admire this gesture of the gods.'

*   *   *

While the battles I have described were going on politics raged around Badoglio. Roosevelt was being clamorously pressed to support major changes in the Italian Government. He suggested that we might yield to the pressure of opinion.

Prime Minister to President Roosevelt   8 Mar 44

Your cable causes me concern. It is a departure from your agreement with me of February 11, which you kindly re-affirmed in your [later] cable as 'finished business'. On the strength of the first assurances I made my statement to Parliament.

My advices do not lead me to believe that any new facts of importance have arisen or that the Allied forces are not capable of maintaining order in the regions they have occupied as the result of the 'unconditional surrender' of Italy. It would be a very serious mistake to give way to [local] agitation, especially when accompanied by threats on the part of groups of office-seeking politicians. We should then be liable to set up in Italy an Administration which might not command the allegiance of the armed forces, but which would endeavour to make its position with the Italian people by standing up to the Allies. In fact, we should have another but more intractable version of the de Gaullist Committee. Meanwhile, in the midst of a heart-shaking battle we are to get rid of the helpful Government of the King and Badoglio, which is doing its utmost to work its passage and aid us in every way.

I readily admit that the course you recommend would be the more popular and would have at least a transitory success. But I am sure that for the victorious conquerors to have their hands forced in this way by sections of the defeated population would be unfortunate. So also would be the obvious open division between you and me and between our two Governments. I gave you and the State Department loyal and vigorous support over the Darlan affair. Unity of action between our two Governments was never more necessary than at the present time, considering the great battles in which we are engaged and which lie ahead.

His reply on the same day encouraged me to believe that we were in agreement. 'It is my strongest wish,' he said, 'that you and I should continue to work in complete harmony in this matter as in all others. We may differ on timing, but things like that can be worked out, and on the big objectives like self-determination we are as one.'

The pressures however continued. The idea of making a bargain with the six Italian Opposition parties gained support in the Supreme Headquarters at Algiers, and General Wilson telegraphed in this sense to the Combined Chiefs of Staff in Washington and London. This he was entitled to do as he served both countries. Nevertheless my views remained unchanged, and my colleagues in the War Cabinet, who saw all that was passing, were in broad agreement with them.

Prime Minister to President Roosevelt   13 Mar 44
 I fear that if we drive out the King and Badoglio at this stage we shall only have complicated the task of the Armies. I see that this is also the Soviet view. They are certainly realistic, but of course their aim may be a Communist Italy, and it may suit them to use the King and Badoglio till everything is ready for an extreme solution. I can assure you that this danger is also in my mind. My idea remains that we should try to construct a broadly based Government, taking into account the opinion of the democratic North of Italy and seeking representatives from there. Of course if we cannot get Rome for several months we shall have to act earlier, but without the favourable conditions which will be open to us once we are in possession of the capital. We shall then have much better chances of finding a really representative footing.

The President's reply disappointed me.

President Roosevelt to Prime Minister   13 Mar 44
 I am sorry if earlier messages were not clear. I did not at any time intend to convey to you agreement that we postpone all political decisions until after Rome had been taken. The political situation in Italy has developed rapidly since our earlier messages; the military situation has not kept pace. The capture of Rome is still remote and major political decisions must be taken.
 I do not like having to use stern measures against our friends in Italy, except for good reason. In the present situation the Commander-in-Chief and his political advisers, both British and American, have recommended that we give immediate support to the programme of the six Opposition parties. Thus

we have, happily, for once, our political and military considerations entirely in harmony.

We do not need to intervene beyond informing the executive junta of our support of their programme and confirming this to the King if necessary. The Italians can present the solution to the King and work out the programme among themselves.

I cannot for the life of me understand why we should hesitate any longer in supporting a policy so admirably suited to our common military and political aims. American public opinion would never understand our continued tolerance and apparent support of Victor Emmanuel.

The Russians now complicated the position by sending an official representative to the Badoglio Government without consulting us.

Prime Minister to President Roosevelt   14 Mar 44

The Russians have announced that they have sent a fully accredited Ambassador to the present Italian Government, with whom we are still technically at war. I do not think it would be wise, without further consideration, to accept the programme of the so-called Six Parties and demand forthwith the abdication of the King and installation of Signor Croce as Lieutenant of the Realm. I will however consult the War Cabinet upon what you justly call a 'major political decision'. Our war with Italy has lasted since June 1940, and the British Empire has suffered 232,000 casualties in men, as well as our losses in ships. I feel sure that in this matter our view will receive consideration from you. We ought to make every effort to act together. Pray remember that I have committed myself in public, and that any divergence will certainly become known.

The War Cabinet considered these messages, and I reported their conclusions to the President.

15 Mar 44

I consulted the War Cabinet this morning on the proposal that the British and American Governments should accept the Six Party programme without further delay. The War Cabinet asked me to assure you that they agree fully with your wish to establish a more broadly based Government in Italy, and that the future form of government of the Italian people can only be settled by self-determination. They also agree with you that the point to consider is the timing. On this they have no doubt that it would be far better to wait till we are masters

of Rome before parting company with the King and Bado
glio, because from Rome a more representative and solidly
based Administration can be constructed than is possible
now. They feel that nothing could be worse for our joint
interests and for the future of Italy than to set up a weak
democratic Government which flopped. Even a settlement
reached at Rome could not be final, because it would be
necessary to review it when the northern provinces and great
industrial centres favourable to us and essential to a demo
cratic solution, like Milan and Turin, have been liberated
They do not consider that the Six Parties are representative in
any true sense of the Italian democracy or Italian nation, or
that they could at the present time replace the existing Italian
Government, which has loyally and effectively worked in our
interests.

In reaching these conclusions the War Cabinet have of
course had before them the telegrams sent by the Allied
Commander-in-Chief [General Wilson], whose views on this
subject they do not share. Meanwhile we should be quite
ready to discuss the suggestions put to the State Department
by the Foreign Secretary. It is also of course recognised that
should the capture of Rome be unduly protracted, say for two
or three months, the question of timing would have to be
reviewed.

Finally, they ask me to emphasise the great importance of
not exposing to the world any divergences of view which may
exist between our two Governments, especially in face of the
independent action taken by Russia in entering into diplo
matic relations with the Badoglio Government without con
sultation with other Allies. It would be a great pity if our
respective viewpoints had to be argued out in Parliament and
the Press, when waiting a few months may make it possible
for all three Governments to take united action.

This was the end of the matter for the moment.

*   *   *

Although Anzio was now no longer an anxiety the campaign
in Italy as a whole had dragged. We had hoped that by this time
the Germans would have been driven north of Rome and that a
substantial part of our armies would have been set free for a
strong landing on the Riviera coast to help the main cross
Channel invasion. This operation, called 'Anvil', had been
agreed in principle at Teheran. It was soon to become a cause of
contention between ourselves and our American Allies. The

campaign in Italy had obviously to be carried forward a long way before this issue arose, and the immediate need was to break the deadlock on the Cassino front. Preparations for the Third Battle of Cassino were begun soon after the February failure, but the bad weather delayed it until March 15.

This time Cassino town was the primary objective. After a heavy bombardment, in which nearly 1,000 tons of bombs and 1,200 tons of shells were expended, our infantry advanced. 'It seemed to me inconceivable,' said Alexander, 'that any troops should be left alive after eight hours of such terrific hammering.' But they were. The 1st German Parachute Division, probably the toughest fighters in all their Army, fought it out amid the heaps of rubble with the New Zealanders and Indians. By nightfall the greater part of the town was in our hands, while the 4th Indian Division, coming down from the north, made equally good progress and next day were two-thirds of the way up Monastery Hill. Then the battle swung against us. Our tanks could not cross the large craters made by the bombardment and follow up the infantry assault. Nearly two days passed before they could help. The enemy filtered in reinforcements. The weather broke in storm and rain. Our attacks gained ground, but the early success was not repeated, and the enemy were not to be overborne in the slogging match.

I wondered why we did not make flank attacks to dislodge the enemy from positions which had twice already proved so strong.

Prime Minister to General Alexander   20 Mar 44

I wish you would explain to me why this passage by Cassino Monastery Hill, etc., all on a front of two or three miles, is the only place which you must keep butting at. About five or six divisions have been worn out going into these jaws. Of course I do not know the ground or the battle conditions, but, looking at it from afar, it is puzzling why, if the enemy can be held and dominated at this point, no attacks can be made on the flanks. It seems very hard to understand why this most strongly defended point is the only passage forward, or why, when it is saturated [in a military sense], ground cannot be gained on one side or the other. I have the greatest confidence in you and will back you up through thick and thin, but do try to explain to me why no flanking movements can be made.

His answer was lucid and convincing. It explained the situation in words written at the moment, and is of high value to the military historian.

General Alexander to Prime Minister   20 Mar 44

I reply to your telegram of March 20. Along whole main battle-front from Adriatic to south coast there is only Liri valley leading direct to Rome which is suitable terrain for development of our superiority in artillery and armour. The main highway, known as Route Six, is the only road, except cart-tracks, which leads from the mountains where we are into Liri valley over Rapido river. This exit into the plain is blocked and dominated by Monte Cassino, on which stands the monastery. Repeated attempts have been made to out-flank Monastery Hill from the north, but all these attacks have been unsuccessful, owing to deep ravines, rocky escarp-ments, and knife-edges, which limit movements to anything except comparatively small parties of infantry, who can only be maintained by porters and to a limited extent by mules where we have managed under great difficulties to make some mule-tracks.

Further, Monastery Hill is cut off almost completely from north by a ravine so steep and deep that so far it has proved impossible to cross it. A wider turning movement is even more difficult, as it has to cross Mount Cairo, which is a precipitous peak now deep in snow. The Americans tried to outflank this Cassino bastion from the south by an attack across the Rapido river, but this, as you know, failed, with heavy losses to the 34th and 36th Divisions. The Rapido is difficult to cross south of Cassino owing to flood-water at this time of year, soft, marshy ground which adds to problems of bridging, lack of any roads to bring up bridging material, and to the strength of enemy's positions on far bank. Again, a crossing of the Rapido river south of Cassino, as already proved, comes under very heavy enfilade artillery fire from German gun positions tucked away at foot of the mountains immedi-ately behind or west of Cassino, and also from foothills of mountains on south of Liri valley.

Freyberg's attack was designed as a direct assault on this bastion, success depending on crushing enemy resistance by surprise and an overwhelming concentration of fire-power. The plan was to rush Cassino town and then to flow round the east and southern slopes of Monastery Hill and take the bastion by storm from a direction where enemy's artillery could not seriously interfere with our movement. It very nearly succeeded in its initial stages, with negligible losses to us. We got, and still have, two bridges over the Rapido river, one on Highway Six and the other over railway bridge ; both are fit for tanks. The Gurkhas got and are still within 200 to 300 yards of monastery. That we have not succeeded in taking our objective within first forty-eight hours may be summarised as follows:

The destruction caused in Cassino to roads and movement by bombing was so terrific that the employment of tanks or any other fighting vehicles has been seriously hampered. The tenacity of these German paratroops is quite remarkable, considering that they were subjected to the whole Mediterranean Air Force plus the better part of 800 guns under greatest concentration of fire-power which has ever been put down and lasting for six hours. I doubt if there are any other troops in the world who could have stood up to it and then gone on fighting with the ferocity they have. I am meeting Freyberg and the Army Commanders to-morrow to discuss the situation.

If we call it off we shall hold on to the two bridges and adjust our positions so as to hold the advantageous key points already gained. The Eighth Army's plan for entering the Liri valley in force will be undertaken when regrouping is completed. The plan must envisage an attack on a wider front and with greater forces than Freyberg has been able to have for this operation. A little later, when the snow goes off mountains, the rivers drop, and the ground hardens, movement will be possible over terrain which at present is impassable.

Prime Minister to General Alexander   21 Mar 44
Thank you very much for your full explanation. I hope you will not have to 'call it off' when you have gone so far. Surely the enemy is very hard pressed too. Every good wish.

The war weighs very heavy on us all just now.

The struggle in the ruins of Cassino town continued until the 23rd, with hard fighting in attacks and counter-attacks. The New Zealanders and the Indians could do no more. We kept hold of a large part of the town, but the Gurkhas had to be withdrawn from their perch high up the Monastery Hill, where supplies could not reach them even by air because of the steep hillside.

*   *   *

In reply to my request General Wilson reported the casualties suffered by the New Zealand Corps during the battle. They totalled:

2nd New Zealand Division		1,050
4th Indian Division: British	401 ⎱	1,160
Indian	759 ⎰	
78th British Division		190
Total		2,400

This was a heavy price to pay for what might seem small gains. We had however established a firm bridgehead at Cassino over the river Rapido, which, with the deep bulge made by the Xth Corps across the lower Garigliano in January, was of great value when the final, successful battle came. Here and at the Anzio bridgehead we had pinned down in Central Italy nearly twenty good German divisions. Many of them might have gone to France.

Before the Gustav Line could be assaulted again with any hope of success our troops had to be rested and regrouped. Most of the Eighth Army had to be brought over from the Adriatic side and two armies concentrated for the next battle, the British Eighth on the Cassino front, the American Fifth on the lower Garigliano. For this General Alexander needed nearly two months.

This meant that the Mediterranean could only help the cross-Channel assault in early June, by fighting south of Rome. The United States Chiefs of Staff still strove for a subsidiary landing in Southern France, and for some weeks there was much argument between us about what orders should be given to General Wilson.

*   *   *

The story must here be told of the Anglo-American argument, first as between 'Overlord' and 'Anvil', and then as between 'Anvil' and the Italian campaign. It will be recalled that in my talk with Montgomery at Marrakesh on December 31 he said that he must have more in the initial punch across the Channel, and that on January 6 I telegraphed to the President that Bedell Smith and Montgomery were convinced that it was better to put in a much heavier and broader 'Overlord' than to expand 'Anvil' beyond what we had planned in outline before Teheran.

This was keenly debated at a conference held by General Eisenhower on January 21, shortly after his arrival in England. Eisenhower himself firmly believed in the vital importance of

'Anvil', and thought it would be a mistake to impoverish it for the sake of strengthening 'Overlord'. As a result of this conference however he sent a telegram to the Combined Chiefs of Staff in Washington, in which he said:

> 'Overlord' and 'Anvil' must be viewed as one whole. If sufficient resources could be made available the ideal would be a five-divisional 'Overlord' and a three-divisional 'Anvil'. If insufficient forces are available for this however I am driven to the conclusion that we should adopt a five-divisional 'Overlord' and a one-divisional 'Anvil', the latter being maintained as a threat until enemy weakness justifies its active employment.

On this telegram the British Chiefs of Staff presented their own views to Washington, namely:

(a) That the first onfall of 'Overlord' should be increased to five divisions, whatever the cost to 'Anvil'.

(b) That every effort should be made to undertake 'Anvil' by using two divisions or more in the assault.

(c) That if these divisions could not be carried landing-craft in the Mediterranean should be reduced to the requirements for a lift of one division.

The American Chiefs of Staff were unable to agree. They considered that a threat in lieu of an actual operation was inadequate and insisted on a two-divisional assault. On this telegram I minuted, 'Apparently the two-division lift for "Anvil" is given priority over "Overlord". This is directly counter to the views of Generals Eisenhower and Montgomery.'

On February 4 the British Chiefs of Staff, in full consultation with me, sent a lengthy telegram to their American colleagues, in which they emphasised that the paramount consideration was that 'Overlord' should succeed, and that the right solution was to build up 'Overlord' to the strength required by the Supreme Commander and then to allocate to the Mediterranean whatever additional resources could be found. They questioned the wisdom of undertaking 'Anvil' at all, in view of the way things were going in Italy, and pointed out that when 'Anvil' first found favour at Teheran we expected that the Germans would withdraw to a line north of Rome. But now it was clear beyond all doubt that the Germans intended to resist our advance in Italy to the utmost. They also pointed out that the distance between the South of France and the beaches of Normandy was nearly five hundred miles, and that a diversion could be created from Italy or other points just as well as through the Rhone valley. 'Anvil' in fact was too far away to help 'Overlord'.

On this the United States Chiefs of Staff proposed that the issue should be decided at a conference between General Eisenhower, who would be their representative, and the British Chiefs of Staff. To this we readily assented, but several weeks were to pass before agreement was reached. General Eisenhower was still reluctant to abandon 'Anvil', but he was beginning to doubt whether it would still be possible to withdraw trained divisions from Italy. On March 21 General Wilson was asked for his opinion. He said he was strongly opposed to withdrawing troops from Italy until Rome had been captured, and he advised that 'Anvil' should be cancelled and that we should only land in the South of France if the Germans cracked.

This turned the scale. The British Chiefs of Staff telegraphed to Washington that it was clear that 'Anvil' could not be carried out on the prescribed date, since it was impossible to withdraw either troops from the battle in Italy or landing-craft from the Anzio bridgehead. The American Chiefs of Staff assented, and agreed that General Wilson should prepare to land in the South of France in July, and also to contain and destroy as many German troops in Italy as possible if it were decided to fight it out there. It was thought that early June would be time enough to decide which plan should be carried out.

That I myself was strongly in favour of maintaining the thrust in Italy can be seen from this telegram:

Prime Minister to General Marshall (Washington)   16 Apr 44
   It is of course very painful to us to forgo the invaluable addition to our landing-craft in the Mediterranean which you so kindly offered under certain conditions and had no doubt great trouble to obtain. What I cannot bear is to agree beforehand to starve a battle or have to break it off just at the moment when success, after long efforts and heavy losses, may be in view. Our forces in Italy are not much larger than those of the enemy. They comprise seven or eight different races, while the enemy is all German. The wet weather has hitherto restricted the full use of our superiority in artillery, in armour, and in the air. Alexander tells me that he strikes out *north-east*, not south-east, from the Anzio beach-head shortly after his main thrust across the Rapido. Thus there

will not necessarily be a moment when we shall pause and say, 'Halt here. Go over to the defensive. All aboard for "Anvil".' Nor will there necessarily be an exact moment when the cutting of supplies for the Italian battle for the sake of 'Anvil' can be fixed beforehand in imagination. A half-hearted undercurrent sets in with an army which has a divided objective, part to the front and part to the rear. This infects all the rearward services, who cannot help knowing. Remember the terrible bleeding the armies in Italy got when their seven best divisions were taken for 'Overlord'.

2. Of course, if the battle goes wrong early and we are hung up before other enemy lines of defence and forced to go over to a general defensive no doubt strong forces could then be spared, but the drain of feeding the bridgehead would continue to press on our landing-craft, and without your Pacific landing-craft there will be no two-division lift for any amphibious operations, 'Anvil' or other.

3. Therefore it seems to me we must throw our hearts into this battle, for the sake of which so many American and British lives have already been sacrificed, and make it, like 'Overlord', an all-out conquer or die. It may well be that by May 31 we shall see many things which are now veiled from us. I regret having to forgo such an hour of choice.

4. Dill tells me that you had expected me to support 'Anvil' more vigorously in view of my enthusiasm for it when it was first proposed by you at Teheran. Please do me the justice to remember that the situation is vastly changed. In November we hoped to take Rome in January, and there were many signs that the enemy was ready to [retire] northwards up the Italian peninsula. Instead of this, in spite of our great amphibious expedition, we are stuck where we are, and the enemy has brought down to the battle south of Rome the eight mobile divisions we should have hoped a full-scale 'Anvil' would have contained. Thus there has been cause for rejoicing as well as bitter disappointment.

5. The whole of this difficult question only arises out of the absurd shortage of the L.S.T.s. How it is that the plans of two great empires like Britain and the United States should be so much hamstrung and limited by a hundred of two of these particular vessels will never be understood by history. I am deeply concerned at the strong disinclination of the American Government even to keep the manufacture of L.S.T.s at its full height so as to have a sufficient number to give to us to help you in the war against Japan. The absence of these special vessels may limit our whole war effort on your left flank, and I fear we shall be accused unjustly of not doing our best, as we are resolved to do.

The instructions Wilson received reflected my views, and in a telegram to the President on April 24 I said:

> I am very glad at what has happened in Italy. It seems to me that we have both succeeded in gaining what we sought. The only thing now lacking is a victory. I had long talks with Alexander when he was here for a few days' consultation. He defended his actions, or inactions, with much force, pointing out the small plurality of his army, its mixed character, there being no fewer than seven separate nationalities against the homogeneous Germans, the vileness of the weather, and the extremely awkward nature of the ground. At latest by May 14 he will attack and push everything in as hard as possible. If this battle were successful, or even raging at full blast, it would fit in very well with other plans.

*   *   *

Political events in Southern Italy again came to a head. A constitutional compromise was reached whereby the King would hand over his powers to his son, the Crown Prince Umberto, as Lieutenant-Governor of the Realm. The fate of the monarchy would then await a plebiscite after the ultimate victory. The royal decree was signed on April 12, and was to take effect at the moment when the Allies entered Rome. At the end of the month Badoglio reconstructed his Government to include leading political figures in the South, of whom Croce and Sforza were the most prominent.

*   *   *

While our armies were preparing to attack General Wilson used all his air-power to impede and injure the enemy, who, like us, were using the pause for reorganising and replenishing themselves for further battle. The potent Allied Air joined in attacking enemy land communications in the hope that these could be kept cut and their troops forced to withdraw for lack of supplies. This operation, optimistically called 'Strangle', aimed at blocking the three main railway lines from Northern Italy, the principal targets being bridges, viaducts, and other bottle-necks. They tried to starve the Germans out of Central Italy.

The effort lasted more than six weeks, and did great damage. Railway movement was consistently stopped far north of Rome, but it failed to attain all that we hoped. By working their coastal shipping to full capacity, transferring loads to motor transport, and making full use of the hours of darkness the enemy contrived to maintain themselves. But they could not build enough reserve stocks for protracted and heavy fighting, and in the severe land battles at the end of May they were much weakened. The junction of our separated armies and their capture of Rome took place more rapidly than we had forecast. The German Air Force suffered severely in trying to defend its communications. By early May it could muster only a bare seven hundred against our thousand combat aircraft.

Here then we may leave the Italian theatre, where much was ripening, for the supreme operation across the Channel.

CHAPTER 12

The Mounting Air Offensive

Our Progress in Bomber Expansion – Early Failures in the Accuracy of Our Bombing – Radar Aids to Target-Finding – The Germans Forced to Turn to Fighter Production – The Americans Join in the Bombing of Axis Europe in 1943 – The Casablanca Directive – British Night Bombing of the Ruhr – The Air Battle at Hamburg – The Onslaught on Berlin – Heavy American Losses at Schweinfurt, October 14, and Their Sequel – British Losses in the Attack on Nuremberg – American Fortresses At Last Provided with Long-Range Fighters – Increase in the Power of British Bombs – Lord Cherwell's Inquiry – Aluminised Explosives – Effect of our Air Offensive on German War Economy – Part to be Played by the Allied Air Force in 'Overlord' – British War Cabinet's Distress at Heavy French Civilian Casualties – We Accept President Roosevelt's Decision – The Valour and Devotion of British and American Bomber Crews.

Bomber Command played an ever-growing part in all our war plans, and eventually made a decisive contribution to victory. Some review of its activities is required at this point in the story.

It was not till 1943 that we possessed sufficient and suitable aircraft for striking heavy and continuous blows, and in the same year the bombers of the American Eighth Air Force joined in our strategic air offensive. Ever since 1940 I had encouraged the expansion of our bomber strength. The difficulties were numerous. Production lagged behind forecasts; other theatres of war and the campaign against the U-boats made heavy demands; and when the Americans came into the war their output was of course at first largely diverted to their own needs. Although growth in numbers had been slow, our new four-engined planes carried a far heavier weight of bombs. In the opening months of 1942 the average load per aircraft was 2,800 lb.; by the end of that year it was 4,400 lb.; during 1943 it rose to 7,500 lb.

Early in the war both we and the Germans had found that bombers, even in close formation, could not fight their way in daylight through an efficient fighter defence without over-heavy casualties. Like the enemy we had had to turn to night attacks. We were too confident at first about the accuracy of our bombing, and our attempts in the winter of 1940–41 to destroy German oil plants, paramount but small targets, proved a failure. In the spring of 1941 Bomber Command was called to join in the Battle of the Atlantic, and not till July was the offensive against Germany resumed. The targets now chosen were industrial cities and their railway centres, especially the Ruhr, and Hamburg, Bremen, Hanover, Frankfurt, and Stuttgart. However, neither our means nor our methods sufficed. Our losses mounted, and during the winter months we had to reduce our effort. In February 1942 'Gee', the new position-finder already described,* was brought into use, and with its help the Ruhr became our primary goal. Under the vigorous leadership of Air Marshal Harris dramatic results were achieved. His operations included fire-raising attacks on Lübeck and Rostock, the thousand-bomber assault on Cologne in May, and the daylight attack on the submarine Diesel engine works at Augsburg, when Squadron-Leader Nettleton won the Victoria Cross.

In August the Pathfinder Force was formed, under Air Commodore Bennett. Radar aids were playing a growing part in navigation and target-finding, and it was a wise measure to entrust the scarce and complicated apparatus to specialists whose duty was to find the way and point the target to others.

Although accurate night bombing, denied so long, thus came gradually into being, the bomber offensive of 1942 did not lower Germany's war production or civilian morale. The strength of her economy had been under-estimated. Productive capacity and labour were drawn extensively from the occupied countries, and German armament production seems to have actually increased. Under the iron discipline imposed by Goebbels, who was in charge of relief measures, civilian morale stood firm and local disasters were prevented from having a national effect. But the German leaders had become deeply alarmed and were forced on to the defensive in the air. German aircraft production was increasingly devoted to fighters rather than bombers. This was the beginning of defeat for the Luftwaffe, and a turning-point in our struggle for the air supremacy which we gained in 1944, without which we could not have won

* Details of the several devices mentioned in this chapter are given in Book 7, Chapter 16.

the war. Second only in importance to this moral victory over the minds of Hitler and his air commanders was the dangerous Third Air Front created for Germany in the West, to the advantage of the Russians, and of ourselves in the Mediterranean.

Thus we come to the year 1943, when the Americans joined in the bombing of Axis Europe. They had different ideas about method. Whereas we had adopted and were now bringing to efficiency our night-bombing technique, they were convinced that their heavily armed Fortress bombers in close formation could penetrate deeply into Germany by daylight without fighter escort. I was doubtful whether this was a practicable system, and have recorded in a previous volume how at Casablanca I discussed my misgivings with General Eaker, commanding the U.S. air forces in England, and withdrew my opposition.* The Casablanca directive, issued to the British and American Bomber Commands in the United Kingdom on February 4, 1943, gave them their task in the following terms:

> Your primary object will be the progressive destruction and dislocation of the German military, industrial, and economic system, and the undermining of the morale of the German people to a point where their capacity for armed resistance is fatally weakened.
>
> Within that general concept your primary objectives ... will for the present be in the following priority:
>
> (a) German submarine yards.
> (b) The German aircraft industry.
> (c) Transportation.
> (d) Oil plants.
> (e) Other targets in enemy war industry.

General Eaker, with the American Eighth Air Force, aimed at destroying six groups of targets by daylight precision bombing. He did not receive the reinforcements for which he had asked, but made many gallant and costly attacks. Air Marshal Harris, bombing only at night, concentrated from March to July 1943 mainly upon the Ruhr, beginning on the night of March 5–6 with the heavily defended town of Essen. Eight Mosquitoes dropped target indicators, using the blind-bombing device of 'Oboe'; then twenty-two heavy bombers of the Pathfinder Force further illuminated the target for an intense attack by 392 aircraft. Essen was severely damaged for the first time

* Book 8, Chapter 15.

in the war. As the power and activities of Bomber Command developed Goebbels became more and more despairing of the outcome, and his diaries bitterly reproach the Luftwaffe for its failure to stop the British bombers. Speer, the most capable of German Ministers of Production, in an address to Gauleiters in June 1943, referred to the serious losses in production of coal and iron and crank-shafts, and to the decision to double the anti-aircraft defences of the Ruhr and draft in 100,000 men for repair duties.

While the British were at last succeeding in wrecking the Ruhr munitions centres the American Fortresses were meeting with serious opposition from German day fighters, and General Eaker soon realised that if his plan was to succeed he must first defeat the German Air Force. In the greatly improved state of the U-boat war a change in the priorities of targets was accepted by the Combined Chiefs of Staff. In a directive known as 'Point-blank', issued on June 10, 1943, they amended the Casablanca decisions so as to give first emphasis to the attack on the German fighter forces and the German aircraft industry.

On July 24–25 the very heavy British attacks on Hamburg began. Hamburg was beyond the range of 'Oboe', and the fullest use was made of the blind-bombing device of H_2S, which was carried in the aeroplane and did not depend on signals from home. This instrument gave an outline of the main ground features on a screen in the aircraft which resembled a television screen of to-day. The picture was particularly good where the land was broken up by water, as it is in the dock area of Hamburg. Bomber Command had been gaining experience of H_2S since its first use in January, and for the assault on Hamburg an additional device called 'Window' which we had long held in reserve, was used for the first time. As is explained in Book 7, this simply consisted of strips of metallised paper dropped by the bombers. A cloud of such strips, tuned to the German wavelength and weighing only a few pounds, looked like an aircraft on the enemy's Radar screens, and thus made it very difficult for either their night fighters to be guided to our bombers or for the A.A. guns and searchlights to be aimed at them.*

The four attacks against Hamburg from July 24 to August 3 caused greater destruction than had ever been suffered by so large a city in so short a time. The second attack delivered such a concentration of incendiary bombs mixed with high explosive

Book 7, Chapter 16.

that there arose a fire tornado which raged through the city with a terrifying howl and defied all human counter-measures. The Air Battle of Hamburg has been described by many Germans as 'the great catastrophe'. Speer himself admitted after the war that he had calculated that if similar attacks had been delivered in quick succession against six other major German cities it would have led to a breakdown of war production. Germany was saved from this fate in 1943 partly because H_2S was found to be difficult to use, even for area bombing, if there were no prominent water features within the target, and partly because of the resolute defence put up by Germany's ever-resourceful night fighters.

Our third great air onslaught of 1943 was upon Berlin. It lasted from November 1943 to March 1944. If this great industrial centre could have been paralysed like Hamburg German war production as well as morale might have been given a mortal blow.

Bomber Command pressed home its attacks with undaunted courage and determination in the face of fearful difficulties. The weather was appalling, and most of the bombing had to rely on the Radar eye of H_2S. The night photographs taken by the bombers at the moment of bomb release showed nothing but clouds. The same disappointment befell the daylight flights over Berlin of the Photographic Reconnaissance Unit. We knew from the admissions of Germans themselves that great destruction was being caused, but we could not judge the relative success of our sixteen major attacks by comparing the photographic evidence of each. We had to wait until March 1944 to obtain photographs clear enough for the damage to be assessed. It fell short of what had been achieved at Hamburg.

Meanwhile the U.S. Eighth Air Force in its assault on the enemy's fighter forces and aircraft industry in accordance with the 'Point-blank' directive was enduring increasing losses at the hands of the German day fighters, which met them with mounting strength and efficiency. The culmination was reached on October 14, 1943. In their attack on the ball-bearing plants at Schweinfurt, which were vital to the German aircraft industry, the Americans had sixty of their large Fortress aircraft destroyed out of 291. It was thereafter accepted that unescorted daylight bombers could not gain air superiority over Germany, and their offensive was suspended until long-range fighters could be produced to cover them in sufficient strength.

Something very like a dispute arose upon whether British Bomber Command should attack Schweinfurt by their own methods. In the end it was decided that the attack should be made by both Air Forces in daylight and in darkness. The American Eighth Air Force, aided at last by the long-range fighters for which they had waited a long time, attacked with 266 bombers by daylight on February 24, 1944, and on the same night Bomber Command sent 734 aircraft. Here was a really combined offensive directed towards the common aim. Unfortunately, the discussion had lasted so long that this tremendous attack was robbed of much of its effectiveness. Warned by the American daylight attack four months earlier, Speer had dispersed Schweinfurt's industry.

* * *

Prolonged and obstinate technical argument on the policy of night or day bombing, and generous rivalry in trying out the opposing theories with the utmost sacrifice and heroism by both the British and American Air Forces, reached its climax after the last attack on Berlin. On March 30–31, 1944, out of 795 aircraft dispatched by British Bomber Command against Nuremberg ninety-four did not return. This was our heaviest loss in one raid, and caused Bomber Command to re-examine its tactics before launching further deep-penetration attacks by night into Germany. This was proof of the power which the enemy's night fighter force, strengthened by the best crews from other vital fronts, had developed under our relentless offensive. But by forcing the enemy to concentrate his strength on defending inner Germany the Western Allies gained the complete air superiority which they needed for the approaching cross-Channel invasion.

* * *

All this time the Americans were intent on bringing their Fortress bombers into action by day as soon as they could be protected by fighters of sufficiently long range to seek out and destroy the enemy's fighters in the air or go down and attack them on their airfields. After long delay this vital need was met. First the Thunderbolt, then the Lightning, and finally the Mustang gave them day fighters which had auxiliary fuel tanks and a radius of action which was increased from 475 miles to 850. On February 23, 1944, there began a week of concentrated

bomber attacks by day on the German aircraft industry. Th
American long-range fighters at last mastered the enemy's, an
the day bombers delivered precision attacks without undue in
terference or loss.

This was a turning-point in the air war against German
From now onwards the U.S. Eighth Air Force was able to bom
targets in Germany by day with high accuracy and ever
increasing freedom. Germany, through her loss of air superi
ority by day, exposed her vitals to our strategic offensive. Th
German night fighters, with the cream of their pilots, remaine
formidable till the end of the war; but this, by lowering th
standard of the day fighters, aided the new developments in th
American Air Force, and in 1944 daylight air superiority ove
Germany was gained. By April new measures of deception an
new tactics to confuse the enemy's defences enabled the Britis
to resume their full-scale night offensive against German citie
The U.S. Eighth Air Force, having got the measure of th
enemy's day fighters, was ready to complete this offensiv
'round the clock'. Such was the position at the advent of 'Over
lord'.

*   *   *

The ever-growing preponderance of our attack on Ger
many received an appreciable reinforcement from the new ex
plosive power given to our bombs. This arose as an incident i
our anxious discussions in 1943 about the threat of the rocket
and the 'doodle-bugs'. Those experts who were taking the mor
gloomy view of our danger made a number of pessimisti
assumptions in comparing the effect of our bombs in German
with the expected effects of rockets in England. German houses
they said, were very much stronger than English houses, so tha
we might expect twice as many to be destroyed per ton of ex
plosives in England as in Germany. In stating this case they inci
dentally took for granted that the enemy bombs were nearl
twice as powerful as the British, since the Germans mixe
aluminium powder with the high explosive. Lord Cherwe
pointed out this statement to me, and I ordered a searchin
inquiry to be conducted under his guidance. The results aston
ished everyone concerned.

Prime Minister to Minister of Production   12 Oct 4
I recently invited Lord Cherwell to inquire into and repor
on the relative efficiency of the high explosives used by th

German and British forces respectively. His preliminary report had shown the undoubted superiority of the German explosive charges.

The Chiefs of Staff strongly recommend that we should change over to aluminised explosives without waiting for the result of further trials. I agree. Pray let me have a report of what this change will involve in the course of the next week.

The question of how this state of affairs has been allowed to arise should be the subject of an inquiry held under the authority of the Minister of Defence. Pray propose three members, with reference. The whole matter is to be kept most secret.

Action was taken accordingly. It appeared that in the early days when aluminium was scarce it had been decided to use all the aluminium powder which could be spared for making depth-charges, and that this custom had persisted, although aluminium had now become more plentiful. Orders were immediately given to improve our explosive—in the first place in our heavy bombs—by adding aluminium powder, and their efficiency during the whole latter half of the war was thus increased by about half as much again. I thought these revelations deserved the attention of my colleagues, and sent out the following in February 1944:

ALUMINISED EXPLOSIVES

17 Feb 44

At the end of September 1943, during discussions about the German long-range rocket, doubts were expressed about the efficiency of our high explosives as compared with those of the Germans. The Paymaster-General immediately discussed the matter with the Chief of the Air Staff, and the latter proposed to the Chiefs of Staff Committee, who supported his proposals strongly, that urgent action should be taken to establish the true facts, and that if a substantial inferiority was revealed the competent authorities should be called upon to give an explanation and a proposed remedy.

2. At the suggestion of the Chiefs of Staff Committee the Paymaster-General undertook the inquiry suggested, and on October 6 submitted a report to the Chiefs of Staff Committee which clearly established that our explosives were inferior to the Germans' and that an improvement estimated by various authorities as between 40 per cent. and 100 per cent. could be made if aluminised explosives were used instead of the existing types. Lord Cherwell recommended that the most urgent possible preparations to change over should

be made without waiting for the result of further trials. With this recommendation the Chiefs of Staff Committee and I agreed, and immediate action was taken to effect the change-over.

3. I also appointed a committee consisting of Sir Walter Monckton (chairman), Sir Alan Barlow, and Sir Robert Robertson 'to consider the report on the efficiency of our blast bombs, to examine the course of our experimental and development work on this subject during the present war, and to report whether, and if so why, there has been any failure to prosecute research to a successful conclusion or to apply the results of that research in practice'.

Briefly, an unfortunate experiment in 1941 gave a misleading result, chiefly owing to the unsatisfactory methods of measuring blast pressures in use at that time. In addition, the impression that in any event no aluminium could be obtained discouraged those in charge from repeating the experiment until midsummer 1943. It was only when the Paymaster-General's attention was drawn to an alleged superiority of German explosives, as stated above, that the necessary impetus was given to turn the lessons of fresh experiments to account.

4. There is no doubt that the power of aluminised explosives is very much greater than that of the types which were being used earlier, and I have thought it right to bring to the notice of my colleagues the important service rendered by the Paymaster-General in calling attention to a most unsatisfactory state of affairs, which might have continued for some time, with serious detriment to our war effort, unless he had intervened.

This episode shows how useful it is in great organisations to have a roving eye.

*   *   *

It is difficult to say to what extent German war economy and armaments production had so far been damaged by the Anglo-American bomber offensive. Bomber Command's three great area battles of 1943—the Ruhr, Hamburg, and Berlin—had created widespread havoc and caused consternation and alarm throughout Germany, and especially in the minds of the German leaders. But they were able to use factories and forced labour from the occupied countries, and under the brilliant control of Speer these were mobilised with extraordinary speed and efficiency. The morale of the people in the bombed cities, though severely shaken, was not allowed to degenerate into a nation-wide panic.

In the reports submitted to Hitler, which must of course be taken with reserve, it was claimed that German armament production was doubled in 1942. Remembering our own loss of output under much less severe bombing, this assertion is difficult to credit. The Germans admitted that production was almost stationary in 1943, and this is evidence of the increasing power of Bomber Command. In the spring of 1944 the Allied strategic bombers were required for 'Overlord', and the weight of attack on Germany itself was inevitably reduced. But by now we were the masters in the air. The bitterness of the struggle had thrown a greater strain on the Luftwaffe than it was able to bear. By being forced to concentrate on building fighters it had lost all power of strategic counter-attack by bombing back at us. Unbalanced and exhausted, it was henceforth unable to defend either itself or Germany from our grievous blows. For our air superiority, which by the end of 1944 was to become air supremacy, full tribute must be paid to the U.S. Eighth Air Force, once it gained its long-range fighters.

*   *   *

As 'Overlord' approached a momentous question confronted us. What part was the mighty weapon of the air to play in the supreme operation? After prolonged technical controversy among the air authorities of both countries, the plan which prevailed was to destroy German railway communications in France, Belgium, and Western Germany by discharging 66,000 tons of bombs during the three months before D-Day, thus creating a 'railway desert' around the German troops in Normandy. This plan had already entered its early stages. The principal targets were the repair and maintenance depots and the locomotives in ninety-three key railway centres on the many approaches to Normandy. The tactical air forces assisted in this general plan, and were given in addition the special task as D-Day drew near of destroying bridges and rolling-stock.

I wrote to General Eisenhower on April 3:

> The Cabinet to-day took rather a grave and on the whole an adverse view of the proposal to bomb so many French railway centres, in view of the fact that scores of thousands of French civilians, men, women, and children, would lose

their lives or be injured. Considering that they are all our
friends, this might be held to be an act of very great severity,
bringing much hatred on the Allied Air Forces. It was decided
that the Defence Committee should consider the matter during this week, and that thereafter the Foreign Office should
address the State Department and I should myself send a
personal telegram to the President.

The argument for concentration on these particular targets
is very nicely balanced on military grounds.

General Eisenhower replied on the 5th:

We must never forget that one of the fundamental factors
leading to the decision for undertaking 'Overlord' was the
conviction that our overpowering Air Force would make
feasible an operation which might otherwise be considered
extremely hazardous, if not foolhardy. ... The weight of the
argument that has been brought against the bombing of
transportation centres in occupied territories is heavy indeed ;
but I and my military advisers have become convinced that
the bombing of these centres will increase our chances for
success in the critical battle. ... I personally believe that
estimates of probable casualties have been grossly exaggerated.

* * *

As the air offensive against the railways developed the losses
among French and Belgian civilians, though far less than the
prior estimates, caused the British War Cabinet distress and
anxiety.

Prime Minister to President Roosevelt   7 May 44
The War Cabinet have been much concerned during the
last three weeks about the number of Frenchmen killed in
the raids on the railway centres in France. We have had
numerous Staff meetings with our own officers, and I have
discussed the matter with Generals Eisenhower and Bedell
Smith. There were and are great differences of opinion in the
two Air Forces—not between them, but criss-cross—about
the efficacy of the 'railway plan' as a short-term project. In
the end Eisenhower, Tedder, Bedell Smith, and Portal all
declare themselves converted. I am personally by no means
convinced that this is the best way to use our Air Forces in
the preliminary period, and still think that the German Air
Force should be the main target. ...

2. When this project was first put forward a loss of 80,000
French civilian casualties, including injured, say 20,000 killed,

was mentioned. The War Cabinet could not view this figure without grave dismay on account of the apparently ruthless use of the Air Forces, particularly of the Royal Air Force, on whom the brunt of this kind of work necessarily falls, and the reproaches that would be made upon the inaccuracy of night bombing. The results of the first, say, three-sevenths of the bombing have however shown that the casualties to French civil life are very much less than was expected by the commanders. . . .

3. I am satisfied that all possible care will be taken to minimise this slaughter of friendly civilian life. Nevertheless the War Cabinet share my apprehensions of the bad effect which will be produced upon the French civilian population by these slaughters, all taking place so long before 'Overlord' D-Day. They may easily bring about a great revulsion in French feeling towards their approaching United States and British liberators. They may leave a legacy of hate behind them. It may well be that the French losses will grow heavier on and after D-Day, but in the heat of battle, when British and United States troops will probably be losing at a much higher rate, a new proportion establishes itself in men's minds. It is the intervening period that causes me most anxiety. . . .

4. The Cabinet ask me to invite you to consider the matter from the highest political standpoint and to give us your opinion as a matter between Governments. It must be remembered, on the one hand, that this slaughter is among a friendly people who have committed no crimes against us, and not among the German foe, with all their record of cruelty and ruthlessness. On the other hand, we naturally feel the hazardous nature of Operation 'Overlord' and are in deadly earnest about making it a success. I have been careful in stating this case to you to use only the most moderate terms, but I ought to let you know that the War Cabinet is unanimous in its anxiety about these French slaughters, even reduced as they have been, and also in its doubts as to whether almost as good military results could not be produced by other methods. Whatever is settled between us, we are quite willing to share responsibilities with you.

The President replied on the 11th:

I share fully with you your distress at the loss of life among the French population incident to our air preparations for 'Overlord'.

I share also with you a satisfaction that every possible care is being and will be taken to minimise civilian casualties. No possibility of alleviating adverse French opinion should be overlooked, always provided that there is no reduction of our effectiveness against the enemy at this crucial time.

However regrettable the attendant loss of civilian lives is, I am not prepared to impose from this distance any restriction on military action by the responsible commanders that in their opinion might militate against the success of 'Overlord' or cause additional loss of life to our Allied forces of invasion.

This was decisive. Meanwhile the rate of the casualties to French civilians continued to be less than had been feared. The sealing off of the Normandy battlefield from reinforcements by rail may well have been the greatest direct contribution that the bomber forces could make to 'Overlord'. The price was paid.

*   *   *

This chapter has been dominated by technical matters. The British and United States rival themes of air attack by night or day have been shown under the hard test of results. The improvements in our explosives and the intricacies of Radar and all its variants have been presented, I trust, in a form intelligible to the lay reader. But it would be wrong to end without paying our tribute of respect and admiration to the officers and men who fought and died in this fearful battle of the air, the like of which had never before been known, or even with any precision imagined. The moral tests to which the crew of a bomber were subjected reached the extreme limits of human valour and sacrifice. Here chance was carried to its most extreme and violent degree above all else. There was a rule that no one should go on more than thirty raids without a break. But many who entered on their last dozen wild adventures felt that the odds against them were increasing. How can one be lucky thirty times running in a world of averages and machinery? Detective-Constable McSweeney, one of the Scotland Yard officers who looked after me in the early days of the war, was determined to fight in a bomber. I saw him several times during his training and his fighting. One day, gay and jaunty as ever, but with a thoughtful look, he said, 'My next will be my twenty-ninth.' It was his last. Not only our hearts and admiration but our minds in strong comprehension of these ordeals must go out to these heroic men, whose duty to their country and their cause sustained them in superhuman trials.

I have mentioned facts like 'the Americans had sixty of their large Fortress aircraft destroyed out of 291', and on another occasion 'out of 795 aircraft dispatched by British Bomber Command against Nuremberg ninety-four did not return'. The American Fortresses carried a crew of ten men, and the British night bombers seven. Here we have each time six or seven hundred of these skilled, highly trained warriors lost in an hour. This was indeed ordeal by fire. In the British and American bombing of Germany and Italy during the war the casualties were over a hundred and forty thousand, and in the period with which this chapter deals there were more British and American air-crew casualties than there were killed and wounded in the great operation of crossing the Channel. They never flinched or failed. It is to their devotion that in no small measure we owe our victory. Let us give them our salute.

CHAPTER 13

The Greek Torment

Greek and Jewish Inspiration – Greece under German Occupation – Formation of E.A.M. and E.L.A.S. – Our Missions to Greece – Political Designs of the Communist Guerrilla Bands – General Smuts' Advice – Danger of a Communist Coup d'État – The Question of the Monarchy – Our Ambassador's Views on the Situation – M. Tsouderos Tenders His Resignation – King George's Decision to Return to Cairo – My Telegrams to Mr. Leeper of April 7 and 8 – Mutiny in the Greek Navy and of the Greek Brigade in Egypt – Our Policy Towards the Greeks – The Mutinous Brigade Surrounded – Arrival of the King in Cairo – My Telegram to President Roosevelt of April 16 – His Most Helpful Message – Climax of the Greek Mutinies – General Paget's Skilful Methods – Surrender of the Mutineers – Formation of a New Greek Government under M. Papandreou – My Statement to the House, May 24.

The Greeks rival the Jews in being the most politically-minded race in the world. No matter how forlorn their circumstances or how grave the peril to their country, they are always divided into many parties, with many leaders who fight among themselves with desperate vigour. It has been well said that wherever there are three Jews it will be found that there are two Prime Ministers and one leader of the Opposition. The same is true of this other famous ancient race, whose stormy and endless struggle for life stretches back to the fountain springs of human thought. No two races have set such a mark upon the world. Both have shown a capacity for survival, in spite of unending perils and sufferings from external oppressors, matched only by their own ceaseless feuds, quarrels, and convulsions. The passage of several thousand years sees no change in their characteristics and no diminution of their trials or their vitality. They have survived in spite of all that the world could do against them, and all they could do against themselves, and each of them from angles so different have left us the inheritance of their genius and wisdom. No two cities have counted more with mankind than Athens and Jerusalem. Their messages in religion, philosophy, and art have been the main guiding lights of modern faith and culture. Centuries of foreign rule and indescribable, endless oppression leave them still living, active communities and forces in the modern world, quarrelling among themselves with insatiable vivacity. Personally I have always been on the side of both, and believed in their invincible power to survive internal strife and the world tides threatening their extinction.

*   *   *

After the withdrawal of the Allies in April 1941 Greece was occupied by the Axis Powers. The collapse of the Army and the retirement of the King and his Government into exile revived the bitter controversies of Greek politics. Both in the country and in Greek circles abroad there was hard criticism of the monarchy, which had sanctioned the dictatorship of General Metaxas, and thereby directly associated itself with the *régime* which had now been defeated. When King George II left Crete in May 1941 he took with him a Government which was mainly Royalist, headed by M. Tsouderos. Their long journey by Cairo and South Africa to London provided ample time for political discussion among Greek communities abroad. The constitution had been suspended in 1936, and the debate upon the future *régime* when Greece would finally be liberated had to be conducted among refugees on Allied soil.

I had long realised the importance of this issue, and in October 1941 addressed a letter to the Greek Prime Minister, congratulating him on his first broadcast from London to occupied Greece, and expressing my gratification that Greece had been declared to be a democratic country under a constitutional monarchy. The King himself broadcast in the New Year to his country on the same lines. If a united nation was to rise out of the war it was essential that links should be maintained between the exiles and Greek opinion at home.

During the first winter of Axis occupation Greece suffered severely from famine, partially relieved by Red Cross shipments, and also from the exhaustion of the fighting which had ended in the destruction of her Army. But at the time of the surrender arms were hidden in the mountains, and in sporadic fashion, and on a minor scale, resistance to the enemy was planned. In the towns of Central Greece starvation provided plenty of recruits. In April 1942 the body calling itself the National Liberation Front (known by its initials in Greek as

E.A.M.), which had come into being in the previous autumn, announced the formation of the People's Liberation Army (E.L.A.S.). Small fighting groups were recruited during the following year, particularly in Central and Northern Greece, while in Epirus and the mountains of the north-west remnants of the Greek Army and local mountaineers gathered round the person of Colonel Napoleon Zervas. The E.A.M.-E.L.A.S. organisation was dominated by a hard core of Communist leaders. The adherents of Zervas, originally Republican in sympathy, became as time passed exclusively anti-Communist. Around these two centres Greek resistance to the Germans gathered. Neither of them had any direct contact with the Greek Government in London, nor any sympathy for its position.

On the eve of Alamein we decided to attack the German supply lines leading down through Greece to the Piræus, the port of Athens and an important base on the German route to North Africa. In the autumn of 1942 the first British Military Mission, under Lieut.-Colonel Myers, was accordingly dropped by parachute into Greece and made contact with the guerrillas. With their aid a vital viaduct on the main Athens railway line was destroyed. Simultaneously brilliant and daring sabotage operations were carried out by Greek agents against Axis shipping in the Piræus. The success of these operations encouraged Middle East Headquarters to send more British parties with supplies of explosives and arms. Thus direct contact with occupied Greece was established.

During the summer of 1943 the British missions were strengthened. We had an added motive for stimulating activities in this area as a cover for our pending operations in Sicily. Special efforts were made to convince the enemy that, following on their defeat in Tunisia, the Allies were planning a major landing on Greek soil. Combined Anglo-Greek parties blew another railway bridge on the main Athens line, and other sabotage operations were successful. The result was that two German divisions were moved into Greece which might have been used in Sicily. This however was the last direct military contribution which the Greek guerrillas made to the war, and henceforward the scene was dominated by the struggle to gain political power at the end of hostilities.

Political quarrels hampered guerrilla warfare, and we soon found ourselves in a complicated and disagreeable situation It was becoming clear that there were three divergent elements:

E.L.A.S., now numbering 20,000 men, and predominantly under Communist control; the Zervas bands, known as E.D.E.S., totalling 5,000; and the Royalist politicians, grouped in Cairo or in London round the King, to whom we had a special obligation as the head of a State which had fought as our Ally in 1941. All now thought that the Allies would probably win the war, and the struggle among them for political power began in earnest, to the advantage of the common foe. In March 1943 a group of prominent politicians in Athens signed a manifesto enjoining the King not to return after the war until a plebiscite had been held. It was important that the King should make clear where he stood. On July 4 he therefore made a conciliatory broadcast to the Greek people promising that a General Election would be held as soon as the country was liberated and that the Greek Government abroad would resign when it arrived in Athens in order that a broadly based Administration could be formed. But opinion inside Greece sought more immediate action. Shortly afterwards a minor mutiny took place in the small Greek forces which we had assembled in the Middle East, where E.A.M. propaganda was now spreading. In August a delegation of six leaders from the main resistance groups in Greece was brought to Cairo, and they too urged that a plebiscite should be held before the King returned, and that three places in the exiled Government should be held by politicians inside Greece. Neither the King nor his Prime Minister would agree.

While I was in Quebec I had received the following message from King George about these developments.

King of Greece (Cairo) to Prime Minister and President Roosevelt   19 Aug 43

On July 4 I declared to my people that after their liberation they will be invited to determine by means of free election the form of their Government.

I am now suddenly faced by the most curious situation, of the unexpected arrival of certain individuals from Greece who are supposed to represent various guerrilla bands; in addition, a representative of certain old political parties, who wish to press me to declare that I should only return after a plebiscite which would decide the form of the future *régime*. ... In these circumstances I would much appreciate your advice as to the policy which would at this time best serve the cause of Greece and the United Nations.

My present personal inclination is to continue the policy

agreed between us before I left England. I feel very strongly that I should return to Greece with my troops, even if I left my country after a short period to work for its national interests among our Allies, should subsequent developments make it politic for me to do so.

I had minuted on this:

Prime Minister to Foreign Secretary 19 Aug 43
If substantial British forces take part in the liberation of Greece the King should go back with the Anglo-Greek Army. This is much the more probable alternative. If however the Greeks are strong enough to drive out the Germans themselves we shall have a good deal less to say in the matter. It follows that the King should demand equal Royalist representation with the Republicans now proposed. In any case he would make a great mistake to agree in any way to remain outside Greece while the fighting for the liberation is going on and while conditions preclude the holding of a peaceful plebiscite.

Smuts, who followed Greek fortunes attentively, also sent a prescient comment.

General Smuts to Prime Minister 20 Aug 43
There appears to be strong suspicion that British Intelligence agents who brought Greek Patriots and other party representatives to Cairo are anti-Royalist, and that Patriot representatives even have Communist leanings. King George has always been strongly pro-Ally, and sacrificed much for Allied cause, and we have every good reason to stand by him in this crisis. It seems to me sound policy that you should once more make it quite clear to the Greek Government that the United Kingdom Government stands by the King, at least until such time as Greek people, under proper conditions of public tranquillity, are able to decide on their future *régime*. A plebiscite or General Election on the *régime* immediately on the Allied occupation of Greece should be ruled out as likely to lead to civil strife, if not to civil war, in the existing bitterness of feeling. Allied administration under military occupation should be continued until public opinion has settled down and safe conditions of public tranquillity have been established. During this interim period of Allied administration King George and Royal Family might well return to Greece to lend their moral support and authority to the Allied administration.
I very much fear that, in the inflamed conditions of public feeling, not only in Greece but also in other Balkan countries,

chaos may ensue after the Allied occupation unless a strong hand is kept on the local situation. With politics let loose among those peoples we may have a wave of disorder and wholsesale Communism set going all over those parts of Europe. This may even be the danger in Italy, but certainly in Greece and the Balkans. It should therefore be made plain at this stage that we mean to maintain public order and authority under Allied control until the situation is safe for local self-determination. The Greek situation brings matters to a head, and you may now consider it proper to raise this matter with the President, as a very important question of future policy is involved. The Bolshevisation of a broken and ruined Europe remains a definite possibility, to be guarded against by supply of food and work and interim Allied control.

* * *

The Italian surrender in September 1943 affected the whole balance of forces in Greece. E.L.A.S. was able to acquire most of the Italian equipment, including the weapons of an entire division, and thus gained military supremacy. The danger of a Communist *coup de'état* in the event of German withdrawal, which now became a practical possibility, needed careful attention. On September 29 I sent a minute to the Chiefs of Staff:

Prime Minister to General Ismay, for C.O.S. Committee
29 Sept 43

I am in full agreement with the Foreign Secretary in this essentially political question. Should the Germans evacuate Greece we must certainly be able to send 5,000 British troops with armoured cars and Bren gun carriers into Athens. They need have no transport or artillery. The Greek troops in Egypt would accompany them. Their duty would be to give support at the centre to the restored lawful Greek Government. The Greeks would not know how many were coming behind them. There may be some bickering between the Greek guerrilla bands, but great respect will be paid to the British, more especially as the saving of the country from famine depends entirely on our exertions in the early months of liberation. The troops need not be organised to contend with more than rioting in the capital or incursion into the capital from the countryside. . . .

Once a stable Government is set up we should take our departure.

This was the first suggestion that we might be forced to intervene in Greek internal affairs at the moment of liberation.

The pace of events now increased as E.L.A.S. developed its plans to take over political power as soon as the Germans withdrew and before an ordered constitutional Government could be established. During the winter there was little activity against the enemy. In October E.L.A.S. forces attacked E.D.E.S. (Zervas), and the British Headquarters in Cairo suspended all shipments of arms to the former. Every effort was made by our missions on the spot to limit and bring to an end the civil war which had now broken out in the ruined and occupied country.

*   *   *

The decisions of the Conferences in Cairo and in Teheran indirectly affected the position in Greece. There would never be a major Allied landing there, nor was it likely that any considerable British forces would follow a German retreat. The arrangements to prevent anarchy had therefore to be considered. The one figure presented to us as above party rancour was Damaskinos, Archbishop of Athens. While in Cairo Mr. Eden had impressed on the King the advantages of a temporary Regency. At the same time we hoped by sending the Greek Brigade in the Middle East to fight in Italy to raise the prestige of the exiled Government, and also to have loyal troops to send into Western Greece if need be.

The King would not agree to a Regency and returned to London. By now E.A.M., with its military component E.L.A.S., had formed a State within a State in the mountains of Central and Northern Greece. In February 1944 British officers succeeded in establishing an uneasy truce between E.L.A.S. and E.D.E.S. But the Soviet armies were now on the borders of Roumania. The chances of a German evacuation of the Balkans increased, and with them the possibilities of a return of the Royal Government, with British support. Assuming that both these events might take place in April, the E.A.M. leaders decided to act.

On March 26 a Political Committee of National Liberation was set up in the mountains, and the news broadcast to the world. This was a direct challenge to the future authority of the Tsouderos Government. An alternative Communist-controlled Administration was thus formed as a rallying-point for all Greeks. This was the signal for trouble in the Greek armed forces in the Middle East and in Greek Government circles abroad. On March 31 a group of officers from the Army, Navy, and Air

Force called on Tsouderos in Cairo to demand his resignation. Matters had now come to a head, but the Greek King in London did not appreciate their urgency. Mr. Leeper, our Ambassador to the Greek Government located in Cairo, telegraphed on April 6: 'I feel I must express myself with some bluntness. The King of Greece is playing with fire. He is endangering not only the interests of the monarchy but those of his country by not realising in time the rapid trend of events. ... E.A.M. have realised the danger to them of a united front between politicians in Athens and the Greek Government in Cairo. They have realised that the outcome of an agreement would be the reinforcement of the Government here and the end of their experiment to set up a separate Government in the mountains. They have therefore used the interval to strike at the Greek Government by subverting the Greek forces. Their agitation has had some success, and within the next few days it may have more.' 'M. Tsouderos,' wrote the Ambassador, 'finds himself in a dilemma. He had secured a good basis of collaboration with his colleagues as a result of messages of support from the Archbishop and politicians in Athens, but this agreement was based on his being able to induce the King to sign a Constitutional Act appointing the Archbishop as Regent. Some weeks have now passed, during which time M. Tsouderos has received no final reply from the King, but merely a preliminary view from him of a negative character. This he concealed from his colleagues in order to avoid an explosion. ... The situation could have been held but for recent E.A.M. agitation in the Army.'

Later in the day M. Tsouderos resigned, and recommended M. Venizelos, the Minister of Marine in his Government, as his successor. On April 4 disorders broke out in the Greek Army, the 1st Brigade of which I was hoping could take part in the Italian campaign. On the 5th the office of the Greek Provost-Marshal in Cairo was occupied by a hundred mutineers, who had to be surrounded by British troops and Egyptian police and were removed without trouble in lorries to an isolation camp. At Alexandria a leader of the Greek seamen's union had barricaded himself in his house with thirty supporters, and was defying the police. Five ships of the Royal Hellenic Navy declared themselves in favour of a republic and demanded the resignation of every member of the existing Government. All the members of the Greek Government tendered their resignations to the

King, but agreed to remain in office pending acceptance.

*   *   *

I was at this time in charge of the Foreign Office, owing to Mr. Eden's absence. I thus had all the threads directly in my hands.

I had sent the following to the Supreme Allied Commander in the Mediterranean:

Prime Minister to General Wilson ; repeated to General Alexander   5 Apr 44

It is now more than three months since we agreed that a Greek Brigade, if necessary without its vehicular equipment, should be sent from Egypt to Italy to take part in the Allied offensive. I am told that one company has already got there, and that the others will be there during the month. Why is there all this delay and difficulty in moving this handful of men? They are very liable in Egypt to be contaminated by revolutionary and Communist elements there. Satan finds some mischief still for idle hands to do. Now do please try to get them shipped off out of Egypt as soon as possible and assembled in some suitable town in Southern Italy. I feel this small matter, which has large political significance, ought not to have hung fire so long.

I also sent the following message to M. Tsouderos on April 7:

I was much shocked to hear of your resignation, which seems to leave Greece forlorn at a moment of peril for her national life. The King, whom I have just seen, tells me he has not accepted your resignation. He is coming out to Alexandria next week. Surely you can await his arrival.

The situation in the Greek Army and Navy had by now further deteriorated, and Venizelos announced that he could no longer accept office. M. Tsouderos replied on April 7: 'I shall remain at my post as the laws of Greece require and as you desire until this present crisis has found lawful solution. If the King waits until he returns to Egypt before he resolves this crisis I fear that by that time there may be no longer any opportunity of resolving it.'

Mr. Leeper telegraphed to the Foreign Office on April 7:

'What is happening here among the Greeks is nothing less than a revolution. It is under such conditions that a makeshift Greek Government in exile, suffering from all the weakness which that implies, has been trying to cope with the situation.

It has failed completely, but has been handicapped by being able to make no legal change without the sanction of the King at a distance. . . .'

Our Ambassador hoped however that the situation could be settled in Cairo without the King's presence. 'The King of Greece's return here at present would certainly provoke fresh trouble. Tsouderos and all his colleagues are strongly of this opinion. He would find himself isolated and unable to do anything, and would be a grave embarrassment to us.' He asked the Foreign Office to do everything in their power to stop his return. 'In the circumstances in which we are living here at the moment the advice of people on the spot should, I submit, be accepted. My views are shared by everybody here.'

* * *

The King of Greece came to luncheon with me in London on this day. I showed him the Ambassador's telegram without comment. He said he would go to Cairo at once. I thought he was quite right.

Prime Minister to Mr. Leeper 7 Apr 44
I have discussed the situation with the King. He is resolved to return to Cairo, leaving by air Sunday evening, and notwithstanding your telegram (which I have shown the King) I consider he is right to do so. If, as you say, what is happening in Cairo is a Greek revolution, I cannot advise him to stay away and allow the issue to be decided in his absence. . . . All local Greek politicians and agitators should at the same time be warned that we shall not hesitate to take adequate measures of security to prevent agitation and demonstrations which might threaten law and order in Egypt and the position and authority of the King and the Greek Government. . . . You should inform M. Tsouderos that I count on him to remain at his post until the present crisis has found a lawful solution. . . .

This is an occasion for you to show those qualities of imperturbability and command which are associated with the British Diplomatic Service.

And the next day I added:

Prime Minister to Mr. Leeper 8 Apr 44
Weather permitting, the King will leave Sunday night. Meanwhile it is M. Tsouderos's duty to stand to his post. Of course if he can get M. Sophocles Venizelos to stay with him

all the better. When the King arrives the British Security Service must ensure his personal safety. He may require a few days to make up his mind, and must on no account be hustled. I am asking the military commanders to move the Greek Brigade as fast as possible to Italy. They will of course weed out recalcitrant elements. In the same way the Admiral is expected to preserve the discipline of all ships under his command, using no more force than is necessary.

For you yourself there is a great opportunity. You should stick to the line I have marked out and not be worried about the consequences. You speak of living on the lid of a volcano. Wherever else do you expect to live in times like these? Please however be careful to follow very exactly the instructions you are receiving from me, namely, first in priority, order and discipline to be maintained in the armed forces ; secondly, the safety of the King's person to be ensured ; thirdly, every effort to be made to induce Tsouderos to hold office till the King returns and has had time to look around ; fourthly, try to get Venizelos to remain with Tsouderos ; fifthly, celebrate Easter Sunday in a manner pious and becoming.

* * *

On April 8 a Greek destroyer refused to obey orders to proceed to sea unless a Government was formed which would include E.A.M. representatives. The mutinous Greek Brigade had taken up defensive positions round their camp, and trouble was expected in the small Greek Air Force units as well. I was forced to give up my hopes of getting the Greek Brigade sent to Italy. Later I telegraphed to General Paget, who commanded the British forces in Egypt :

Prime Minister to General Paget   8 Apr 44

A mutinous brigade threatening its officers should certainly be surrounded and forced to surrender by stoppage of all supplies. Why do you leave out water? Will this not bring the desired result quicker? Obviously these troops should be disarmed. I agree that the hope of getting them to Italy may have to be abandoned. Keep me fully informed of plans for disarming. We cannot tolerate political revolutions carried out by foreign military formations for which we are ultimately responsible. In all cases large numbers of British troops should be used so as to overawe, and thus minimise bloodshed.

I also sent Mr. Leeper a full statement of our policy for use with the Greeks.

9 Apr 44

Our relations are definitely established with the lawfully constituted Greek Government headed by the King, who is the ally of Britain and cannot be discarded to suit a momentary surge of appetite among ambitious *émigré* nonentities. Neither can Greece find constitutional expression in particular sets of guerrillas, in many cases indistinguishable from banditti, who are masquerading as the saviours of their country while living on the local villagers. If necessary I shall denounce these elements and tendencies publicly in order to emphasise the love Great Britain has for Greece, whose sufferings she shared in a small measure, being, alas, not then armed as we are now. Our only desire and interest is to see Greece a glorious, free nation in the Eastern Mediterranean, the honoured friend and ally of the victorious Powers. Let all therefore work for this objective, and make it quite clear that any failure in good conduct will not be overlooked.

I had been working very hard to arrange the movement of the Greek Brigade to Italy. Here they might still take part in the entry into Rome which is to be expected during the summer. This Brigade, the 1st Greek Brigade, representatives of the army which had beaten back the Italian invader and were only felled by the treacherous and brutal intervention of the German hordes, had and still has the chance of raising the name of Greece high in the world. It is a lamentable fact that they should have signalised this opportunity by an undignified, even squalid, exhibition of indiscipline, which many will attribute to an unworthy fear of being sent to the front.

In the same way the Greek Navy, which is full of daring seamen and is playing a worthy part upholding its country's good name, should not suddenly have tried to meddle with politics and presume to dictate a constitution to the Greek people. I believe that both of these two forces can be brought back to a high sense of national honour and duty if courageous leadership is forthcoming, backed by overwhelming force in reserve.

All the time I have been planning to place Greece back high in the councils of the victorious nations. Witness how we have included them in the Italian Advisory Council and tried to send a brigade to take part in the impending victories in Italy. Greeks who are in safety in Egypt under our protection, equipped with our vessels or armed with our weapons or otherwise in security under the military authority of the British Commander-in-Chief Middle East, will place themselves in an abject and shameful position before all history if they allow their domestic feuds to mar their performance of the solemn duties to their country of which they have become the heirs. They may easily, by selfish, excitable be haviour, reduce Greece to a country without expression eith at home or abroad, and their names will be stained as long a history is written.

The King is the servant of his people. He makes no claim rule them. He submits himself freely to the judgment of th people as soon as normal conditions are restored. He plac himself and his Royal House entirely at the disposition of th Greek nation. Once the German invader has been driven o Greece can be a republic or a monarchy, entirely as the peop wish. Why then cannot the Greeks keep their hatreds for th common enemy, who has wrought them such cruel injuri and would obliterate them as a free people, were it not for th resolute exertions of the Great Allies?

*   *   *

General Paget now reported to me that as the 1st Gree Brigade had mutinied against its officers and refused to hand its arms under specific orders from him he proposed to ta direct action to carry out such orders. I telegraphed on April 'These small-scale events are developing rapidly, and I ful concur with the action you are taking. . . . *You will have achieve success if you bring the Brigade under control without bloo shed. But brought under control it must be. Count on my su port.*'

The Greek Brigade was now surrounded by superior Brita forces. Its strength was 4,500 men, with over fifty guns, whi were all deployed in defensive positions against us. On April I sent further directions to Mr. Leeper and all others concerne 'There can be no question of making terms with mutineers abo political matters. They must return to their duty unconditio ally. They must submit to be disarmed unconditionally. It wou be a great pity to give any assurances about the non-punis ment of ringleaders. . . . The question of clemency would re with the King. Let me know how this stands before taking a decisive action.'

And further:

Prime Minister to Mr. Leeper and all Principals   14 Apr 4
concerned (Cairo)
     Surely you should let lack of supplies work its part both the camp and the harbour before resorting to firing. Y should use the weapon of blockade to the full and defer yourselves against attempts to break out. Do not worry t

much about the external effects. Do not show yourself over-eager to parley. Simply keep them rounded up by artillery and superior force and let hunger play its part. On no account accept any assistance from American or Russian sources, otherwise than as specially enjoined by me. You have ample force at your disposal and plenty of time. It is much more important that the [mutineers] should be reduced to proper discipline than that any particular Greek Government should be set up. It would even be harmful if a brigade and a flotilla had been permitted to meddle in political issues.

My latest information reports that the situation of the Greek Brigade shows signs of improving and that they have finished their rations. You should take full advantage of these tendencies and keep me informed.

And the next day:

Prime Minister to Mr. Leeper   15 Apr 44
Do not be influenced by possible anti-British sentiment among the local Greeks. It would be a great mistake to end this grave business up in a pleasant kiss all round. That might come later as an act of clemency from the King and his new Government. We have got to get these men into our hands disarmed, without conditions, and I trust without bloodshed.

*   *   *

Meanwhile the King had arrived in Cairo, and on April 12 had issued a proclamation stating that a representative Government composed largely of Greeks from within Greece would be formed. The next day Venizelos took office in succession to Tsouderos, and steps were taken in secret to bring out representatives from metropolitan Greece.

I now reported the whole position to the President, who was sympathetic to my view and to King George of Greece.

Prime Minister to President Roosevelt   16 Apr 44
The outbreak in the Greek Army and Navy followed closely on the establishment in the mountains of Greece of the Political Committee sponsored by E.A.M., and there is little doubt that the extremist elements who have long been working to subvert the allegiance of the Greek forces to their legitimate King and Government seized on this as a heaven-sent opportunity for open and violent action. The dissident elements are undoubtedly opposed to the King and in favour of a republic, but throughout the disturbances there have been almost no direct attacks on the King's personal position,

and the only specific demand put forward is that the Greek Government should take immediate and effective steps to recognise and associate with themselves the Political Committee in Greece.

This crisis came at a particularly unfortunate moment, since M. Tsouderos had already sent an invitation to a number of moderate politicians in Athens urging them to come to Cairo to join the Government. He had also invited representatives of E.A.M., the Communist-controlled organisation which has created and now dominates the Political Committee. Tsouderos was thus doing everything in his power to create a truly representative Greek Government.

In this programme he had the support of his colleagues, and they appear to have had no hand in provoking the disturbances in the Greek forces. But they were extremely jealous of Tsouderos's position, and used the trouble in the Greek Army, which was at first on a small scale, to get rid of him. Feeling that he had lost control of the situation, Tsouderos resigned and proposed Venizelos for the Premiership. The trouble in the Greek Army rapidly spread to the Navy, and assumed the proportions of a full-scale mutiny in both forces. The politicians in Cairo realised that the matter had gone beyond one of personal rivalries or ambitions, and their only thought was to find some candidate for the Premiership sufficiently notorious for his Left Wing views to be acceptable to the mutinous elements in the forces.

The King of Greece was reluctant to accept a new Government whose composition was in effect dictated by the mutineers. He considered that order in the Greek armed forces must be restored before any lawful reconstruction of the Government could be undertaken. I entirely agreed with him, and instructed our Ambassador to the Greek Government to do his utmost to induce the Greek Ministers to remain at their posts until the King could get back to Cairo and take stock of the situation. This, I am glad to say, they agreed to do. I also gave instructions to the military authorities in the Middle East to deal firmly with indiscipline in the Greek forces under their command. Order in the Greek Army and Navy has not been completely re-established, but the dissident elements are being isolated, and once the ringleaders are under arrest the mutiny should rapidly subside.

The King of Greece has now reached Cairo, and, after studying the position for himself, has formed a Government under M. Venizelos.

The President sent me the following most helpful message:

President Roosevelt to Prime Minister   18 Apr 44
   Thank you for the information regarding recent difficulties
encountered in Greek participation in our Allied effort.
   I join with you in a hope that your line of action toward the
problem may succeed in bringing the Greeks back into the
Allied camp and to a participation against the barbarians that
will be worthy of traditions established by the heroes of Greek
history. Frankly, as one whose family and who personally has
contributed by personal help to Greek independence for over
a century, I am unhappy over the present situation, and hope
that Greeks everywhere will set aside pettiness and regain
their sense of proportion. Let every Greek think of their
glorious past and show a personal unselfishness which is so
necessary now. You can quote me if you want to in the above
sense.

Prime Minister to President Roosevelt   18 Apr 44
   Thank you so much. I have told our people to make use of
your message to the King and his new Ministers, and to read
it to the mutinous brigade and recalcitrant ships. It may have
a most salutary effect.

*   *   *

As matters reached a climax at Alexandria I telegraphed to
the Naval Commander-in-Chief:

17 Apr 44
   You should leave the senior member of the *Averoff** in no
doubt that his guarantee that the use of firearms will be
avoided will not be reciprocated by us. We shall fire on
mutineers whenever it is necessary. No officers or sailors of
the Greek Navy have the slightest right to meddle in the
formation of the new Government. Their duty is to obey the
orders they receive from the Greek Government recognised
by the Great Allies.

The mutiny in the Greek Brigade was also approaching a
crisis.

Prime Minister to General Paget   22 Apr 44
   If you find it necessary to open fire on the mutineers' camp
you should consider whether you might not start with a few
ranging shots directed on their batteries which are aiming at
you. If they make no reply, after an appropriate interval let
them have a stiffer dose, and at the same time tell them the
weight of fire which you are ready to direct on them if they

* Greek cruiser.

persist. We are prepared to use the utmost force, but let us avoid slaughter if possible. It is proposed that the onus should lie to the account of the British rather than of the slender, tottering Greek Government.

I received by return the following reply:

General Paget to Prime Minister   23 Apr 44

My plan is in line with your suggestions. In order to get close observation of their camp we must first capture two Greek posts on high ground. This will be done, by infantry only, just before dawn. When it is light we will lay a smoke-screen over their camp for ten minutes. Then there will be a pause for the smoke to clear away, after which leaflets will be dropped. They will state that there will be a further smoke-screen for half an hour, under cover of which all who wish should leave camp and come over to our lines. If mutineers are still holding out after this a few shells will be fired at one of their batteries, followed by a further pause to allow for surrender. We shall continue this process until all their guns are knocked out. If the mutineers still will not surrender it will be necessary to make an infantry assault on the camp under covering fire from artillery and tanks ; but tanks will be used in sniping *rôle* and will not advance into the camp, as the mutineers are known to be well supplied with anti-tank weapons. They are undoubtedly now very short of food, but they have managed to get some from the local Arabs. It has not proved possible to invest the camp closely enough to stop this.

On the evening of the same day the mutinous Greek ships were boarded by loyal Greek sailors, and with about fifty casualties the mutineers were collected and sent ashore. General Paget now hoped to obtain the surrender of the Greek Brigade by parley and without bloodshed. The handling of the affair was completely successful, and I was able to inform the President the next day that British troops had occupied key positions on the ridge overlooking the Greek camp after slight opposition. There were no Greek casualties, but one British officer was killed. The Greek Brigade surrendered and laid down its arms, and was evacuated to a prisoner-of-war cage, where the ringleaders were arrested. The naval mutineers had surrendered unconditionally twenty-four hours earlier.

To General Paget I said: 'I congratulate you on the satisfactory outcome of your firm and well-devised action.'

The President shared my relief.

President Roosevelt to Prime Minister   26 Apr 44

I am very pleased indeed by your success in handling the Greek naval and military mutiny. I will hope for a similar success in your efforts with the Egyptian political problem. Our prospects of assisting 'Overlord' by vigorous action in Italy do look much better with a fixed date upon which we may expect all our pressure against the enemy. In view of our postponement of 'Anvil' a real success in Italy now seems essential.

Everything goes well here in my vacation residence. The doctor agrees with me that I am better.

*   *   *

We had also kept the Russians informed of these events, both by messages to Molotov and through the Soviet Embassy in Cairo. The Soviet Government confined itself to criticism of our actions, and when on May 5 a formal request to Russia for co-operation in Greek affairs was made in Moscow the reply was that it would be improper to join in any public pronouncement on political matters in Greece.

*   *   *

With the end of the mutiny the question of the formation of a Greek Government became acute. It was not felt that Venizelos was suitable for this task, and the leader of the Greek Social Democratic Party, Papandreou, who had been specially brought out of Greece, took office on April 26. The following day he issued a proclamation which was to form the agenda for a conference of all parties, including leaders from the Greek mountains. These delegates met at a mountain resort in the Lebanon on May 17, where it was agreed, after a fierce debate lasting three days, to set up an Administration in Cairo in which all groups would be represented under the Premiership of Papandreou, while in the mountains of Greece a united military organisation would continue to struggle against the Germans. This arrangement held promise for the future.

On May 24 came the announcement of the new Greek Government. I reported these events to the House of Commons on the same day.

After prolonged discussion complete unity was reached at the Lebanon conference, and all parties will be represented in the new Government, which will devote itself to what is after all the only purpose worthy of consideration, namely, the formation of a national Army in which all the guerrilla bands will be incorporated, and the driving, with this Army, of the enemy from the country, or, better still, destroying him where he stands.

On Monday there was published in the newspapers the very agreeable letter which I received from the leaders of the [Greek] Communists and the extreme Left Wing party. There is published to-day in the papers the letter I have received from M. Papandreou expressing the hopes which he has for the future of his Government, and thanks for the assistance we have given in getting round these troubles—what I call the diseases of defeat, which Greece has now a chance of shaking off. I believe that the present situation—I hope and pray that it may be so—indicates that a new and fair start will come to Greece in her struggle to cleanse her native soil from the foreign invader. I have therefore to report to the House that a very marked and beneficial change has occurred in the situation in Greece, which is more than I could say when I last spoke upon this subject.

Thus this dangerous episode, which, although on a small scale compared with the vast movement of the war, might have been the cause of endless discussions detrimental to our affairs, came to a satisfactory conclusion. I have recorded it in detail because of the very direct personal responsibility which I assumed. I circulated all my telegrams to the War Cabinet as they were sent, and my colleagues in no way hampered my freedom of action. It was certainly an achievement that our military commanders were able by overwhelming force, firmness, and patience to quell these political mutinies among such fiery troops without bloodshed, except for the loss of a single British officer, Major J. R. Copeland, of the 2nd Battalion Rifle Brigade, who certainly did not die in vain.

The difficulties and struggles which lay before us all in this nerve-centre of Europe and the world will be recounted in their proper place. I consider however that, taken by and large, my policy was vindicated by events; and this is true not only of the period of the war, but up to the present time of writing.

Burma and Beyond

The reader must now be asked to hark back nearly a year in order that a summary may be presented to him of the war against Japan in the Pacific, which was at this time the main effort of the United States and of the Commonwealth of Australia.

By the latter half of 1943 the Japanese had lost the eastern end of New Guinea. Before he could attack the Philippines General MacArthur had first to reoccupy all its northern shore. Part of the 41st U.S. Division worked their way towards Salamaua, and at the end of June other troops landed near it from the sea. They were joined by the 3rd Australian Division from Wau, and began their attack on Salamaua. It was purposely deliberate, so as to draw reinforcements from Lae, the next major objective. The attack on Lae began on September 4, 1943, when the 9th Australian Division, of Alamein fame, landed on the coast ten miles east of the town. Next day American parachutists dropped on Nadzap, in the Markham valley, and, with the help of Australian pioneers, rapidly made an airfield. The 7th Australian Division flew in, and immediately advanced. Attacked from two sides, Lae was taken on September 16. Salamaua had fallen a few days before, and Finschhafen fell on October 2. All were fiercely defended. The Markham valley, running north-west from Lae, had many potential airfields, and the 7th Australian Division, swift to exploit success, occupied its length in a series of airborne assaults. All the operations were well conceived and skilfully executed, and the co-operation of all three fighting Services was brought to a high pitch.

The Australian capture of Finschhafen was followed by fierce Japanese counter-attacks, and there was much fighting during the last fortnight of October. By mid-November the 5th Australian Division was moving forward through the mountains of the Huon peninsula, overcoming a series of strongly held positions, while the 9th Australian Division was clearing the heights overlooking the Markham valley. Part of the 32nd U.S. Division made an amphibious landing at Saidor early in January 1944, where they were joined on February 11 by the 5th Australian Division. It had taken five months to clear the Huon peninsula. Out of 12,000 Japanese who had been engaged there not more than 4,200 survived.

In April General MacArthur made an amphibious leap of four hundred miles. He by-passed 50,000 Japanese around Wewak, and landed an American division at Aitape and two more near Hollandia. The Japanese Air Force had been thoroughly pounded, and 380 machines were found destroyed. Allied superiority by sea and air was henceforward so decisive that MacArthur could select whatever objectives suited him best and leave behind him large pockets of Japanese to be dealt with later. His final bound was to Biak Island, where the 41st U.S. Division had a fierce struggle against an enemy garrison nearly ten thousand strong. A convoy of a dozen Japanese warships was destroyed or crippled by air attack as they tried to bring reinforcements, and the island was effectively in American possession before the end of June 1944. This marked the end of the two-year struggle in New Guinea, where the stubborn resistance of the enemy, the physical difficulties of the country, the ravages of disease, and the absence of communications made the campaign as arduous as any in history.

*　　　*　　　*

Farther east, at the beginning of July 1943, and simultaneously with General MacArthur's attack on Salamaua, Admiral Halsey had struck in New Georgia. After several weeks of severe fighting both this and the adjacent islands were won. Air fighting again dominated the scene, and the ascendancy of the American airmen soon proved decisive. Japanese losses in the air now exceeded those of the Americans by four or five to one.

In July and August a series of naval actions gave the Americans

New Guinea

command of the sea. By September the backbone of Japanese resistance had been broken, and although severe fighting continued at Bougainville and other islands the campaign in the Solomons was ended by December 1943. Such positions as remained in enemy hands had been neutralised and could now be safely by-passed and left to wilt.

Rabaul itself, in New Britain, became the next centre of attack. During November and December it was heavily and repeatedly struck by Allied air forces, and in the last days of 1943 General MacArthur's amphibious forces landed on the western extremity of New Britain at Cape Gloucester. It was now decided to bypass Rabaul. An alternative base was therefore needed to sustain the advance to the Philippines, and this was within MacArthur's grasp at Manus Island, in the Admiralty Group. In February 1944 the first stage of this envelopment was accomplished by the seizure of Green Island, 120 miles east of Rabaul. This was followed by the brilliant capture of the whole Admiralty Group, to the westward. In March Emirau Island, immediately to the north, was taken by Admiral Halsey, and the isolation of Rabaul was complete. The air and sea surrounding these islands thus passed entirely under American control.

*   *   *

Meanwhile the main American maritime forces, under Admiral Nimitz, began to concentrate for his drive through the island groups near the equator, which were the outposts defending the Japanese fleet base at Truk, in the Carolines. The most easterly of these groups, the Gilberts, seized from the British in 1941, was chosen for the first attack. In October 1943 Admiral Spruance, who had gained fame at Midway, was appointed to command the Central Pacific force. In November, while Halsey was attacking Bougainville, Spruance struck at Tarawa, in the Gilberts. The island was strongly fortified, and was held by about 3,500 Japanese troops. The landing by the 2nd Marine Division was bitterly contested, in spite of heavy preliminary air attacks. After four fierce days, in which casualties were severe, the island was captured.

With Tarawa eliminated the way was clear for attack on the Marshall Group, to the north and west of the Gilberts. In February 1944 they were the object of amphibious operations on the greatest scale yet attempted in the Pacific, and by the end of the month the Americans were victorious. Without pause Spruance began the next phase of his advance, the softening by air attack of Japanese defences in the Carolines and Marianas. The flexibility of seaborne attack in an ocean area is the most remarkable feature of these operations. While we in Europe were making our final preparations for 'Overlord' with immense concentration of force 'in the narrow waters of the Channel, Spruance's carriers were ranging over huge areas, striking at islands in the Marianas, the Palau group, and the Carolines, deep within the Japanese defensive perimeter, and at the same time helping MacArthur in his attack on Hollandia. On the eve of 'Overlord' Japan's strength was everywhere on the wane; her defence system in the Central Pacific had been breached at many points and was ripe for disruption.

Summing up these operations in the South-West Pacific, General Marshall could report that in a little over twelve months the Allies had 'pushed 1,300 miles closer to the heart of the Japanese Empire, cutting off more than 135,000 enemy troops beyond hope of rescue'.

*   *   *

The curtain must now rise on a widely different scene in South-East Asia. For more than eighteen months the Japanese had been masters of a vast defensive arc covering their early conquests. This stretched from the jungle-covered mountains of Northern and Western Burma, where our British and Indian troops were at close grips with them, across the sea to the Andamans and the great Dutch dependencies of Sumatra and Java, and thence in an easterly bend along the string of lesser islands to New Guinea.

The Americans had established a bomber force in China which was doing good work against the enemy's sea communications between the mainland and the Philippines. They wanted to extend this effort by basing long-range aircraft in China to attack Japan itself. The Burma Road was cut, and they were carrying all supplies for them and the Chinese armies by air over the southern spurs of the Himalayas, which they called 'The Hump'. This was a stupendous task. I had always advocated air aid to China and the improvement of the air route and protection of the airfields, but I hoped this might be done by forces essentially airborne and air-sustained on the Wingate model, but on a larger scale. The American wish to succour China not

The Pacific Theatre

only by an ever-increasing air-lift, but also by land, led to heavy demands upon Britain and the Indian Empire. They pressed as a matter of the highest urgency and importance the making of a motor road from the existing roadhead at Ledo through five hundred miles of jungles and mountains into Chinese territory. Only one metre-gauge, single-line railway ran through Assam to Ledo. It was already in constant use for many other needs, including the supply of the troops who held the frontier positions ; but in order to build the road to China the Americans wanted us to reconquer Northern Burma first and quickly.

Certainly we favoured keeping China in the war and operating air forces from her territory, but a sense of proportion and the study of alternatives were needed. I disliked intensely the prospect of a large-scale campaign in Northern Burma. One could not choose a worse place for fighting the Japanese. Making a road from Ledo to China was also an immense, laborious task, unlikely to be finished until the need for it had passed. Even if it were done in time to replenish the Chinese armies while they were still engaged it would make little difference to their fighting capacity. The need to strengthen the American air bases in China would also, in our view, diminish as Allied advances in the Pacific and from Australia gained us airfields closer to Japan. On both counts therefore we argued that the enormous expenditure of man-power and material would not be worth while. But we never succeeded in deflecting the Americans from their purpose. Their national psychology is such that the bigger the Idea the more wholeheartedly and obstinately do they throw themselves into making it a success. It is an admirable characteristic provided the Idea is good.

We of course wanted to recapture Burma, but we did not want to have to do it by land advances from slender communications and across the most forbidding fighting country imaginable. The south of Burma, with its port of Rangoon, was far more valuable than the north. But all of it was remote from Japan, and for our forces to become side-tracked and entangled there would deny us our rightful share in a Far Eastern victory. I wished, on the contrary, to contain the Japanese in Burma, and break into or through the great arc of islands forming the outer fringe of the Dutch East Indies. Our whole British-Indian Imperial front would thus advance across the Bay of Bengal into close contact with the enemy, by using amphibious power at every stage. This divergence of opinion, albeit honestly held and frankly discussed, and with decisions loyally executed, continued. It is against this permanent background of geography, limited resources, and clash of policies that the story of the campaign should be read.

* * *

The Washington standpoint was clearly set forth to me by the President.

President Roosevelt to Prime Minister   25 Feb 44

My Chiefs of Staff are agreed that the primary intermediate objective of our advance across the Pacific lies in the Formosa–China coast–Luzon area. The success of recent operations in the Gilberts and Marshalls indicates that we can accelerate our movements westward. There appears to be a possibility that we can reach the Formosa–China–Luzon area before the summer of 1945. From the time we enter this vital zone until we gain a firm lodgment in this area it is essential that our operations be supported by the maximum air-power that can be brought to bear. This necessitates the greatest expansion possible of the air strength based in China.

I have always advocated the development of China as a base for the support of our Pacific advances, and now that the war has taken a greater turn in our favour time is all too short to provide the support we should have from that direction.

It is mandatory therefore that we make every effort to increase the flow of supplies into China. This can only be done by increasing the air tonnage or by opening a road through Burma.

Our occupation of Myitkyina will enable us immediately to increase the air-lift to China, by providing an intermediate air transport base, as well as by increasing the protection of the air route.

General Stilwell is confident that his Chinese-American force can seize Myitkyina by the end of this dry season, and, once there, can hold it, provided Mountbatten's IVth Corps from Imphal secures the Shwebo–Monywa area. I realise this imposes a most difficult task, but I feel that with your energetic encouragement Mountbatten's commanders are capable of overcoming the many difficulties involved.

The continued build-up of Japanese strength in Burma requires us to undertake the most aggressive action within our power to retain the initiative and prevent them from launching an offensive that may carry them over the borders into India. ... I most urgently hope therefore that you back to the maximum a vigorous and immediate campaign in Upper Burma.

* * *

The campaign had been opened in December, when General Stilwell, with two Chinese divisions, organised and trained by himself in India, crossed the watershed from Ledo into the jungles below the main mountain ranges. He was opposed by the renowned Japanese 18th Division, but forged ahead steadily, and by early January had penetrated forty miles, while the road-makers toiled behind him. In the south the British XVth Corps, under General Christison, began their advance down the Arakan coast on January 19. At the same time the Allied air forces re-doubled their efforts, and, with the aid of newly arrived Spit-fires, gained a degree of air superiority which was shortly to prove invaluable.

On February 4 our advance was suddenly halted. The Japanese also had a plan. Since November they had increased their strength in Burma from five divisions to eight, and they pro-posed to invade Eastern India and raise the flag of rebellion against the British. Their first stroke was a counter-offensive in the Arakan towards the port of Chittagong, which would draw our attention and our reserves to that front. Holding our 5th Division frontally on the coast, they passed the better part of a division through the jungle and round the flank of the 7th Divi-sion, which was farther inland. Within a few days it was sur-rounded and the enemy threatened to cut the coastal road behind the 5th Division. They fully expected both divisions to withdraw, but they had reckoned without one factor, supply by air. The 7th Division grouped themselves into perimeters, stood their ground, and fought it out. For a fortnight food, water, and ammunition were delivered to them, like manna, from above. The enemy had no such facilities; they had taken with them only ten days' supply, and the obstinacy of the 7th Division prevented more reaching them. Unable to overwhelm our for-ward troops, pressed from the north by our 26th Division, which had been brought from reserve, they broke up into small parties to fight their way back through the jungle, leaving five thousand dead behind.

The XVth Corps resumed their advance, proud of an achieve-ment which put an end to the legend of Japanese invincibility in the jungle.

Prime Minister to Admiral Mountbatten   1 Mar 44

I sent you to-day my public congratulations on the Arakan fighting. I am so glad this measure of success has attended it. It is a sign of the new spirit in your forces, and will, I trust, urge everyone to keep closer to the enemy. Looking at the maps from here, I do not see why you should not continue your advance along the coast in the direction of Akyab.

*   *   *

In February there were sure signs that the enemy were also preparing an attack on the central front against Imphal, thereby forestalling our own projected advance to the Chindwin. The now famous Chindits* operation was a part of our offensive plan. Although it was clear that the Japanese would get their blow in first, it was decided that Wingate's brigades should carry on with their task. This was principally to cut the enemy's communications near Indaw, thereby dislocating their supply system, and notably that of the Japanese 18th Division, with whom Stilwell was at close grips. The enemy would moreover be forced to detach troops to deal with the menace behind his fighting front. One Chindits brigade, the 16th British, had already started on February 5 from Ledo. They marched across 450 miles of mountain and jungle and were supplied solely from the air.

On March 5, sustained by an American 'Air Commando' of 250 machines, the fly-in of the 77th and 111th Brigades, British and Gurkha troops, began. After assembly at their rallying-point they set out upon their task and cut the railway north of Indaw.

I sent a full account of all this to the President.

14 Mar 44

I feel you will be interested to hear about the flying in of two of Wingate's Long-Range Penetration brigades. Landing strips in two areas were selected from which the brigades could advance westwards primarily to interrupt the Japanese lines of communication, and so assist the American-Chinese operations taking place farther north. The strips were 100 miles inside enemy territory and 260 miles from the transport base.

The first landings were made by gliders, whose occupants then prepared the strips to receive transport aircraft. Between March 6 and March 11 seven thousand five hundred men, with all their gear and with mules, were successfully

* 'Chindits', the familiar name for Wingate's Long-Range Penetration Force.

Burma

landed. The only losses were a number of the gliders, and some of these should be repairable. The brigades have now started their advance, but a small holding party has been left at one of the strips to receive a flight of Spitfires and a squadron of Hurricane fighter-bombers which were to fly in to protect the base and provide air support.

The only serious mishap occurred on the first night. One of the strips in the northern area was found to have been obstructed by the Japanese, and the surface of the remaining strip was much worse than was expected, causing crashes which blocked the strip and prevented further landings that night. A few of the gliders had to be turned back in the air, and failed to reach our territory. Another strip was immediately prepared in this area, and was ready for landing two days later. The total of killed, wounded, and missing is at most 145.

The operation appears to have been a complete surprise for the Japanese. There has been no enemy air action against the strips in the northern area, and the one in the south was only bombed on March 10 after our men had left it. As it happened, the enemy were concentrating aircraft at airfields in the Mandalay area as part of their own plans. In consequence the strong air forces we had collected to protect the landings had a very good bag, and in two days destroyed sixty-one enemy aircraft for the loss of only three of our own.

We are all very well pleased that Wingate's venture has started so well, and the success of this flying-in operation augurs well for the future. Your men have played an important part both in the transport squadrons and in the supporting air operations.

'I am thrilled,' replied Roosevelt the next day, 'by the news of our success under Wingate. If you wire him please give him my hearty good wishes. May the good work go on. This marks an epic achievement for the airborne troops, not forgetting the mules.'

Wingate did not live long to enjoy this first success or to reap its fruits. On March 24, to my great distress, he was killed in the air. He insisted on starting. The facts are unknown. Probably the pilot lost his way in thick weather. The aircraft crashed into a hillside, and it was long before it was discovered. With him a bright flame was extinguished.

*　　　*　　　*

On March 8 three Japanese divisions began their expected

ttack on our central front. General Scoones withdrew his IVth
Corps, also of three divisions, to the Imphal plateau, so as to
ight concentrated on ground of his own choosing. If the enemy
cut the road to the railhead at Dimapur he would have to depend upon the air until the battle was won. The Japanese repeated the tactics they had used with misfortune in the Arakan.
They counted on capturing our stores at Imphal to feed themselves. They also intended to cut not only the road to Dimapur,
but also the railway there, and thus sever the supply route
maintaining Stilwell's force and the United States air-lift to
China. Important issues were therefore at stake.

The key lay again in transport aircraft. Mountbatten's resources, though considerable, were not nearly enough. He
ought to retain twenty United States aircraft already bor-
owed from 'the Hump' traffic, and asked for seventy more.
This was a hard requirement to make or to procure. In the
anxious weeks that followed I gave him my strongest support.
'Chiefs of Staff and I,' I told him, 'are backing you up to the
ull. I have telegraphed to the President. In my view nothing
matters but the battle. Be sure you win.' In the end Mountbatten's needs were largely met by the temporary loan of seventy-
nine aircraft from the Mediterranean.

By the end of March the Japanese had cut the road to Dimapur and were pressing hard on the fringes of the Imphal plain
from three sides. The 5th Indian Division was flown into Imphal
from the Arakan front, where operations were halted, and the
7th Indian Division was flown into Dimapur. Thither by rail
came the headquarters of the XXXIIIrd Corps, under General
Stopford, the 2nd British Division, an independent Indian
brigade, and also the last remaining brigade of Wingate's force.

At Kohima, a roadside township that commanded the pass to
the Assam valley, the Japanese northern attack was held. Here
the garrison consisted of a battalion of the Royal West Kent, a
Nepalese battalion, and a battalion of the Assam Rifles, with
every man, and even convalescents from the hospital, who could
bear arms. They were attacked on April 4 by the Japanese 31st
Division, slowly forced back into a diminishing area, and finally
on to a single hill. They had no supplies except what was
dropped on them by parachutes. Attacked on every side, they
held on steadfastly, supported by bombing and cannon-fire from
the air, until they were relieved on the 20th by the 161st Indian
Brigade, which, with the 2nd British Division, was fighting its

way up from Dimapur. Four thousand Japanese were killed
The valiant defence of Kohima against enormous odds was a
fine episode.

*   *   *

We had the command of the air, but we depended upon
having enough transport planes. The climax came in May. Sixty
thousand British and Indian soldiers, with all their modern
equipment, were confined in a circle on the Imphal plain. I could
feel the stress amid all other business. On the principle 'Nothing
matters but the battle' I used my authority.

Prime Minister to Admiral Mountbatten   4 May 4
(South-East Asia)
Let nothing go from the battle that you need for victory.
will not accept denial of this from any quarter, and will back
you to the full.

Prime Minister to General Ismay, for C.O.S.   9 May 4
Committee
The gap must be filled at all costs, either by delaying the
return of the seventy-nine transport aircraft to the Mediter
ranean, or by drawing twenty plus fifty-nine from 'the Hump'
or by a combination of both. We cannot on any accoun
throw away this battle. I am quite willing to telegraph to the
President pointing out to him the disastrous consequences to
his own plans for helping China which would follow the cast
ing away of this battle.

Prime Minister to General Ismay and General   14 May 4
Hollis, for C.O.S. Committee
Whatever happens Admiral Mountbatten is not to send
away the seventy-nine aircraft to the Mediterranean excep
as they are replaced in his command by suitable American
aircraft either from United States or 'the Hump'. His argu
ment seems to me unanswerable.
I have not been given any sufficient reasons to show tha
General Alexander's battle will be hampered if the date of th
arrival of these aircraft in the Mediterranean is postponed
General Wilson has already an overwhelming superiority in
the air, and these aircraft are not needed so much for th
battle as for amphibious operations following its success
whereas they are vital to the operations proceeding in Burma
General Hollis should therefore prepare me a short note
which I will discuss with him at midnight to-night. Mean

while this minute should be brought to the attention of the Chiefs of Staff. I am determined that Mountbatten's battle shall not be ruined by the folly of flying 150 aircraft 5,000 miles in opposite directions, and I will appeal to the President to-morrow unless I am satisfied that the needs are met.

* * *

Meanwhile on the northern front Stilwell was making good progress towards the line Mogaung–Myitkyina, against the stubborn resistance of the Japanese 18th Division. He was anxious about his eastern flank, where their 56th Division, along the Chinese frontier, might turn upon him. The President persuaded Chiang Kai-shek to send Stilwell another Chinese division, but it was not till April 21 that the Generalissimo agreed to order his troops in Yunnan to advance into Burma. On May 10 four Chinese divisions crossed the Salween at and above Kunlong, thus worrying the Japanese flank.

The Chindits, operating on the enemy communications, had been reinforced in early April by two more brigades, so that five were now in action. They worked northwards up the railway, preventing the passage of reinforcements and destroying dumps as they went. Despite the havoc they caused, the Japanese withdrew nothing from the Imphal front and only one battalion from Stilwell's. They brought their 53rd Division from Siam and tried, at the cost of over 5,400 killed, but without success, to quell the nuisance.

On May 17 Stilwell sprung a surprise both on the Japanese and ourselves by capturing the airfield at Myitkyina by a swift advance of General Merrill's U.S. brigade. Reinforcements were flown in to assault the town, but the Japanese held it obstinately till early August. At the end of May Mogaung, Stilwell's other main objective, was invested by the leading Chindits brigade, the 77th, and finally fell to them on June 26. These successes were largely due to Stilwell's leadership, energy, and pertinacity ; but his troops were exhausted by their efforts and many had to be withdrawn.

* * *

Around Imphal the situation was still at full strain. Our Air Force was dominant, but the monsoon was hindering the air supply, on which our success depended. All our four divisions were slowly pushing outwards from their encirclement. Along

the Kohima road the relieving force and the besieged were fight
ing their way towards each other. It was a race against time
We marked their progress with tense feelings.

Prime Minister to Admiral Mountbatten   22 June 4
(South-East Asia)

The Chiefs of Staff have expressed anxiety about the situa
tion in Imphal, particularly in respect of reserves of supplie
and ammunition. You are absolutely entitled to ask for al
aircraft necessary to maintain the situation, whether the
come from 'the Hump' or any other source. 'The Hump
must be considered the current reserve, and should be draw
upon whenever necessary. The Americans have by a brillian
feat of arms landed us in Myitkyina, but neither Myitkyin
nor Imphal can be held without drawing on 'the Hump'. I
you fail to make your demands in good time, invoking me i
necessary to help from here, it will be no good complainin
afterwards if it is not a success. Keep your hand close on th
job, which seems to me both serious and critical. Every goo
wish.

The finale came while this message was on the way. I quot
Admiral Mountbatten's report:

In the third week in June the situation was critical, and i
seemed possible, after all the efforts of the previous tw
months, that early in July the IVth Corps would finally ru
out of reserves. But on June 22, with a week and a half i
hand, the 2nd British and 5th Indian Divisions met at a poin
twenty-nine miles north of Imphal and the road to the plai
was open. On the same day the convoys began to roll in.

Mountbatten was justified in adding, 'The Japanese bid fo
India was virtually over, and ahead lay the prospect of the firs
major British victory in Burma.'

CHAPTER 15

Strategy Against Japan

*The Choice Before Us – My Minute of January 24, 1944 –
Arrival of Admiral Mountbatten's Mission – The New Plan –
United States Objections – A Powerful Japanese Fleet Moves
to Singapore – Prevention of Amphibious Operations – We Lose
Local Naval Superiority – My Telegram to the President of
March 10 – The President's Reply – I Give a Ruling to the
Chiefs of Staff, March 20 – The 'Middle Strategy'.*

While the fierce and critical fighting by land and air described
in the last chapter was raging in Burma and the Pacific the
whole future policy of the conduct of the war against Japan
was being hotly debated among ourselves in London, among the
Americans in Washington, and between London and Washington. I have already mentioned the report of the Combined Chiefs
of Staff at the Cairo Conference on the long-term policy in the
Pacific, and the British share in it, and how this had been initialled by the President and me without our being able in the
pressure of events to study it, or discuss it together or with our
advisers. It was only when at Marrakesh I received a request to
transmit a dispatch on the subject to the Dominions that I became aware how far the British Chiefs of Staff had developed
their opinions. I found myself immediately in disagreement,
and thus arose the only considerable difference which I and the
War Cabinet had with our trusted military colleagues.

Briefly the following choice lay before us. Should we send
our naval forces and any troops or air-power we could spare or
transport to act with the left flank of the United States forces
in the South-West Pacific, basing ourselves upon Australia? Our
Chiefs of Staff thought we should, and they had had no difficulty
in reaching agreement with their American comrades in Cairo.
I, on the other hand, and my colleagues, held that we should
advance eastwards to the Malay peninsula and the Dutch islands,
using India as our base. The Chiefs of Staff contended that
whereas Mountbatten could not carry out amphibious operations on a major scale until six months after a German defeat,

their Pacific reinforcement plan, to which they suggested we were committed, could be begun much sooner.

As soon as I got home I convened a meeting of the Defence Committee, where the whole subject was for the first time effectively examined and thrashed out between us.

A few days later I wrote the following minute:

Prime Minister to General Ismay, for C.O.S.   24 Jan 44
Committee

All my Ministerial colleagues who were present at the meeting on the 19th have spoken to me about the projects then expounded by the Planners in a strongly adverse sense. I myself am not in agreement with these plans, and the issue will have to be debated as between Governments. It must also be remembered that this plan is entirely different from that expounded to us by General MacArthur's Chief of Staff, so that evidently there is a great difference of opinion even among the Americans themselves upon it.

2. No one would object to sending the handful of ships proposed to work with the American Fleet in any June operation they may have in view, and of course we should always be ready to build up a fleet in the Pacific. But no plan of war in these theatres could be considered satisfactory which provided no outlet in 1944–5, before Hitler is defeated, for the very large air and military forces we have standing in India and around the Bay of Bengal.

3. For these forces the only effectual operation is Sumatra ['Culverin']. I have long been convinced that this is the most practicable manner of drawing off very large numbers of Japanese aircraft, and possibly of troops, or, in the alternative, of regaining important territory and securing bases from which we may strike equally at Singapore, at Bangkok, in the Malacca Straits, and along the Japanese communications with Burma. My colleagues agree with me in thinking that it is upon this that we should concentrate our efforts, making it clear to the Americans that if we help them in the Pacific, as we shall do, we shall expect them to assist us with a proper supply of landing-craft in time to attack Sumatra in October, November, or December. This they can perfectly well do from the immense new construction of L.S.T.s, which will be continuous throughout the year. . . .

4. We must await the arrival of the officers whom Admiral Mountbatten is sending, to go into the matter fully with them, and we cannot send any telegrams to the Dominions until we have at least formed our own view.

In mid-February 1944 Mountbatten's mission arrived, headed

by his able American Deputy Chief of Staff, General Wede-meyer. Mountbatten did not believe the American project for a through road from Northern Assam to China could be completed for two-way traffic before June 1946. He therefore advised dropping it and expanding the existing air route instead. If this were done he would not have to capture so large a part of Northern Burma. With the resources thus released he wished to penetrate the enemy perimeter of Malaya and the Dutch East Indies, and push rapidly north-eastwards from base to base along the Asiatic coast. This would open better communication with China by sea, and would be a direct help to the American advances on Japan from the Central Pacific and New Guinea. Sumatra would have to be captured first, and he proposed to do this as amphibious resources were released from North-West Europe. 'Culverin' was thus revived.

This strategy was however opposed to the recommendations which the Combined Chiefs of Staff had agreed upon at Cairo. It raised our differences about long-term policy in an immediate and practical form. Having long been an advocate of the Sumatra enterprise, I liked Mountbatten's new plan. I still believed that the size of the forces considered necessary for Sumatra was excessive, but nevertheless there would be a surplus over the needs of the Burma land campaign, as proposed by Mountbatten, and I was against sending them to play a minor part in MacArthur's operations. In this I was fully supported by the Foreign Office, who thought that the British *rôle* in the Far East should not be a mere minor contribution to the Americans ; this was not likely to appeal to the British people. Moreover, the peoples of Asia were little interested in the Pacific islands as compared with the wide regions which meant most to them. In contrast, the strategy advocated by South-East Asia Command would have immediate psychological and political effects which would hasten the defeat of Japan.

I was quite sure that American minds would move in a different direction. I was not therefore surprised at a passage in President Roosevelt's telegram to me of February 25, 1944 :

> I am gravely concerned over the recent trends in strategy that favour an operation toward Sumatra and Malaya in the future rather than face the immediate obstacles that confront us in Burma. I fail to see how an operation against Sumatra and Malaya, requiring tremendous resources and forces, can possibly be mounted until after the conclusion of the war in

Europe. Lucrative as a successful 'Culverin' might be, there appears much more to be gained by employing all the resources we now have available in an all-out drive into Upper Burma, so that we can build up our air strength in China and ensure the essential support for our westward advance to the Formosa–China–Luzon area.

This did not augur well for the success of Wedemeyer's mission. They presented themselves in Washington in March to the American Chiefs of Staff. They were not the first in the field. Admiral Mountbatten's Commanders-in-Chief had fully supported his plans, but not so his Deputy, the American General Stilwell. This was understandable, as Stilwell combined the office of Deputy with several others, notably that of Chief of Staff to Chiang Kai-shek. It was not a good arrangement on the part of the Americans, but we had had no option but to consent. Stilwell favoured every measure which might conceivably aid China, and believed that supply by road could begin sooner than South-East Asia Command expected. He was entitled to urge his views on Admiral Mountbatten, and when they were not accepted to represent them, with Mountbatten's consent, to his superiors in Washington. But he also permitted himself, without Mountbatten's knowledge, to send a mission to Washington to state his case there.

The American Chiefs of Staff had recently decided that though General MacArthur's advance towards the Philippines should continue the main attack should be made by Admiral Nimitz from the Central Pacific against Formosa. They therefore thought the strategic value of liberating Malaya and the Dutch East Indies would be small and tardy. They saw no need for any attack on Sumatra. Their hearts were still set on flying more supplies to China over 'the Hump' and building the Burma Road. They also had a new plan for basing long-range bombers in China to attack Japan, which would need more supply tonnage than they had so far required. Wedemeyer marshalled the arguments for Mountbatten's proposals with great skill, but he failed to convince his auditors and masters.

* * *

However, at this very time an unexpected event of the first importance occurred. A powerful Japanese fleet, including seven battleships, moved from the Central Pacific to Singapore. Their purpose was uncertain, but we now know that it was partly to seek temporary shelter from American air attack, and also to bring them nearer to their oil supplies in the Dutch East Indies. None the less, they might break into the Bay of Bengal, and this possibility put a stop for the time being to 'Culverin' or other amphibious adventures in Indian waters. We no longer had even local naval superiority. I immediately recognised this unpleasant fact.

Prime Minister to General Ismay, for C.O.S.   7 Mar 44
Committee
   The plan for Sumatra was made on the assumption that no considerable detachment would be made from the Japanese main Fleet. This was of course pure assumption, based on what it would be reasonable for the enemy to do, and there never could be any guarantee that the enemy would not do unreasonable things. However, at that time the Japanese were believed to be concerned in defending Truk and Rabaul and other outposts against the United States and in holding themselves in readiness for the possibilities of a fleet action. They have now abandoned any such intentions, if they had them, and, falling back from their outpost line, are able to make defensive dispositions of their Fleet, which includes the stationing of a strong force at Singapore. While that Fleet is there it is evident that we could not do Sumatra, or anything like it, unless our own naval forces were built up to the point where we should welcome a fleet action. It is very much to the advantage of the United States that the Japanese should be held at Singapore. The longer they are there the greater the opportunities for Admiral Nimitz to act with freedom and advance with rapidity. How long the Japanese can afford to remain at Singapore depends upon the progress of the American advance. It seems quite certain they will have to reunite their Fleet, and, having reunited it, will have again to contemplate the idea of a general engagement for the sake of the Philippines or nearer home. The probabilities of their coming back to Singapore, should they leave it, can only be assessed in relation to the situation prevailing at the time. The longer we can detain them in their present position at Singapore the greater the help we can give the United States. This will be achieved by continued preparations for large amphibious attacks the moment they are forced by the United States' main advance to reunite their Fleet and withdraw into the Pacific.
   2. Make sure this minute is put before the Joint Planners.

*   *   *

Meanwhile our discussions with our Chiefs of Staff were long and sometimes tense. The policy of helping General MacArthur or Admiral Nimitz depended on what size of force could be based on Australia, and whether on the east or north and west coasts. We had insufficient information, and further investigation was admittedly needed. It would obviously be a very great strain on our shipping. In March we seemed to have reached a deadlock among ourselves at home. The Chiefs of Staff felt that the Americans were expecting us to send a fleet to the Pacific for operations which might occur in June. I therefore thought it necessary to clear up this point with the President, and also to inform him of the whole position.

Prime Minister to President Roosevelt   10 Mar 44
In the final report of the Cairo Conference the Combined Chiefs of Staff reported that they had 'approved in principle as a basis for further investigation and preparation' an overall plan for the defeat of Japan. This plan contemplated the dispatch to the Pacific of a detachment of the British Fleet which was provisionally scheduled to become operational in the Pacific in June 1944. Although you and I both initialled the final report neither of us had had the opportunity of going into these matters personally, as we were concerned with affairs of more immediate urgency. Since then the War Cabinet and Chiefs of Staff have been 'investigating', and we have not so far reached united conclusions. Meanwhile the Japanese Fleet has arrived at Singapore, which constitutes in my mind a new major fact.

2. After the surrender of the Italian Fleet in September 1943 I was very keen on sending a detachment of our Fleet as quickly as possible to the Pacific, but when I opened this to Admiral King he explained to me how very strong the United States Navy was already in those waters compared with the Japanese, and I formed the impression that he did not need us very much. I have also seen several telegrams from our naval representatives in Washington which tend to confirm the above impression. On the other hand, I am told that Admiral King has informed the First Sea Lord that he would like to have our detachment, provided it did not arrive until August or September, when its logistic requirements could more easily be met. I am, in the upshot, left in doubt about whether we are really needed this year.

3. Accordingly I should be very grateful if you could let me know whether there is any specific American operation in the Pacific (*a*) before the end of 1944 or (*b*) before the

summer of 1945 which would be hindered or prevented by the absence of a British Fleet detachment.

4. On the other hand, the movement of the Japanese Fleet to Singapore, which coincided, *inter alia*, with their knowledge of the movement of our battleship squadron into the Indian Ocean, seems to show their sensitiveness about the Andamans, Nicobars, and Sumatra. It would surely be an advantage to you if, by keeping up the threat in the Bay of Bengal, we could detain the Japanese Fleet or a large portion of it at Singapore, and thus secure you a clear field in the Pacific to enable your by-passing process and advance to develop at full speed.

5. General Wedemeyer is able to unfold all Mountbatten's plans in the Indian theatre and the Bay of Bengal. They certainly seem to fit in with the kind of requests which Chiang Kai-shek was making, which you favoured, but which we were unable to make good before the monsoon on account of the Mediterranean and 'Overlord' operations. I am personally still of opinion that amphibious action across the Bay of Bengal will enable all our forces and establishments in India to play their highest part in the next eighteen months in the war against Japan. We are examining now the logistics in detail, and, *prima facie*, it seems that we could attack with two or three times the strength the islands across the Bay of Bengal, and thereafter the Malay peninsula, than we could by prolonging our communications about 9,000 miles round the south of Australia and operating from the Pacific side and on your southern flank. There is also the objection of dividing our Fleet and our effort between the Pacific and Indian Oceans and throwing out of gear so many of our existing establishments from Calcutta to Ceylon and way back in the Suez Canal zone.

6. Before however reaching any final conclusions in my mind about this matter I should like to know what answer you would give to the question I posed in paragraph 3, namely, would your Pacific operations be hindered if, for the present at any rate and while the Japanese Fleet is at Singapore, we kept our centre of gravity in the Indian Ocean and the Bay of Bengal and planned amphibious operations there as resources came to hand?

The President's reply to my direct question was conclusive.

President Roosevelt to Prime Minister　　　　13 Mar 44
(a) There will be no specific operation in the Pacific during 1944 that would be adversely affected by the absence

of a British Fleet detachment. (b) It is not at the present time possible to anticipate with sufficient accuracy future developments in the Pacific to be certain that a British Fleet detachment will not be needed there during the year of 1945, but it does not now appear that such a reinforcement will be needed before the summer of 1945.

In consideration of recent enemy dispositions it is my personal opinion that unless we have unexpected bad luck in the Pacific your naval force will be of more value to our common effort by remaining in the Indian Ocean.

All of the above estimates are of course based on current conditions, and are therefore subject to change if the circumstances change.

*   *   *

Thus fortified upon the distressing controversy in which I and my Cabinet colleagues were engaged with the Chiefs of Staff, I felt it my duty to give a ruling. In this case I addressed myself to each of the Chiefs of Staff personally, and not collectively to them as a committee.

Prime Minister to First Sea Lord, C.I.G.S., and   20 Mar 44
C.A.S.

I have addressed the attached minute to each of the Chiefs of Staff personally.

1. My question and the President's reply are directed ... solely to the point as to whether there is any obligation to the American authorities that we should send a detachment of the British Fleet to the Pacific before the summer of 1945, and whether their operations would be hampered if we stood out. We now know that there is no obligation and that their operations will not be hampered, also that they will not in any case require our assistance (barring some catastrophe) before the autumn of 1945. We are therefore free to consider the matter among ourselves and from the point of view of British interests only. ...

3. The serious nature of the present position has been brought home to me by the reluctance of the Chiefs of Staff to meet with their American counterparts for fear of revealing to the United States their differences from me and my Cabinet colleagues. The Ministers on the Defence Committee are convinced, and I am sure that the War Cabinet would agree if the matter were brought before them, that it is in the interest of Britain to pursue what may be termed the 'Bay of Bengal strategy', at any rate for the next twelve months. I

therefore feel it my duty, as Prime Minister and Minister of Defence, to give the following rulings:

(a) Unless unforeseen events occur, the Indian theatre and the Bay of Bengal will remain, until the summer of 1945, the centre of gravity for the British and Imperial war effort against Japan.

(b) All preparations will be made for amphibious action across the Bay of Bengal against the Malay peninsula and the various island outposts by which it is defended, the ultimate objective being the reconquest of Singapore.

(c) A powerful British fleet will be built up, based on Ceylon, Addu Atoll, and East Indian ports, under the shield of our strong shore-based aircraft. The fleet train for this Eastern Fleet must be developed as fast as possible, subject to the priority needs of 'Overlord' and the Mediterranean, and the necessary feeding of this country on its present rations.

(d) The plans of South-East Asia Command for amphibious action across the Bay of Bengal will be examined, corrected, and improved, with the desire of engaging the enemy as closely and as soon as possible.

(e) The Reconnaissance Mission to Australia should be sent as soon as I have approved the personnel. They should report promptly upon the existing facilities in Australia and on the recaptured islands to the north of it, and propose measures for carrying the Eastern Fleet and its fleet train, with any additions that may be required, into the South-West Pacific and basing it on Australian ports should we at any time wish to adopt that policy.

4. I should be very ready to discuss the above rulings with the Chiefs of Staff in order that we may be clear in our minds as to the line we are going to take in discussions with our American friends. Meanwhile, with this difference on long-term plans settled, we may bend ourselves to the tremendous and urgent tasks which are now so near, and in which we shall have need of all our comradeship and mutual confidence.

Nevertheless the scene was melting and reshaping so rapidly that I preferred to keep the options open, and we continued to study other plans. As the Japanese Fleet might stop us attacking across the Bay of Bengal, and we could not mount any large amphibious operation in the East until six months after Germany had been defeated, a middle course was considered. This 'middle strategy', as it was termed in our circle, was to advance northwards from Australia, help General MacArthur to liberate Borneo, and then strike either at Singapore and Malaya or at Hong Kong and the China coast. This could be done by forming a British and Australian force under an Australian commander, who would be subordinate to MacArthur.

The disadvantages were obvious. The 'middle strategy' would do little to help the Americans in the Central Pacific. If their plans went well we should not reach Borneo in time to take part even in the assault against Hong Kong, and we should probably find ourselves shut out from the main fighting in the Pacific, in which we were determined to share. The Australians welcomed the idea of establishing an Imperial Command which would relieve American predominance over the whole zone, but the bases on their east coast were already fully engaged. A new organisation to meet British needs might cause dislocation. Moreover, it was a much longer sea voyage to Australia than to India, and this would be a heavy strain on our shipping.

At the time the answers to most of these puzzles were unknown, but the broad problems were laid before a conference of Dominion Premiers which assembled in London on May 1. The Australian and New Zealand Prime Ministers were assured that their own countries would not be expected to increase the sum of their war effort, and pronounced themselves in favour of the 'middle strategy'. They also agreed to find the troops and most of the aircraft. The proposal offered a useful opportunity for Dominion effort. However, in the end these plans did not mature. The course of events soon changed fundamentally the conditions which prevailed or could be foreshadowed at the Cairo Conference or in the months which followed ; and anyhow the war with Japan ended in a manner and at a date which no one dreamed of at the time of the discussion.

CHAPTER 16

Preparations for 'Overlord'

*Hard Memories – The Cross-Channel Plan – The Commanders
– Increased Weight of the Assault – The Mulberry Harbours –
Plans for the Airborne Attack – 'Waterproofing' of Vehicles –
Fire Plan of the Naval Bombardment – My Telegram to General
Marshall of March 11 – Training the Troops in Amphibious
Operations – D Day and H Hour – Final Dispositions and First
Objectives – The Navy's Task – The Air Offensive – Deception
Devices – The Germans Misled – All Southern England One
Vast Camp.*

Thought arising from factual experience may be a bridle or a
spur. The reader of these volumes will be aware that while I
was always willing to join with the United States in a direct
assault across the Channel on the German sea-front in France,
I was not convinced that this was the only way of winning the
war, and I knew that it would be a very heavy and hazardous
adventure. The fearful price we had had to pay in human life
and blood for the great offensive of the First World War was
graven in my mind. Memories of the Somme and Passchendaele
and many lesser frontal attacks upon the Germans were not to
be blotted out by time or reflection. It still seemed to me, after
a quarter of a century, that fortifications of concrete and steel
armed with modern fire-power, and fully manned by trained,
resolute men, could only be overcome by surprise in time or
place by turning their flanks, or by some new and mechanical
device like the tank. Superiority of bombardment, terrific as it
may be, was no final answer. The defenders could easily have
ready other lines behind their first, and the intervening ground
which the artillery could conquer would become impassable
crater-fields. These were the fruits of knowledge which the
French and British had bought so dearly from 1915 to 1917.

Since then new factors had appeared, but they did not all
tell the same way. The fire-power of the defence had vastly increased. The development of minefields both on land and in the
sea was enormous. On the other hand, we, the attackers, held
air supremacy, and could land large numbers of paratroops

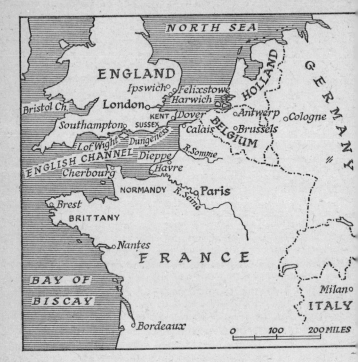

The Coast of North-West Europe

behind the enemy's front, and above all block and paralyse the
communications by which he could bring reinforcements for a
counter-attack.

Throughout the summer months of 1943 General Morgan
and his Allied Inter-Service Staff had laboured at the plan. In a
previous chapter I have described how it was presented to me
during my voyage to Quebec for the 'Quadrant' Conference.
There the scheme was generally approved, but there was one
feature of it which requires comment. The size and scope of the
first assault on the Normandy beaches was necessarily limited
by the numbers of landing-craft available. General Morgan's instructions were to plan an assault by three divisions, with two

divisions as an immediate follow-up. He accordingly proposed to land the three divisions on the coast between Caen and Carentan. He would have liked to land part of the force north of Carentan, nearer to Cherbourg, but he thought it unwise to divide so small a force. The estuary of the river Vire at Carentan was marshy and it would have been difficult for the two wings of the attack to keep in touch. No doubt he was right. I would certainly have preferrred a stronger attack on a broader front, but at that time, ten months before the event, we could not be sure of having enough landing-craft.

It was the absence of important harbours in all this stretch of coast which had impelled Mountbatten's staff to propose the synthetic harbours. The decisions at Quebec confirmed the need and clarified the issues. I kept in touch with the development of this project, which was pressed forward by a committee of experts and Service representatives, summoned by Brigadier Bruce White of the War Office, himself an eminent civil engineer. It was a tremendous undertaking, and high credit is due to many, not least to Major-General Sir Harold Wernher, whose task it was to co-ordinate the many interests concerned.

Here too should be mentioned 'Pluto', the submarine pipelines which carried petrol from the Isle of Wight to Normandy and later from Dungeness to Calais. This idea and many others owed much to Mountbatten's staff. Space forbids description of the many contrivances devised to overcome the formidable obstacles and minefields guarding the beaches. Some were fitted to our tanks to protect their crews ; others served the landing-craft. All these matters aroused my personal interest, and, when it seemed necessary, my intervention.

*   *   *

General Morgan and his staff were well content with the approval given at Quebec to their proposals. The troops could now begin their training and their special equipment could be made. For this Morgan had been given powers greater than a Staff officer usually wields.

The discussions which led to the appointment of General Eisenhower to the Supreme Command and of General Montgomery to command the expeditionary army have already been related. Eisenhower's Deputy was Air Chief Marshal Tedder. Air Marshal Leigh-Mallory was appointed to the Air and Admiral Ramsay to the Naval Command. General Eisenhower brought with him General Bedell Smith as his Chief of Staff, to whom General Morgan was appointed Deputy.

Eisenhower and Montgomery disagreed with one important feature of the plan. They wanted an assault in greater strength and on a wider front, so as to gain quickly a good-sized bridgehead in which to build up their forces for the break-out. Also it was important to capture the docks at Cherbourg earlier than had been planned. They wanted a first assault by five divisions instead of three. Of course this was perfectly right. General Morgan himself had advocated an extension of the initial landing, but had not been given enough resources. But where were the extra landing-craft to come from? South-East Asia had already been stripped. There were sufficient in the Mediterranean to carry two divisions, but these were needed for 'Anvil', the seaborne assault on Southern France which was to take place at the same time as 'Overlord' and draw German troops away from the North. If 'Anvil' were to be reduced it would be too weak to be helpful. It was not until March that General Eisenhower, in conference with the British Chiefs of Staff, made his final decision. The American Chiefs of Staff had agreed that he should speak for them. Having recently come from the Mediterranean, he knew all about 'Anvil', and now as Supreme Commander of 'Overlord' he could best judge the needs of both. It was agreed to take the ships of one division from 'Anvil' and to use them for 'Overlord'. The ships for a second division could be found by postponing 'Overlord' till the June moon period. The output of new landing-craft in that month would fill the gap. As for the additional troops, Britain and the United States would each contribute one division to bring the total up to five. The United States also agreed to provide naval support for their extra division. Thus the naval forces allocated to the operation were roughly 80 per cent. British and 20 per cent. American. Planning now went ahead on this revised and greatly improved foundation.

*   *   *

As soon as I returned from Marrakesh I busied myself with the many technical matters of the 'Overlord' preparations. Across the Channel the whole front bristled with obstacles; defences had been built and manned. The enemy expected us, but did they know *where* or *when* or *how*? They had no flanks that could be turned, at any rate within the range of our fighter air cover. Ships were more vulnerable than ever to shore batteries, which could aim by Radar. Once our troops were landed they still had to be supplied and the enemy's air and tank counter-attacks beaten off. I never ceased to search for means to overcome the perils which lay before us.

Prime Minister to General Ismay and Sir Edward   23 Jan 44
Bridges

In view of the many repercussions which 'Overlord' preparations will make on our life, and in order to keep the whole matter under constant survey, I propose to set up a weekly committee, over which I will preside myself. This committee will be a substitute for the Anti-U-boat Warfare Committee, which can now be put on a two-monthly basis.

Pray let me have your suggestions for the personnel of this new committee.

*   *   *

The 'Mulberry' harbours, I now heard, were meeting with difficulties. I therefore summoned a conference on January 24. It was intended to plant a breakwater ('Gooseberry') in each divisional assault area. This now meant a total of five 'Gooseberries', two of which would in due course be absorbed into the 'Mulberries'. On the suggestion of Admiral Tennant, who was in charge of the operational side of the 'Mulberry' plan, it was agreed that all the 'Gooseberries' should be composed of blockships, although this meant using many more vessels. Moving under their own power, they could quickly reach the scene and be sunk in the right place, thus providing a certain amount of shelter almost at once. All could be laid in four or five days. The 'Phœnix' concrete caissons to complete the 'Mulberries' would be towed over by instalments, but this would take at least a fortnight. There was a shortage of tugs, and I gave instructions for a census. The Admiralty needed eight thousand yards of blockships. Nearly all were provided by using seventy old merchant ships and four obsolete warships. As the British were building most of the 'Mulberries' I thought we could reasonably expect the Americans to help with the blockships. At my suggestion they did so, contributing nearly half. For the rest, the twenty-three 'Whale' floating pier units were progressing well, but the steel 'Bombardons', for the outer breakwaters were meeting technical troubles, which the Admiralty had to solve.

*   *   *

The plans for airborne attack seemed to me to deserve special attention and support.

Prime Minister to General Ismay, for C.O.S.   28 Jan 44
Committee

I am not at all satisfied with the provision that, on existing plans, is being made for the carriage of airborne troops for 'Overlord'. There are four airborne divisions available, but I am told that there are only sufficient aircraft to lift one of these divisions. This is not on account of lack of production, but because the date by which everything must be ready has been set at March 15. The production of Stirlings and Albemarles between March 15 and May 15 will be 110 aircraft—seventy Stirlings and forty Albemarles. All these should be available for the battle. I have also asked you to examine how many aircraft can be made available from Coastal Command. It is clear to me that if strenuous effort is made much more ample resources could be secured for General Eisenhower.

2. General Eisenhower should be asked to state the maximum airborne forces he desires to launch simultaneously at the opening of 'Overlord'. At the same time I should be glad to receive a statement of what we are giving him under present plans. I will preside at a meeting next week to review the position and see how we can meet General Eisenhower's requirements.

*   *   *

The appointment of the commanders gave a fresh impetus. 'D.D.' tanks which could swim ashore had already been successfully used in the Mediterranean, and would certainly be wanted again. There was also a process of 'waterproofing' ordinary tracked and wheeled vehicles to enable them to drive ashore under their own power through several feet of water. But, as usual, the Army's demands for vehicles of all kinds seemed wildly extravagant.

Prime Minister to Minister of Production and   25 Jan 44
Minister of Supply

Pray let me have the report upon the possibilities of producing 300 D.D. tanks by the end of April.

2. What is the position of waterproofing material?

3. I understand that General Montgomery has given a list of some of his priorities to the Ministry of Supply. Let me see this list, with comments upon the possibility of meeting his wishes.

Prime Minister to General Montgomery   31 Jan 44

You spoke to me about waterproofing materials, and every effort is being made to produce what is necessary. Surely however the whole 200,000 vehicles with their one hundred varieties, each of which is a separate proposition, do not require to be waterproofed. Many of these vehicles will not come in till three or four months after the landing has begun, and we hope that by that time the troops will not have to wade ashore. It is very necessary that selective processes and refinements should play their part in the preparations for 'Overlord' at this stage in the war, when one need can usually be met only at the expense of another. I know you will bear this in mind.

2. I am most anxious that you should have, if possible, a two-division lift for your airborne force. This would be helped if a firm date could be fixed. The Air Ministry and Ministry of Aircraft Production have been given target dates —for instance, March 15 as the date for providing certain aircraft, such as Albemarles, etc., of which 180 are to be available. If however without prejudice to the above a two-months later date were acceptable, then in this batch alone instead of 180 there would be 270 by May 15. I cannot doubt that similar expansions could be obtained in the case of many other requisitions. I am well aware of the arguments about training, but it is the crews and not the machines which need training. If highly skilled crews can be obtained (from, say, the Fleet Air Arm) they can practise on the existing stock of machines so as to have a redundancy of troops to be taken, up till zero hour, over the outflow of machines. Talk to me about this when we meet.

I was most interested in the fire plan of the opening bombardment, particularly its naval aspect.

Prime Minister to First Sea Lord   20 Feb 44

As you will remember, I have several times stressed in my minutes to the Chiefs of Staff the great importance of a bombarding squadron or fleet in Operation 'Overlord'. Once the air shield has been established the power of the warships is liberated. High-velocity guns are particularly suited for the smashing of concrete pill-boxes. You have told me of the arrangements that you are making, and I consider they should be pressed to the fullest possible extreme.

2. I had a talk yesterday with Admiral Cooke [U.S.N.], who showed me photographs of the Kwaijalein attack in the Marshalls. He also stressed the great value of short-range bombardment, at, say, 2,000 yards. The beaches in our case will

not be convenient for that, I presume. Nevertheless the greater the power that can be brought to bear the better. Here is the time to use the *Ramillies* class ; and, as I have said, men can be taken off other ships in order to work up a bombardment for the actual event of the landing, after which they can return to their duties.

3. I propose to have a Defence Committee meeting on Monday week, February 28, to discuss this aspect of 'Overlord'. Meanwhile I shall be glad to have a paper from you.

In the event naval bombarding forces included six battleships, two large monitors, and twenty-two cruisers, besides large numbers of destroyers and smaller vessels. Two-thirds of these were British.

* * *

I was anxious that General Marshall should realise the efforts I was making to sustain the plan he had so long desired. I accordingly telegraphed:

Prime Minister to General Marshall (*Washington*)   11 Mar 44
    Since I got home from Marrakesh I have looked carefully into the following aspects of 'Overlord', namely:
    (i) 'Mulberry' and all connected with it ;
    (ii) airborne assault lift, including method of glider attack ;
    (iii) inshore bombarding squadrons ; and
    (iv) Air Command arrangements.
I have presided at a series of meetings at which either Ike or Bedell has been present, and I am satisfied that everything is going on well. Ike and Bedell will probably tell you they are well pleased. I am hardening very much on this operation as the time approaches, *in the sense of wishing to strike if humanly possible, even if the limiting conditions we laid down at Moscow are not exactly fulfilled.** I hope a chance may come for us to have a talk before long. Every good wish.

* * *

Once the size of the expedition had been determined it was possible to go ahead with intensive training. Not the least of our difficulties was to find enough room. A broad partition was arranged between British and American forces, whereby the British occupied the south-eastern and the Americans the south-western parts of England. The inhabitants of coastal areas

* Author's subsequent italics.

accepted all the inconveniences in good part. One British division with its naval counterpart did all its earlier training in the Moray Firth area in Scotland. The winter storms prepared them for the rough-and-tumble of D Day.

The theory and practice of amphibious operations had long been established by the Combined Operations Staff, under Admiral Mountbatten, who had been succeeded by General Laycock. It had now to be taught to all concerned, in addition to the thorough general training needed for modern warfare. This of course had long been going on in Britain and America in exercises great and small with live ammunition. Many officers and men entered into battle for the first time, but all bore themselves like seasoned troops.

Lessons from previous large-scale exercises, and of course from our hard experience at Dieppe, were applied in final rehearsals by all three Services, which culminated in early May. All this activity did not pass unnoticed by the enemy. We did not object, and special pains were taken that they should be remarked by watchers in the Pas de Calais, where we wanted the Germans to believe we were coming.

Our plans had to be altered and kept up to date as fresh information came in about the enemy. We knew the general layout of his troops and his principal defences, the gun positions, the strong-points and entrenchments along the coast, but after Rommel took command in late January great additions and refinements began to appear. In particular we had to discover any new types of obstacle that might be installed, and contrive the antidote.

Constant air reconnaissance kept us informed of what was going on across the Channel. And of course there were other ways of finding out. Many trips were made by parties in small craft to resolve some doubtful point, to take soundings inshore, to examine new obstacles, or to test the slope and nature of a beach. All this had to be done in darkness, with silent approach, stealthy reconnaissance, and timely withdrawal.

*   *   *

An intricate decision was the choice of D Day and H Hour, the moment at which the leading assault craft should hit the beach. From this many other timings had to be worked backwards. It was agreed to approach the enemy coast by moonlight, because this would help both our ships and our airborne

Normandy

troops. A short period of daylight before H Hour was also needed
to give order to the deployment of the small craft and accuracy
to the covering bombardment. But if the interval between first
light and H Hour was too long the enemy would have more time
to recover from their surprise and fire on our troops in the act
of landing.

Then there were the tides. If we landed at high tide the under-
water obstacles would obstruct the approach ; if at low tide the
troops would have far to go across the exposed beaches. Many
other factors had to be considered, and it was finally decided
to land about three hours before high water. But this was not
all. The tides varied by forty minutes between the eastern and
western beaches, and there was a submerged reef in one of the
British sectors. Each sector had to have a different H Hour,
which varied from one place to another by as much as eighty-
five minutes.

Only on three days in each lunar month were all the desired
conditions fulfilled. The first three-day period after May 31,
General Eisenhower's target date, was June 5, 6, and 7. Thus

was June 5 chosen. If the weather were not propitious on any of those three days the whole operation would have to be postponed at least a fortnight—indeed, a whole month if we waited for the moon.

*　　*　　*

By April our plans were taking final shape. The Second British Army, under General Dempsey, was to land three divisions on beaches north and north-west of Caen. One airborne division was to be dropped, a few hours before, north-east of Caen to capture the bridges over the lower Orne and protect the eastern flank. On the British right the First U.S. Army, under General Omar Bradley, was to land one division on the coast east of the Vire estuary and one division north of it. The latter would be aided by a previous drop of two airborne divisions a few miles inland. Each Army had one division in ships for immediate reinforcement.

The first objectives of the attack included Caen, Bayeux, Isigny, and Carentan. When these were gained the Americans would advance across the Cotentin peninsula, and also drive northward to capture Cherbourg. The British would protect the American flank from counter-attack from the east, gaining ground south and south-east of Caen, where we could create airfields and use our armour. It was hoped to reach the line Falaise-Avranches three weeks after the landing, and, with the strong reinforcements by that time ashore, to break out eastwards towards Paris, north-eastwards towards the Seine, and westwards to capture the Brittany ports.

These plans depended on our ability to maintain a rapid build-up over the beaches. To co-ordinate all the intricate shipping movements a special organisation was established at the Supreme Commander's headquarters at Portsmouth, with subordinate inter-Service bodies at the embarkation ports. This enabled the commanders on the far shore to control the flow of supplies to their beaches. A similar organisation controlled supplies from the air. The nourishing and expanding of the numerous organisations on the beaches of France was a prime feature. They would soon be as busy as a major port.

The Navy's task would be to carry the Army safely across the Channel and support the landing with all available means; thereafter to ensure the timely arrival of reinforcements and supplies, despite all the hazards of the sea and the enemy.

240

Admiral Ramsay commanded two Task Forces, one Britis
and the other American. The Eastern Task Force, unde
Admiral Vian, would control all naval operations in the Britis
sector. Admiral Kirk, U.S.N., operated similarly for the Amer
can First Army. These two commands contained five assau
forces, each carrying the fighting elements of a division an
each having its own specialised craft to give close support 1
the troops in the landings. Here was the hard core of the attacl
Surrounding and protecting the assault forces would be tl
powerful Allied Navies and Air Forces.

From the embarkation ports, stretching from Felixstowe o
the east to the Bristol Channel on the west, shipping would b
brought coastwise in convoy to a rendezvous near the Isle o
Wight. From here the vast armada would sail to Normandy
Because of the great congestion in our southern ports and t
help our deception plans, the heavy naval bombarding force
would assemble in the Clyde and at Belfast.

Mines were the chief danger during the approach, althoug
U-boats and light surface craft would also present a threa
and minesweeping was of vital concern. A mine barrier extende
across our line of approach, and we could not tell what mor
the enemy might do at the last moment in the assault are
itself. Ten separate channels through the barrier must b
swept for the assault convoys, and thereafter the whol
area must be searched. Twenty-nine flotillas of minesweeper
were assembled, amounting to about three hundred and fift
craft.

The mighty offensive assigned to Bomber Command an
described in an earlier chapter had already been in progress fo
many weeks. The Allied tactical air forces, under Air Chie
Marshal Leigh-Mallory, not only helped the heavy bombers t
destroy enemy communications and isolate the battle area, bu
also had to defeat the enemy's Air Force before the battl
began on land. German airfields and installations were attacke
for three weeks before D Day in growing weight of bombard
ment, while fighter sweeps tempted the reluctant enemy t
battle. For the assault itself the initial task was to protect ou
naval forces and convoys from attack by sea or air; then t
neutralise the enemy's Radar installations, and, while joining i
the joint bombardment plan, additionally to provide fighte
cover over the anchorages and beaches. Three airborne division
were to be delivered safely and in darkness on to their objec

tives, together with a number of special parties to stir and encourage the seething Resistance Movement.

*　　　*　　　*

The bombardment to cover the first landing was a prime factor. Before D Day preliminary air attacks had been delivered on many coastal batteries, not merely those covering the invasion beaches, but, for the sake of deception, all along the French shore. On the night before D Day a great force of British heavy bombers would attack the ten most important batteries that might oppose the landings. At dawn their place was to be taken by medium bombers and ships' gunfire, directed by spotting aircraft. About half an hour after first light the full weight of the U.S. heavy and medium bombers would fall upon the enemy defences. A great variety of guns and rockets mounted in naval assault craft would join in a crescendo of fire.

*　　　*　　　*

Of course we had not only to plan for what we were really going to do. The enemy were bound to know that a great invasion was being prepared; we had to conceal the place and time of attack and make him think we were landing somewhere else and at a different moment. This alone involved an immense amount of thought and action. Coastal areas were banned to visitors; censorship was tightened; letters after a certain date were held back from delivery; foreign embassies were forbidden to send cipher telegrams, and even their diplomatic bags were delayed.

Our major deception was to pretend that we were coming across the Straits of Dover. It would not be proper even now to describe all the methods employed to mislead the enemy, but the obvious ones of simulated concentrations of troops in Kent and Sussex, of fleets of dummy ships collected in the Cinque Ports, of landing exercises on the near-by beaches, of increased wireless activity, were all used. More reconnaissances were made at or over the places we were *not* going to than at the places we were. The final result was admirable. The German High Command firmly believed the evidence we put at their disposal. Rundstedt, the Commander-in-Chief on the Western Front, was convinced that the Pas de Calais was our objective.

*　　　*　　　*

The concentration of the assaulting forces—176,000 men, 20,000 vehicles, and many thousand tons of stores, all to be shipped in the first two days—was in itself an enormous task. It was handled principally by the War Office and the railway authorities, and with great success. From their normal stations all over Britain the troops were brought to the southern counties, into areas stretching from Ipswich round to Cornwall and the Bristol Channel. The three airborne divisions which were to drop on Normandy before the sea assault were assembled close to the airfields whence they would set out. From their concentration areas in rear troops were brought forward for embarkation in assigned priority to camps in marshalling areas near the coast. At the marshalling camps they were divided up into detachments corresponding to the ship- or boat-loads in which they would be embarked. Here every man received his orders. Once briefed, none were permitted to leave camp. The camps themselves were situated near to the embarkation points. These were ports or 'hards'—*i.e.*, stretches of beach concreted to allow of easy embarkation on smaller craft. Here they were to be met by the naval ships.

It seemed most improbable that all this movement by sea and land would escape the attentions of the enemy. There were many tempting targets for their Air, and full precautions were taken. Nearly seven thousand guns and rockets and over a thousand balloons protected the great masses of men and vehicles. But there was no sign of the Luftwaffe. How different things were four years before! The Home Guard, who had so patiently waited for a worth-while job all those years, now found it. Not only were they manning sections of anti-aircraft and coast defences, but they also took over many routine and security duties, thus releasing other soldiers for battle.

All Southern England thus became a vast military camp, filled with men trained, instructed, and eager to come to grips with the Germans across the water.

Rome

The Regrouping of the Allied Armies – Alexander's Great Offensive Begins, May 11 – General Juin Takes Ausonia – The Poles Capture the Cassino Monastery – General Advance of the Allies – My Telegram to Alexander of May 17, and His Reply – Report from General Wilson – The Climax Approaches – The Canadian Corps in the Liri Valley – Capture of Cisterna – Alexander's Report, May 24 – The Anzio Army under General Truscott Advances to the Alban Hills, but Fails to Take Valmontone – My Telegrams of May 28 to Alexander – Stubborn German Resistance – Alexander's Telegram of May 30, and My Reply – Valmontone Captured by the Americans, June 2 – The Allied Entry into Rome, June 4 – The War Cabinet Send Congratulations to All – I Send the Good Tidings to Stalin – The Magnificent Achievements of the Russian Armies – Hitler Faces Impending Doom on Three Fronts.

The regrouping of our forces in Italy was undertaken in great secrecy. Everything possible was done to conceal the movements from the enemy and to mislead him. By the time they were completed General Clark of the Fifth Army, had over seven divisions, four of them French, on the front from the sea to the river Liri ; thence the Eighth Army, now under General Leese, continued the line through Cassino into the mountains with the equivalent of nearly twelve. Six divisions had been packed into the Anzio beach-head ready to sally forth at the best moment ; the equivalent of only three remained in the Adriatic sector. In all the Allies mustered over twenty-eight divisions.

Opposed to them were twenty-three German divisions, but our deception arrangements, which included the threat of a landing at Civitavecchia, the seaport of Rome, had puzzled Kesselring so well that they were widely spread. Between Cassino and the sea, where our main blows were to fall, there were only four, and reserves were scattered and at a distance. Our

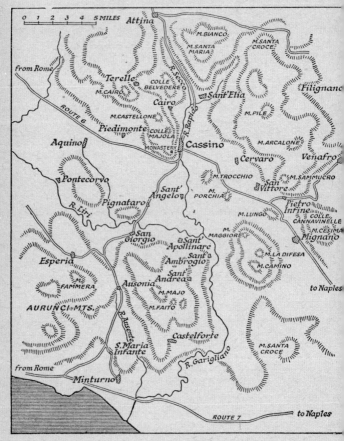

Cassino

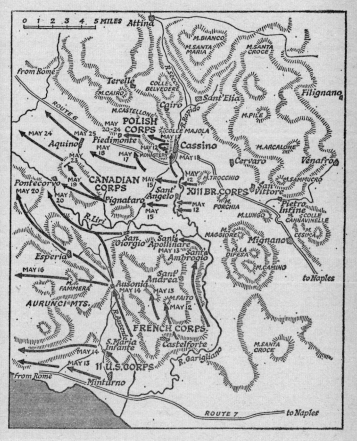

Cassino, May 11–25

attack came unexpectedly. The Germans were carrying out reliefs opposite the British front, and one of their Army Commanders had planned to go on leave.

On the morning of May 11 Alexander and I exchanged telegrams.

Prime Minister to General Alexander   11 May 44
All our thoughts and hopes are with you in what I trust and believe will be a decisive battle, fought to a finish, and having for its object the destruction and ruin of the armed force of the enemy south of Rome.

General Alexander to Prime Minister   11 May 44
All our plans and preparations are now complete and everything is ready. We have every hope and every intention of achieving our object, namely, the destruction of the enemy south of Rome. We expect extremely heavy and bitter fighting, and we are ready for it. I shall signal you our private code-word when the attack starts.

The great offensive began at 11 p.m. that night, when the artillery of both our armies, 2,000 guns, opened a violent fire, reinforced at dawn by the full weight of the tactical air force. North of Cassino the Polish Corps tried to surround the monastery on the ridges that had been the scene of our previous failures, but they were held and thrown back. The British XIIIth Corps, with the 4th British and 8th Indian Divisions leading, succeeded in forming small bridgeheads over the Rapido river, but had to fight hard to hold them. On the Fifth Army front the French soon advanced to Monte Faito, but on the seaward flank the IInd U.S. Corps ran into stiff opposition and struggled for every yard of ground. After thirty-six hours of heavy fighting the enemy began to weaken. The French Corps took Monte Majo, and General Juin pushed his motorised division swiftly up the river Garigliano to capture Sant' Ambrogio and Sant' Apollinare, thus clearing all the west bank of the river. The XIIIth Corps bit more deeply into the strong enemy defences across the Rapido, and on May 14, with the 78th Division coming up to reinforce, began to make good progress. The French thrust forward again up the Ausente valley and took Ausonia, and General Juin launched his Goums* across the trackless mountains westwards from

* Goums: native Moroccan troops, under French officers and N.C.O.s, highly skilled in mountain warfare. They numbered about 12,000.

Ausonia. The American Corps succeeded in capturing Santa Maria Infante, for which they had been fighting for so long. The two German divisions which on this flank had had to support the attack of six divisions of the Fifth Army had suffered crippling losses, and all the German right flank south of the Liri was breaking.

Despite the collapse of their seaward flank the enemy north of the Liri hung on desperately to the last elements of the Gustav Line. But gradually they were overborne. On the 15th the XIIIth Corps reached the Cassino–Pignataro road, and General Leese brought up the Canadian Corps to be ready to exploit his success. Next day the 78th Division broke through the defences in a north-westerly drive which reached Route 6, and on the 17th the Poles attacked north of the monastery. This time they succeeded, and occupied the ridges north-west of it which overlooked the highway.

On the morning of May 18 Cassino town was finally cleared by the 4th British Division, and the Poles triumphantly hoisted their red and white standard over the ruins of the monastery. They greatly distinguished themselves in this their first major engagement in Italy. Later, under their thrustful General Anders, himself a survivor from Russian imprisonment, they were to win many laurels during the long advance to the river Po. The XIIIth Corps had also advanced all along their front, reaching the outskirts of Aquino, with the Canadian Corps driving forward to the south of them. On the other bank of the Liri the French had reached Esperia and were pushing on towards Pico. The U.S. Corps had taken Formia, and they too were getting on splendidly. Kesselring had been sending down reinforcements as fast as he could muster them, but they were arriving piecemeal, only to be thrown into the battle to check the mounting flood of the Allied advance. The Eighth Army had yet to break the Adolf Hitler Line, running from Pontecorvo to Aquina and thence to Piedimonte, but it was now certain that the Germans would soon be forced into a general retreat.

The minds of our commanders were therefore focused on two points: the timing and direction of the Anzio break-out, and the possibility of a final German stand south of Rome, based on the Alban Hills and Valmontone on the high-road.

* * *

Prime Minister to General Alexander   17 May 44

I congratulate you wholeheartedly on the fine advance made along your whole front.

There is some opinion here that it would have been better for the Anzio punch to have been let off first. But C.I.G.S. and I agree with you that it is better to keep the threat of the compressed spring working on the enemy in the present phase. Let me know however what you have in mind.

In your message received this morning you speak of a pause to bring up the artillery. Will this take a few days or a longer period? It seems to me very important to keep close on their heels. It is unusual for a beaten army to stop at a line of entrenchment which has been dug for them in rear unless there is another considerable force already holding this line.

I wonder what your casualties have been since the beginning of this battle. Do not call for any returns which hamper the regular procedure. My own feeling is that seven or eight thousand killed and wounded would cover your losses on the whole front. It suffices to let me know whether your own feeling is that they are higher or lower than this.

All blessings upon you and your men.

Alexander replied the next day:

18 May 44

Many thanks for your congratulations, which we all greatly appreciated.

2. I weighed very carefully the pros and cons of an Anzio break-out, and among many factors two influenced me most. Firstly, the enemy's reserves in that area were too strong, with 90th Division and 26th Division, and I wanted to draw them away first. As you know, 90th Division has been drawn down to main battle area, and part of 26th Division has also been moved. Secondly, the German expected Anzio to be the major thrust, and to gain surprise I did what he did not expect. I have ordered 36th U.S. Division to start moving into bridgehead to-night. I am trying to dribble them in unseen. When right moment comes the Americans will punch out to get astride enemy's communications to Rome. If successful, this may well prove decisive.

3. The intention is not only to keep up the present pressure on the main battle-front, but to step it up. I have ordered Eighth Army to use the utmost energy to break through the Adolf Hitler Line in the Liri valley before the Germans have time to settle down in it. I have also directed that Poles press on at once to Piedimonte, so as to turn this line from north. And I have directed that French Corps, after reaching Pico,

should turn north and come in behind enemy facing Eighth Army. If these manœuvres are successful it will go a long way toward destroying right wing of German Tenth Army. If we get held up in front of the Adolf Hitler Line and are unable to turn it from north or south a full-scale mounted attack will be necessary to break it ; in which case the heavier artillery will have to be moved forward, and this will take several days. But you may be sure that there will be no un-necessary delay. The Germans are very quick to regain their balance, and I have no intention of allowing them to do so.

4. My latest information on casualties is as follows: Eighth Army, 6,000 ; Fifth Army, 7,000 ; total, 13,000.

5. Capture of Cassino means a great deal to me and both my armies. Apart from its Foreign Office value, it seems to me to have great propaganda possibilities.

General Wilson, who had gone to the front from Algiers, also reported:

General Wilson to Prime Minister   18 May 44
Battle continues to progress satisfactorily. I visited Poles to-day. They are elated at their hard-won success at Monte Cassino, where fighting was very severe.

2. Eighth Army and Americans have resources to main-tain impetus of attack, but those of Juin's corps uncertain after eight more days of hard fighting, at present rate of casualties. I discussed this with de Gaulle to-day at Juin's H.Q. He has agreed to send from North Africa one armoured and one infantry regiment at once, and to follow this up with further reinforcements as soon as they have been trained in American weapons.

*   *   *

The Eighth Army found that probing attacks on the Adolf Hitler Line in the Liri valley gave no results, for although the defenders had been hurriedly thrown in they were resolute men and the defences themselves were formidable. A set-piece assault was necessary, which could not be launched until May 23, but in the meantime the French had taken Pico after a stiff fight, and the U.S. IInd Corps were in Fondi. The Germans had good cause to be anxious for their southern flank.

Prime Minister to General Alexander   23 May 44
Your battle seems to be approaching its climax, and all thoughts here are with you. Owing to the enemy pivoting backwards on his left, the advances of the French and the

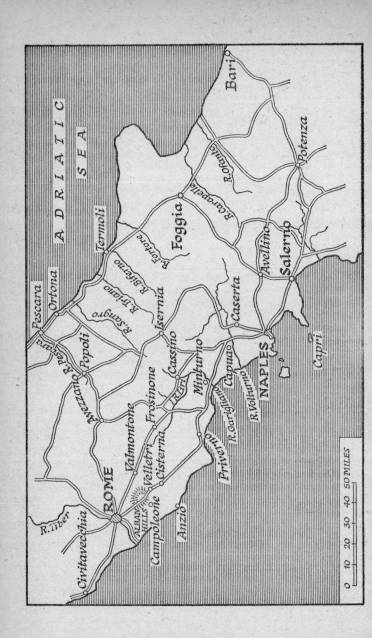

Americans are naturally filling the headlines. Your well-deserved message to the Poles also gained them great prominence.

At Cabinet yesterday some queries were made as to whether the part played by the British troops was receiving proportionate notice. They have been up against the stiffest and most unyielding parts of the line. We do not want anything said that is not justified, but reading the current Press one might well doubt if we were making any serious contribution. I know of course what the facts are, but the public may be upset. Could you therefore bring them a little more into the communiqués, presuming of course you think that such mentions are deserved?

It fell to the Canadian Corps to make the main attack in the Liri valley. By noon of the 24th they had made a clear break-through, and their Armoured Division pierced towards Ceprano. Next day the Germans were in full retreat and hotly pursued on the whole of the Eighth Army front.

* * *

General Alexander had decided that the break-out from the Anzio beach-head should be simultaneous with the onslaught of the Eighth Army. The American General Truscott now struck his blow against Cisterna with two divisions of his Army, still called the VIth Corps. It was captured on the 25th after two days of stiff fighting, and on the same day the beach-head forces gained contact with the leading troops of the U.S. IInd Corps, which had captured and thrust forward from Terracina. At long last all our forces were reunited, and we began to reap the harvest from our winter sowing at Anzio.

General Alexander to Prime Minister   24 May 44
Herewith some interesting and pleasant facts. My usual daily report to C.I.G.S. follows through normal channels.

The Gustav Line, which the enemy has been preparing all winter, and which was guarded by Rapido river, was penetrated by both Armies in the initial assault, and the enemy was driven out of it in first week of battle. Cassino, which was an almost impregnable fortress, was turned by a brilliant pincers movement, which ended by isolating it from the battlefield.

The much-vaunted Adolf Hitler Line, fortified by wire, mines, and concrete and steel pill-boxes, has been smashed on the front of Eighth Army.

The Beach-head enabled us to position a strong force on
T—s.w.w—10—L

the German rear flanks, which is now in operation to complete another larger pincers manœuvre. The deepest penetration up to date is a distance of thirty-eight miles as the crow flies.

In the Anzio sector the Americans have advanced 4,000 yards through heavily prepared fixed defences, and have surrounded Cisterna.

We have taken over 10,000 prisoners, and killed and wounded a large number of the enemy, of which figures are not yet available. Owing to extent of battlefield and rate of advance, it has not been possible yet to check the material captured, but it includes not less than a hundred guns of various types and a great deal of ammunition and other equipment. Much mechanical transport has been destroyed and damaged by our air forces, who claim at least a hundred vehicles destroyed to-day.

Of German divisions that have been engaged, the 71st and 94th Infantry Divisions have been destroyed as fighting formations. 1st Parachute Division, 90th Panzer Grenadier Division, and 15th Panzer Grenadier Division have lost the greater part of their effective strength. Heavy losses have been inflicted on 26th Panzer, 29th Panzer Grenadier Division, 715th and 362nd Infantry Divisions. 576th Regiment, 305th and 131st Regiments, 44th Division, have also been practically wiped out. All enemy reserves, including a division which was believed to have been north of Rome, have been drawn into the battle, and there are strong indications that the Hermann Goering Division, which was in O.K.W. Reserve, is on its way south to try to stem the tide, though this cannot be referred to in public, as this division has not yet been identified in the fighting.

Co-operation between the two Armies and Allied Air Forces has been quite excellent. British, American, French, Canadian, New Zealand, Indian, and Polish troops have all been engaged in fighting. British troops have played a conspicuous part in very bitter fighting, especially for the crossings over the Rapido river and in turning Cassino from the south. I will see that they have their share of publicity in the communiqués. British and American Air Forces have combined in both the close and more distant support of both Armies. Allied naval forces are co-operating by bombardment and by the movement of troops and stores by sea. It is, and will continue to be, in every sense an Allied battle.

Finally, we have freed five hundred square miles of Italy from the grip of the German aggressor in under a fortnight.

*   *   *

General Truscott quickly took advantage of the breach he had made at Cisterna. Under General Clark's orders, he dispatched three divisions, one of them armoured, to Velletri and the Alban Hills, but only one, the 3rd U.S. Division, towards Valmontone, where they would cut the most important escape route of the enemy farther south. This was not in accord with Alexander's instructions, which put Valmontone as the primary objective.

Prime Minister to General Alexander   28 May 44

We are all delighted to hear your good news. At this distance it seems much more important to cut their line of retreat than anything else. I am sure you will have carefully considered moving more armour by the Appian Way up to the northernmost spearhead directed against the Valmontone –Frosinone road. A cop is much more important than Rome, which would anyhow come as its consequence. The cop is the one thing that matters.

Prime Minister to General Alexander   28 May 44

Further to my telegram [above], I have been looking through the tank strength as we get it from various sources. C.I.G.S. furnishes me with figures showing that you have at least 2,500 serviceable. Surely one-half of these could be used, and indeed used up, in making a scythe movement cutting off the enemy's retreat.

I am going to send you and your Armies a public message in a few days, and will back you up whatever happens, but I should feel myself wanting in comradeship if I did not let you know that the glory of this battle, already great, will be measured, not by the capture of Rome or the juncture with the bridgehead, but by the number of German divisions cut off. I am sure you will have revolved all this in your mind, and perhaps you have already acted in this way. Nevertheless I feel I ought to tell you that it is the cop that counts.

But the Hermann Goering Division and elements of others, delayed though they were by damaging attacks from the air, got to Valmontone first. The single American division sent by General Clark was stopped short of it and the escape road remained open. That was very unfortunate.

The enemy in the south were in full retreat, and the Allied Air did its utmost to impede movement and break up concentrations. Obstinate rearguards frequently checked our pursuing forces, and their retirement did not degenerate into a rout. The

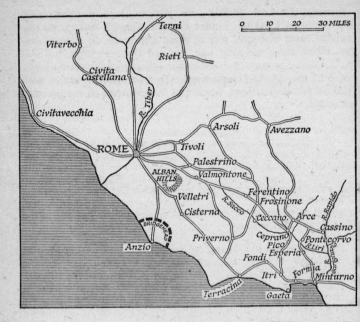

The Roads to Rome

IInd U.S. Corps moved on Priverno, the French to Ceccano, while the Canadian Corps and British XIIIth Corps advanced up the valley to Frosinone and the Xth Corps up the road to Avezzano. The three American divisions dispatched from the Anzio breach towards Velletri and the Alban Hills, later reinforced by a fourth, the 36th, had met very stiff resistance, and for three days could make no ground. They got ready to renew the attack on Valmontone, which Kesselring had been reinforcing with any troops he could find that were fit to fight. However, a brilliant stroke by the 36th U.S. Division must have disconcerted him. They had been fighting hard at the south-west corner of the Alban Hills. On the night of May 30 they found that the Germans had left a commanding height unguarded. Their infantry moved forward in close columns and occupied their key points. Within twenty-four hours the whole 36th Division was firmly established and the last German defence line south of Rome penetrated.

General Alexander to Prime Minister   30 May 44

Thank you for your telegram.

Our serviceable tank strength is about 2,000.

You will see in my Operation Order that my aim is to destroy German Army in the field.

Except for the use of roads through Rome, battle formations are not to go into the city. Further, I am considering the advisability of only mentioning the capture of Rome in my military communiqué among inhabited localities taken by my armies in their stride from day to day. I shall appreciate your advice in this matter.

You will have heard of fresh enemy divisions which are on their way here. I hope our tap will not be turned off too soon, as it was before, and prevent us from gaining full fruits of our present advantageous position.

Prime Minister to General Alexander   31 May 44

I entirely agree with your operational intention, and trust you will execute it.

The capture of Rome is a vast, world-wide event, and should not be minimised. I hope that British as well as Americans will enter the city simultaneously. I would not lump it in with other towns taken on the same day. Nevertheless, as you rightly state, the destruction of the German Army in the field gives us Rome and the rest thrown in.

How lucky it was that we stood up to our United States Chiefs of Staff friends and refused to deny you the full exploitation of this battle! I will support you in obtaining the first priority in everything you need to achieve this glorious victory. I am sure the American Chiefs of Staff would now feel this was a bad moment to pull out of the battle or in any way weaken its force for the sake of other operations of an amphibious character, which may very soon take their place in the van of our ideas.

All good luck.

*   *   *

The success of the 36th U.S. Division did not bear immediate fruit. The enemy hung on desperately both in the Alban Hills and at Valmontone, although the retreat of most of their army had now been deflected northwards towards Avezzano and Arsoli, where they were hunted by the Xth and XIIIth British Corps and the aircraft of the tactical air force. Unhappily, the mountainous country stopped us using our great strength in armour, which otherwise could have been employed to much advantage.

On June 2 the IInd U.S. Corps captured Valmontone and drove westwards. That night German resistance broke, and next day the VIth U.S. Corps in the Alban Hills, with the British 1st and 5th Divisions on its left, pressed on towards Rome. The IInd American Corps led them by a short head. They found the bridges mostly intact, and at 7.15 p.m. on June 4 the head of their 88th Division entered the Piazza Venezia, in the heart of the capital.

On June 9 I sent the congratulations of the War Cabinet to all concerned, and also the following personal telegram to Alexander:

> To these tributes I venture to add my own. We have always been in agreement that the main object was the destruction of the enemy's armed force. It certainly seems that the position which your armies occupy and the superiority they enjoy in the air and in armour gives favourable opportunities by further rapid action of inflicting more heavy losses on Kesselring's disordered army, so that their retreat to the north may cost them dear.
>
> We shall be glad if you will compliment on our behalf the leaders and the troops of the United States, of Britain, Canada, New Zealand, South Africa, India, of France, Poland and Italy, who have distinguished themselves from one end of the line to the other.
>
> We share your hopes for future success in the relentless pursuit and cutting off of the beaten enemy.

*   *   *

I had kept Stalin fully informed from time to time of the progress of these operations, and on June 5, when other things were also going on, sent him our good tidings.

Prime Minister to Premier Stalin   5 June 44

You will have been pleased to learn of the Allied entry into Rome. What we have always regarded as more important is the cutting off of as many enemy divisions as possible. General Alexander is now ordering strong armoured forces northward on Terni, which should largely complete the cutting off of all the divisions which were sent by Hitler to fight south of Rome. Although the amphibious landing at Anzio and Nettuno did not immediately fructify as I had hoped when it was planned, it was a correct strategic move, and brought its reward in the end. First, it drew ten divisions from the following places: one from France, one from Hungary, four from Yugoslavia and Istria, one from Denmark, and three from North Italy. Secondly, it brought on a defensive battle for us in which, though we lost about 25,000 men, the Germans were repulsed and much of the fighting strength of their divisions broken, with a loss of about 30,000 men. Finally, the Anzio landing has made possible the kind of movement for which it was originally planned, only on a far larger scale. General Alexander is concentrating every effort now on entrapping the divisions south of Rome. Several have retreated into the mountains, leaving a great deal of their heavy weapons behind, but we hope for a very good round-up of prisoners and material. As soon as this is over we shall decide how best to use our armies in Italy to support the main adventure. Poles, British, Free French, and Americans have all broken or beaten in frontal attack the German troops opposite them, and there are various important options which will soon have to be considered.

2. I have just returned from two days at Eisenhower's headquarters watching the troops embark [for Normandy]. The difficulties of getting proper weather conditions are very great, especially as we have to consider the fullest employment of the air, naval, and ground forces in relation to tides, waves, fog, and cloud. With great regret General Eisenhower was forced to postpone for one night, but the weather forecast has undergone a most favourable change and to-night we go. We are using 5,000 ships, and have available 11,000 fully mounted aircraft.

From many quarters came messages of warm congratulation. I even got a pat from the Bear.

Marshal Stalin to Prime Minister   5 June 44
I congratulate you on the great victory of the Allied Anglo-American forces—the taking of Rome. This news has been greeted in the Soviet Union with great satisfaction.

*   *   *

Stalin had cause to be in a good mood, for things were going well with him. The scale of the Russian struggle far exceeded the operations with which my account has hitherto been concerned, and formed of course the foundation upon which the British and American Armies approached the climax of the war. The Russians had given their enemy little time to recover from their severe reverses of the early winter of 1943. In mid-January their attacks on the 120-mile front from Lake Ilmen to Leningrad had pierced the defences in front of the city. Farther

The Front in Russia, January–June, 1944

south by the end of February the Germans had been driven back to the shores of Lake Peipus. Leningrad was freed once and for all, and the Russians stood on the borders of the Baltic States.

Successful Russian attacks west of Kiev had forced the Germans back towards the old Polish frontier. The whole southern front was aflame and the German line deeply penetrated at many points. One great pocket of surrounded Germans was left behind at Kersun, from which few escaped.

Throughout March the Russians pressed their advantage all along the line and in the air. From Gomel to the Black Sea the invaders were in full retreat, which did not end until they had been thrust across the Dniester, back into Roumania and Poland. Then the spring thaw brought them a short respite. In the Crimea however operations were still possible. After three days' fighting the Russians broke through the Perekop neck on April 11, joined hands with others that had crossed at Kerch, and set about destroying the Seventeenth German Army and regaining Sebastopol.

The situation of Hitler's armies at the end of May was forlorn. His two hundred divisions on the Eastern Front could not hope to withstand the Russian flood when it was again released. Everywhere he was faced with imminent disaster. Now was the time for him to decide how to regroup his forces, where they should withdraw and where hold. But instead his orders were for them all to stand and fight it out. There was to be no withdrawal, anywhere. The German armies were thus condemned to be broken on all three fronts.

CHAPTER 17

On the Eve

The King Presides at a Final Conference, May 15 – Plenty of Vehicles for the Expedition – Dinner with General Montgomery – Transport for the Leclerc Division – D-Day Tension Grows – I Arrange to Witness the Naval Bombardment Afloat – The King Wishes to Come Too – His Majesty's Letters to Me of May 31 – A Discussion in the Map Room – His Majesty's Letter of June 2 – My Reply – A General Comment – The Weather Begins to Cause Anxiety – Mr. Bevin, Smuts, and I Watch Embarkations at Portsmouth and in the Solent – Worse News about the Weather – Field-Marshal Smuts' Memories – Eisenhower's Decision at 4.15 a.m., June 4, to Postpone for Twenty-four Hours – A Letter from the President – My Reply, June 4 – Mr. Eden Arrives with General de Gaulle – The General's Bristling Mood – Eisenhower's Final Decision at 4 a.m. on June 5: the Die is Cast – The Bad Weather Deceives the Germans – The Armada at Sea – Supreme Climax of the War.

On Monday, May 15, three weeks before D-Day, we held a final conference in London at Montgomery's headquarters in St. Paul's School. The King, Field-Marshal Smuts, the British Chiefs of Staff, the commanders of the expedition, and many of their principal Staff officers were present. On the stage was a map of the Normandy beaches and the immediate hinterland, set at a slope so that the audience could see it clearly, and so constructed that the high officers explaining the plan of operation could walk about on it and point out the landmarks.

General Eisenhower opened the proceedings, and the forenoon session closed with an address by His Majesty. I too spoke, and in the course of my remarks I said, 'I am hardening on this operation.' General Eisenhower in his book* has taken this to mean that in the past I had been against the cross-Channel operation, but this is not correct. If the reader will look back to Chapter 16 he will see that I wrote these very words to General Marshall, and explained that I used them 'in the sense

* *Crusade in Europe*, p. 269.

of wishing to strike if humanly possible, even if the limiting conditions we laid down are not exactly fulfilled'.*

Montgomery took the stage and made an impressive speech. He was followed by several Naval, Army, and Air commanders, and also by the Principal Administrative Officer, who dwelt upon the elaborate preparations that had been made for the administration of the force when it got ashore. The amount of paraphernalia sounded staggering, and reminded me of Admiral Andrew Cunningham's story of dental chairs being landed at Algiers in the first flight of Operation 'Torch'. I was told, for example, that two thousand officers and clerks were being taken across the sea to keep records, and I was given the following statement, which showed that twenty days after the landing— D + 20—there would be one vehicle ashore for every 4.77 men. Each vehicle required a driver and its share of maintenance staff.

—	U.S.		British		Total	
	Vehicles	Person-nel	Vehicles	Person-nel	Vehicles	Personnel
D+20	96,000	452,000	93,000	450,000	189,000	902,000
D+60	197,000	903,000	168,000	800,000	365,000	1,703,000

Plus replacement of casualties.

Although these figures included fighting vehicles such as guns, armoured cars, and tanks, I remembered too well the swarm in the Anzio beach-head, and after reflection I asked Ismay to write to Montgomery and express my concern about what seemed to me an excess of motor-cars and non-fighting vehicles of all kinds. This he did, and we arranged to discuss it when I visited the General's headquarters on Friday, May 19. This interview has been misrepresented. Montgomery is said to have led me into his study and advised me not to speak to his staff, and to have threatened to resign if I insisted on altering the loading plans at the eleventh hour, and I am alleged to have given way, and, after telling his officers that I was not allowed

* See p. 236.

to talk to them, to have walked out. It may be well therefore to state what actually happened.

When I arrived for dinner Montgomery asked to speak to me alone, and I went into his room. I do not remember the actual course of the conversation, but no doubt he explained the difficulties of altering the loading scale at this stage, seventeen days before D-Day. I am sure however that at no time either in this conversation or in any other of the many I had with him during the war did he threaten to resign, and that nothing in the nature of a confrontation with his staff took place. I should not have accepted such behaviour. After our talk we went to dinner, at which only eight or nine persons, mostly the General's personal staff, were present. All our proceedings were of a most friendly character, and when that night the General asked me to put something for him in his private book, as I had done before other great battles, I wrote the following, which has already been published elsewhere:

> On the verge of the greatest adventure with which these pages have dealt, I record my confidence that all will be well, and that the organisation and equipment of the Army will be worthy of the valour of the soldiers and the genius of their chief.

I may add however that I still consider that the proportion of transport vehicles to fighting men in the early phase of the cross-Channel invasion was too high and that the operation suffered both in risk and execution from this fact.

*   *   *

Another project was close to my heart. Our aim was to liberate France, and it seemed both desirable and fitting that a French division should be landed early in the operation and the French people told that their troops were fighting once more on the soil of France. The 2nd French Armoured Division, commanded by General Leclerc, had had a long and distinguished career in North Africa, and as early as March 10 I had told de Gaulle that I hoped they would be with us in the main battle. Since then the matter had been much probed by the Chiefs of Staff. Eisenhower was glad to have the division, and General Wilson did not plan to use it in the attack on the Riviera. The problem was how to get it home and properly mounted in time. The troops could be shifted easily enough, but there was little

room in home-coming ships for their equipment and their
vehicles. After correspondence between the British and United
States Chiefs of Staff and Allied Headquarters in Algiers, much
had been transported in the landing-ships which were sailing
back from the Mediterranean. But on April 4 the Chiefs of
Staff reported that they would still be short of about two thousand vehicles. To give them British ones would seriously complicate Eisenhower's problems of maintenance, and a few days
later his headquarters declared that no American ones could
be provided either from the United Kingdom or the U.S.A.
This meant that the division would not be able to fight until long
after the landing, all for the lack of comparatively few vehicles
out of the immense numbers to be employed. Mr. Eden shared
my disappointment, and on May 2 I made a personal appeal
by letter to General Eisenhower.

2 May 44

Please provide from your vast masses of transport the few
vehicles required for the Leclerc division, which may give
real significance to French re-entry into France. Let me remind you of the figures of Anzio—viz., 125,000 men with
23,000 vehicles, all so painfully landed to carry them, and
they only got twelve miles.

Forgive me for making this appeal, which I know you will
weigh carefully and probe deeply before rejecting.

His answer was reassuring.

10 May 44

I have gone very carefully into the transportation status of
the Leclerc division, and members of my staff have con-
ferred with General Leclerc on the same subject.

I find that about 1,800 vehicles of the division, including
nearly all the track and armoured vehicles, have already
arrived here, or will arrive by May 15. Approximately 2,400
vehicles remain to be shipped, and on the present schedule
all but 400 of these vehicles should be in England by June 12,
the remainder reaching here by June 22. General Leclerc says
that he now has adequate material for training, and he is
being assisted by the American Third Army, to which he is
attached. His general supply situation is good, and the minor
deficiencies which remain after his vehicles arrive, including
provision for maintenance, will be met from American
sources. I believe that the shipping and equipment schedule
of the division will ensure their being properly provided prior
to their entry into combat.

Thus all was arranged, and the march which had begun at Lake Chad ended through Paris at Berchtesgaden.

* * *

As D-Day approached the tension grew. There was still no sign that the enemy had penetrated our secrets. He had scored a minor success at the end of April by sinking two American L.S.T.s which had been taking part in an exercise, but apparently he did not connect this with our invasion plans. We observed some reinforcement of light naval forces at Cherbourg and Havre during May, and there was more minelaying activity in the Channel, but in general he remained quiescent, awaiting a definite lead about our intentions.

Events now began to move swiftly and smoothly to the climax. After the conference on May 15 His Majesty had visited each of the assault forces at their ports of assembly. On May 28 subordinate commanders were informed that D-Day would be June 5. From this moment all personnel committed to the assault were 'sealed' in their ships or at their camps and assembly points ashore. All mail was impounded and private messages of all kinds forbidden except in case of personal emergency. On June 1 Admiral Ramsay assumed control of operations in the Channel, the functions of the naval Commanders-in-Chief in the home ports being subordinated to his requirements.

I thought it would not be wrong for me to watch the preliminary bombardment in this historic battle from one of our cruiser squadrons, and I asked Admiral Ramsay to make a plan. He arranged for me to embark in H.M.S. *Belfast,* in the late afternoon of the day before D-Day. She would call in at Weymouth Bay on her passage from the Clyde, and would then rejoin her squadron at full speed. She was one of the bombarding ships attached to the centre British force, and I would spend the night in her and watch the dawn attack. I was then to make a short tour of the beaches, with due regard to the unswept mine areas, and come back in a destroyer which had completed her bombardment and was to return to England for more ammunition.

Admiral Ramsay felt it his duty however to tell the Supreme Commander of what was in the air. Eisenhower protested against my running such risks. As Supreme Commander he could not bear the responsibility. I sent him word, as he has described, that while we accepted him as Supreme Commander of the British forces involved, which in the case of the Navy were four to one compared with those of the United States, we did not in any way admit his right to regulate the complements of the British ships in the Royal Navy. He accepted this undoubted fact, but dwelt on the addition this would impose upon his anxieties. This appeared to be out of proportion both to the scale of events and to our relations. I too had responsibilities, and felt I must be my own judge of my movements. The matter was settled accordingly.

However, a complication occured which I had His Majesty's permission to recount. When I attended my weekly luncheon with the King on Tuesday, May 30, His Majesty asked me where I intended to be on D-Day. I replied that I proposed to witness the bombardment from one of the cruiser squadrons. His Majesty immediately said he would like to come too. He had not been under fire except in air raids since the Battle of Jutland, and eagerly welcomed the prospect of renewing the experiences of his youth. I thought about this carefully, and was not unwilling to submit the matter to the Cabinet. It was agreed to discuss the matter with Admiral Ramsay first.

Meanwhile the King came to the conclusion that neither he nor I ought to go. He was greatly disappointed, and wrote me the following letter:

BUCKINGHAM PALACE
May 31, 1944

My dear Winston,

I have been thnking a great deal of our conversation yesterday, and I have come to the conclusion that it would not be right for either you or I to be where we planned to be on D-Day. I don't think I need emphasise what it would mean to me personally, and to the whole Allied cause, if at this juncture a chance bomb, torpedo, or even a mine, should remove you from the scene ; equally a change of Sovereign at this moment would be a serious matter for the country and Empire. We should both, I know, love to be there, but in all seriousness I would ask you to reconsider your plan. Our presence, I feel, would be an embarrassment to those responsible for fighting the ship or ships in which we were, despite anything we might say to them.

So, as I said, I have very reluctantly come to the conclusion that the right thing to do is what normally falls to those at the top on such occasions, namely, to remain at home and wait.

I hope very much that you will see it in this light too. The anxiety of these coming days would be very greatly increased for me if I thought that, in addition to everything else, there was a risk, however remote, of my losing your help and guidance.

> Believe me,
> Yours very sincerely,
> GEORGE R.I.

And later:

> BUCKINGHAM PALACE
> *May* 31, 1944

My dear Winston,

I hope you will not send me a reply to my letter, as I shall be seeing you to-morrow afternoon, when you can then give me your reactions to it before we see Ramsay.

> I am,
> Yours very sincerely,
> GEORGE R.I.

At 3.15 p.m. on June 1 the King, with Sir Alan Lascelles in attendance, came to the Map Room at the Annexe, where I and Admiral Ramsay awaited him. The Admiral, who did not then know that there was any idea of the King coming, explained what the *Belfast* would do on the morning of D-Day. It was clear from what he said that those on board the ship would run considerable risks, and also would see very little of the battle. The Admiral was then asked to withdraw for a few minutes, during which it was decided to ask his opinion on the advisability of His Majesty also going to sea in the *Belfast*. The Admiral immediately made it clear that he was not in favour of this. I then said that I should feel obliged to ask the Cabinet and to disclose the Admiral's opinion about the risk, and I said I was sure they would not recommend His Majesty to go. Ramsay then departed. The King said that if it was not right for him to go neither was it right for me. I replied I was going as Minister of Defence in the exercise of my duty. Sir Alan Lascelles, who the King remarked was 'wearing a long face', said that 'His Majesty's anxieties would be increased if he heard his Prime Minister was at the bottom of the English Channel'. I replied that that was all arranged for, and that moreover I considered the risk negligible. Sir Alan said that he had always understood that no Minister of the Crown could leave the country without the Sovereign's permission. I answered that this did not apply as

I should be in one of His Majesty's ships. Lascelles said the ship would be well outside territorial waters. The King then returned to Buckingham Palace.

*   *   *

On the morning of Friday, June 2, I set out in my train for our siding by Eisenhower's headquarters near Portsmouth, with Field-Marshal Smuts, Mr. Ernest Bevin, General Ismay, and my personal staff. Just before we started a further letter arrived.

BUCKINGHAM PALACE
June 2, 1944

My dear Winston,

I want to make one more appeal to you not to go to sea on D-Day. Please consider my own position. I am a younger man than you, I am a sailor, and as King I am the head of all these Services. There is nothing I would like better than to go to sea, but I have agreed to stay at home ; is it fair that you should then do exactly what I should have liked to do myself? You said yesterday afternoon that it would be a fine thing for the King to lead his troops into battle, as in old days ; if the King cannot do this, it does not seem to me right that his Prime Minister should take his place.

There there is your own position. You will see very little, you will run a considerable risk, you will be inaccessible at a critical time, when vital decisions might have to be taken, and however unobtrusive you may be your mere presence on board is bound to be a very heavy additional responsibility to the Admiral and Captain. As I said in my previous letter, your being there would add immeasurably to my anxieties, and your going without consulting your colleagues in the Cabinet would put them in a very difficult position, which they would justifiably resent.

I ask you most earnestly to consider the whole question again, and not let your personal wishes, which I very well understand, lead you to depart from your own high standard of duty to the State.

Believe me,
Your very sincere friend,
GEORGE R.I.

Meanwhile my train lay just outside Southampton, and we were soon connected by telephone with Eisenhower's headquarters. That afternoon we paid him a visit. His tents and caravans were very well concealed in a wood near by. His Majesty was concerned at not having had a reply from me to his letter. At 11.30 p.m., in response to inquiries, I spoke to Lascelles at Windsor Castle on the scrambler telephone, and said that I had cancelled my arrangements in deference to His Majesty's desire. I wrote the following letter in the small hours of the morning and sent it at once by dispatch-rider to Windsor.

June 3, 1944

Sir,

I must excuse myself for not having answered Your Majesty's letter earlier. It caught me just as I was leaving by the train, and I have been in constant movement ever since. I had a dispatch-rider standing by in order to take it to you to-night.

Sir, I cannot really feel that the first paragraph of your letter takes sufficient account of the fact that there is absolutely no comparison in the British Constitution between a Sovereign and a subject. If Your Majesty had gone, as you desire, on board one of your ships in this bombarding action it would have required the Cabinet approval beforehand, and I am very much inclined to think, as I told you, that the Cabinet would have advised most strongly against Your Majesty going.

On the other hand, as Prime Minister and Minister of Defence I ought to be allowed to go where I consider it necessary to the discharge of my duty, and I do not admit that the Cabinet have any right to put restrictions on my freedom of movement. I rely on my own judgment, invoked in many serious matters, as to what are the proper limits of risk which a person who discharges my duties is entitled to run. I must most earnestly ask Your Majesty that no principle shall be laid down which inhibits my freedom of movement when I judge it necessary to acquaint myself with conditions in the various theatres of war. Since Your Majesty does me the honour to be so much concerned about my personal safety on this occasion, I must defer to Your Majesty's wishes, and indeed commands. It is a great comfort to me to know that they arise from Your Majesty's desire to continue me in your service. Though I regret that I cannot go, I am deeply grateful to Your Majesty for the motives which have guided Your Majesty in respect of

Your Majesty's humble and devoted servant and subject,
WINSTON S. CHURCHILL

I may add that the cruiser squadron concerned was, as I had justly estimated, not exposed to any undue danger. In fact, it did not sustain a single casualty. I should not have referred to this matter if it had not been publicised in a friendly but unwittingly inaccurate form by General Eisenhower.

I may here set down the view I have formed over many years on this sort of thing. A man who has to play an effective part in taking, with the highest responsibility, grave and terrible decisions of war may need the refreshment of adventure. He may need also the comfort that when sending so many others to their death he may share in a small way their risks. His field of personal interest, and consequently his forces of action, are stimulated by direct contact with the event. As a result of what I saw and learned in the First World War, I was convinced that generals and other high commanders should try from time to time to see the conditions and aspect of the battle scene themselves. I had seen many grievous errors made through the silly theory that valuable lives should not be endangered. No one was more careful of his personal safety than I was, but I thought my view and theme of the war were sufficiently important and authoritative to entitle me to full freedom of judgment as to how I discharged my task in such a personal matter.

*   *   *

The weather now began to cause anxiety. A fine spell was giving way to unsettled conditions, and from June 1 onwards a commanders' meeting was held twice daily to study the weather reports. At their first meeting poor conditions were predicted for D-Day, with low clouds. This was of prime importance to the Air Forces, affecting both the bombing and the airborne landings. The next evening the first warships sailed from the Clyde, as well as two midget submarines from Portsmouth, whose duty was to mark the assault areas. June 3 brought little encouragement. A rising westerly wind was whipping up a moderate sea; there was heavy cloud and a lowering cloud base. Predictions for June 5 were gloomy.

That afternoon I drove down to Portsmouth with Mr. Bevin and Field-Marshal Smuts and saw a large number of troops embarking for Normandy. We visited the headquarters ship of the 50th Division, and then cruised down the Solent in a launch, boarding one ship after another.

On the way back we stopped at General Eisenhower's camp and wished him luck. We got back to the train in time for a very late dinner. While it was in progress Ismay was called to the telephone by Bedell Smith, who told him that the weather was getting worse and that the operation would probably have to be postponed for twenty-four hours. General Eisenhower would wait until the early hours of June 4 before making a definite decision. Meanwhile units of the great armada would continue to put to sea according to programme.

Ismay came back and reported the bleak news. Those who had seen the array in the Solent felt that the movement was now as impossible to stop as an avalanche. We were haunted by the knowledge that if the bad weather continued and the postponement had to be prolonged beyond June 7 we could not again get the necessary combination of moon and tide for at least another fortnight. Meanwhile the troops had all been briefed. They clearly could not be kept on board these tiny ships indefinitely. How was a leakage to be prevented?

But the anxiety that everyone felt was in no way apparent at the dinner-table in the train. Field-Marshal Smuts was at his most entertaining pitch. He told the story of the Boer surrender at Vereeniging in 1902—how he had impressed on his colleagues that it was no use fighting on and that they must throw themselves on the mercy of the British. He had been assailed as a coward and a defeatist by his own friends, and he had spent the most difficult hour of his life. In the end however he had won through, had gone to Vereeniging, and peace was made. The Field-Marshal then went on to speak about his experiences at the outbreak of the Second World War, when he had to cross the floor of the House and fight his own Prime Minister, who wished to remain neutral.

We went to bed at about half-past one. Ismay told me that he would wait up to hear the result of the morning conference. As there was nothing I could do about it, I said that I was not to be woken to hear the result. At 4.15 a.m. Eisenhower again met his commanders, and heard from the weather experts the ominous report, sky overcast, cloud ceiling low, strong south-westerly wind, with rain and moderate sea. The forecast for the 5th was even worse. Reluctantly he ordered a postponement of the attack for twenty-four hours, and the whole vast array was put into reverse in accordance with a carefully prepared plan. All convoys at sea turned about and small craft sought shelter in covenient anchorages. Only one large convoy, comprising a hundred and thirty-eight small vessels, failed to receive the message, but this too was overtaken and turned round without

ousing the suspicions of the enemy. It was a hard day for the
thousands of men cooped up in landing-craft all round the coast.
The Americans who came from the West Country ports had the
greatest distance to go and suffered most.

At about five o'clock that morning Bedell Smith again tele-
phoned Ismay confirming the postponement, and Ismay went
to bed. Half an hour later I woke up and sent for him. He told
me the news. He says I made no comment.

* * *

The early post brought me a letter from the President
written a fortnight before and withheld for delivery till the
fateful moment came. Alas, I cannot find it. F.D.R. expressed
in the most kindly terms his feelings about our joint work and
comradeship, and his hopes and longings for our success. I
cabled a grateful but somewhat discursive reply.

Prime Minister to President Roosevelt   4 June 44

I was so glad to get your charming letter of May 20. Our
friendship is my greatest stand-by amid the ever-increasing
complications of this exacting war. Averell brought me a
good account of your physical health, and I have sustained
from many quarters impressions that your political health is
also greatly improved. I am here near Ike's headquarters in
my train. His main preoccupation is the weather. There are
wonderful sights to see with all these thousands of vessels.

De Gaulle's Committee by a large majority decided that he
should accept my invitation to come here. He hummed and
hawed, but Massigli and several others threatened to resign
if he did not do so. We expect him on D minus 1. If he
arrives Eisenhower will see him for half an hour and explain
to him the position exclusively in its military aspect. I shall
return to London during the night of D-Day. I do not expect
that very much can be done with de Gaulle, but I still hope
the word 'leadership', which I am told you approved in Hull's
speech, may prove serviceable. I do not expect we shall get
more than a certain number of miles from the beaches, and
probably what we get will be a depopulated area wearing the
aspect of a battlefield. This I can explain to de Gaulle safely
here when he arrives. I will also deliver him your friendly
message to come over to see you. I shall keep you constantly
informed.

I see some of your newspapers are upset at my references in
the House of Commons to Spain. This is very unfair, as all
I have done is to repeat my declaration of October 1940. I

only mentioned Franco's name to show how silly it was identify Spain with him or him with Spain by means of ca catures. I do not care about Franco, but I do not wish to ha the Iberian peninsula hostile to the British after the war. I not know how I can depend on a de Gaullist France. G many would have to be held down by main force, and have a twenty-years alliance with Russia. You must rememb that we are very near to all this pleasant outlook.

We should not be able to agree here in attacking countri which have not molested us because we dislike their tota tarian form of government. I do not know whether there more freedom in Stalin's Russia than in Franco's Spain. I ha no intention to seek a quarrel with either.

After D-Day ought not you and I to send a short messa to Stalin, which can be published? Perhaps it would be w to wait till we are definitely established over the other side.

We this month have the all-time high record for the U-bo war—only four ships of all the United Nations, amounting about 20,000 tons, sunk. In addition we have four U-boa sunk for every ship of ours, and a tremendous plurality enemy ships sunk by our own combined fleets.

I am so glad Alex has not belied your support and impre sions of him. How magnificently your troops have fought! hear that relations are admirable between our armies in eve rank there, and here certainly it is an absolute brotherhood. am looking forward to seeing your Chiefs of Staff. I have bee delighted to receive increasingly good news about Harry. earnestly hope that this will be maintained. I am deep grieved that you cannot come before that very distant [Octe ber] date. Let me know if I can help matters by a journey.

Presently Mr. Eden arrived with General de Gaulle, who ha just flown in from Algiers. I told de Gaulle that I had asked hi to come because of the forthcoming operation. I could not d this by telegraph, and I felt that the history of our two countri required that the liberation of France must not be undertake by the British and Americans without the French being informe I had intended to invite him a little before D-Day, but th weather had forced us to postpone the assault for twenty-fo hours, and it might even be later. This was a grave fact. Thirty five divisions and 4,000 ships had been assembled in the por and camps and 150,000 troops had been embarked for the fir wave of the attack. Many of these had to be kept in conditior of extreme discomfort in small craft. Eleven thousand plane were ready, of which 8,000 would go into action provided th

weather was all right. I then went on to say how much we re-
retted the bombing of the French railways, with its loss of
French life, but we had fewer infantry than the Germans, and it
was the only way we could stop them bringing up overpowering
reinforcements while we built up our front.

The General was bristling. He asked for an absolutely free
right to telegraph to Algiers in his own cipher. As the recognised
head of a great empire he said it was impossible to deny him
free right of communication. I asked him for an assurance that
he would not impart any military information about the forthcoming assault to any of his colleagues, except those actually at
our meeting. De Gaulle said that he must be free to keep in
touch with Algiers about operations in Italy, and I explained
that I was only talking about 'Overlord'. I then unfolded to him
our plan. After he had thanked me for this I asked him if he
would send a public message to France as soon as the armada
had actually sailed. Queen Wilhelmina, King Haakon of Norway, and rulers of other countries which the enemy expected us
to attack had agreed to do so, and I hoped he would do the
same. He said he would.

Mr. Eden now intervened in the conversation, saying that the
great operation impending had taken all our thoughts, but after
it was launched it might be useful to discuss certain political
questions. I explained that I had been in correspondence with
the President for some time, and that while he had begun by
wanting the General to visit the United States he did not seem
so anxious about it now. This was perhaps because of the way
General Giraud had been treated. The President had arranged
with Giraud for the French forces to be equipped, and now
Giraud was dismissed. To this de Gaulle replied that he thought
it was better at this moment to be in England rather than Washington. I warned him that 'liberated France' might for some time
only consist of a few people under fire, and both Eden and I
strongly urged him to visit Mr. Roosevelt soon. De Gaulle said
that he was quite willing to do this, and had so told the President,
but he was anxious about who was to administer liberated
France. This should have been arranged long ago, last September.

This remark made me speak bluntly. The United States and
Great Britain were willing to risk the lives of scores of thou-
sands of men to liberate France. Whether de Gaulle went to
Washington or not was his own affair, but if there was a split

between the Committee of National Liberation and the Unite
States we should almost certainly side with the American
About the administration of liberated French soil, if Gener
de Gaulle wanted us to ask the President to give him the titl
deeds of France the answer was 'No'. If he wanted us to as
the President to agree that the Committee was the princip
body with whom he should deal in France the answer wa
'Yes'. De Gaulle replied that he quite understood that if th
U.S.A. and France disagreed Britain would side with the U.S.A
With this ungracious remark the interview ended.

In a little while I took him to Eisenhower's headquarters i
the woodland, where he was most ceremoniously received. Ik
and Bedell Smith vied with one another in their courtesy
Presently Ike took him to their map tent, and for twent
minutes imparted to him the whole story of what was about t
happen. We then returned to my train. I had expected that d
Gaulle would dine with us and come back to London by thi
the swiftest and most convenient route, but he drew himself u
and stated that he preferred to motor with his French officer
separately.

*   *   *

The hours dragged slowly by until, at 9.15 p.m. on the evenin
of June 4, another fateful conference opened at Eisenhower'
battle headquarters. Conditions were bad, typical of Decembe
rather than June, but the weather experts gave some promise o
a temporary improvement on the morning of the 6th. After thi
they predicted a return of rough weather for an indefinit
period. Faced with the desperate alternatives of accepting th
immediate risks or of postponing the attack for at least a fort
night, General Eisenhower, with the advice of his commanders
boldly, and as it proved wisely, chose to go ahead with th
operation, subject to final confirmation early on the followin;
morning. At 4 a.m. on June 5 the die was irrevocably cast: th
invasion would be launched on June 6.

In retrospect this decision rightly evokes admiration. It wa
amply justified by events, and was largely responsible for gainin;
us the precious advantage of surprise. We now know that th
German meteorological officers informed their High Comman
that invasion on the 5th or 6th of June would not be possibl
owing to stormy weather, which might last for several days
The fact that such a complex series of movements could be ac

complished without detection by a wary and determined enemy is a remarkable tribute to the work of the Allied Air Forces and the excellence of our deception plans.

* * *

All day on June 5 the convoys bearing the spearhead of the invasion converged on the rendezvous south of the Isle of Wight. Thence, in an endless stream, led by the minesweepers on a wide front and protected on all sides by the might of the Allied Navies and Air Forces, the greatest armada that ever left our shores set out for the coast of France. The rough conditions at sea were a severe trial to troops on the eve of battle, particularly in the terrible discomfort of the smaller craft. Yet, in spite of all, the vast movement was carried through with almost the precision of a parade, and, although not wholly without loss, such casualties and delays as did occur, mostly to small craft in tow, had no appreciable effect on events.

Round all our coasts the network of defence was keyed to the highest pitch of activity. The Home Fleet was alert against any move by German surface ships, while air patrols watched the enemy coast from Norway to the Channel. Far out at sea, in the Western Approaches and in the Bay of Biscay, aircraft of Coastal Command, in great strength, supported by flotillas of destroyers, kept watch for possible enemy reactions. Our intelligence told us that over fifty U-boats were concentrated in the French Biscay ports, ready to intervene when the moment came. The hour was now striking.

* * *

Here then we reach what the Western Powers may justly regard as the supreme climax of the war. Nor, though the road might be long and hard, could we doubt that decisive victory would be gained. Africa was cleared. India had been defended from invasion. Japan, over-strained and disillusioned, was recoiling on her homeland. All danger to Australia and New Zealand had passed away. Italy was fighting on our side. The Russian armies had driven the German invaders from their country. All the gains Hitler had acquired so swiftly from the Soviets three years before had vanished, with staggering losses of men and equipment. The Crimea had been cleared. The Polish frontiers had been reached. Roumania and Bulgaria were desperately seeking to escape the vengeance of their Eastern conquerors.

Russia's new offensive, timed with our Continental landing, was about to break. While I sat in my chair in the Map Room of the Annexe the thrilling news of the capture of Rome arrived. The immense cross-Channel enterprise for the liberation of France had begun. All the ships were at sea. We had the mastery of the oceans and of the air. The Hitler tyranny was doomed.

Here then we might pause in thankfulness and take hope, not only for victory on all fronts and in all three elements, but also for a safe and happy future for tormented mankind.